The **OFFICIAL** DSA GUIDE to

DRIVING
GOODS VEHICLES

London: TSO

Written and compiled by Driver and Vehicle Standards Agency Learning Materials.

First published 1994
Twelfth edition 2020
Fifth impression 2023

ISBN 978 0 11 553746 2

A CIP catalogue record for this book is available from the British Library

Other titles in the Driving Skills series
The Official DVSA Guide to Driving – the essential skills
The Official DVSA Theory Test for Car Drivers
The Official DVSA Guide to Learning to Drive
The Official DVSA Guide to Better Driving

The Official DVSA Theory Test Kit iPhone/Android App
The Official DVSA Hazard Perception Practice iPhone/Android App

The Official DVSA Guide to Riding – the essential skills
The Official DVSA Theory Test for Motorcyclists
The Official DVSA Guide to Learning to Ride

The Official DVSA Guide to Driving Buses and Coaches
The Official DVSA Theory Test for Drivers of Large Vehicles
Driver CPC – the official DVSA guide for professional bus and coach drivers
Driver CPC – the official DVSA guide for professional goods vehicle drivers

The Official DVSA Guide to Tractor and Specialist Vehicle Driving Tests (eBook)

Every effort has been made to ensure that the information contained in this publication is accurate at the time of going to press. The Stationery Office cannot be held responsible for any inaccuracies. Information in this book is for guidance only.

All metric and imperial conversions in this book are approximate.

Acknowledgements

The following organisations contributed to previous editions of this publication: Avonline Transport, Bennetts of Malvern, Countrywide PLC, County Building Supplies, David Haynes Commercial Maintenance, DSD Contracting (Bedford), Eurotunnel, Hereford and Worcester Ambulance Service, Home Delivery Network, Picanini Stud, Skills for Logistics, SMH Fleet Solutions Ltd, Volvo Trucks, and Worcester Truck Services.

The Driver and Vehicle Standards Agency (DVSA) would like to thank Logistics UK (was the Freight Transport Association), JAUPT, the Road Haulage Association, and White Logistics and Storage Ltd for their contributions to this edition.

WORLD LAND TRUST™
www.carbonbalancedprint.com
CBP2223

We're turning over a new leaf.

MIX
Paper | Supporting responsible forestry
FSC® C002151
www.fsc.org

Find us online

❯ GOV.UK – Simpler, clearer, faster

GOV.UK is the best place to find government services and information for

- car drivers
- motorcyclists
- driving licences
- driving and riding tests
- towing a caravan or trailer
- medical rules
- driving and riding for a living
- online services.

Visit **www.gov.uk** and try it out.

You can also find contact details for DVSA and other motoring agencies like DVLA at **www.gov.uk**

You'll notice that links to **GOV.UK**, the UK's central government site, don't always take you to a specific page. This is because this kind of site constantly adapts to what people really search for and static links would quickly go out of date. Try it out. Simply search what you need from your preferred search site or from **www.gov.uk** and you should find what you're looking for. You can give feedback to the Government Digital Service from the website.

Driver & Vehicle Standards Agency

The Driver and Vehicle Standards Agency (DVSA) is an executive agency of the Department for Transport.

We improve road safety in Great Britain by setting standards for driving and motorcycling, and making sure drivers, vehicle operators and MOT garages understand and follow roadworthiness standards. We also provide a range of licensing, testing, education and enforcement services.

www.gov.uk/dvsa

The Driver and Vehicle Agency (DVA) is an executive agency within the Department of the Environment for Northern Ireland.

Its primary aim is to promote and improve road safety through the advancement of driving standards and implementation of the government's policies for improving the mechanical standards of vehicles.

nidirect.gov.uk/motoring

⊙ Contents

⊕ A message from the Chief Driving Examiner

As the driver of a goods vehicle, you'll be in control of one of the biggest types of vehicle on our roads. You'll also probably spend more time than the average driver behind the wheel, so you have a particular responsibility to drive safely, and with respect towards other road users.

Becoming a professional driver takes a special kind of approach and attitude. You'll need to understand the theory behind driving a goods vehicle, as well as learning all the skills and techniques for handling a lorry and the goods you carry. And, importantly, you'll need to develop a strong awareness of other, more vulnerable road users and how to behave around them on our increasingly crowded roads.

Unfortunately, recent years have seen a sharp increase in the number of collisions between lorries and cyclists – particularly in London. Of course, it isn't necessarily the driver's fault, but the cyclist almost always comes off worse. So, it's your responsibility as a driver to make sure you have the knowledge and skills to try and make sure these collisions don't happen. Keep up to date with new information, advice and technology and you'll be a better, safer driver.

This edition contains the information you'll need to prepare for the extended theory and practical tests that link to the Driver Certificate of Professional Competence (Driver CPC). Put this information into practice and you should be able to reach the high standards demanded of a safe and responsible lorry driver.

Mark Winn

Mark Winn
Chief Driving Examiner

Section one
➜ Getting started

This section covers

- Your instructor and your licence
- The theory and practical tests
- Medical requirements
- Professional standards
- Driver Certificate of Professional Competence
- Responsibility and attitude
- Work organisation
- Manual handling techniques
- Diet and driving ability

⊕ Your instructor and your licence

Selecting an instructor

It's important that you have the correct training and instruction before you take your heavy goods vehicle (HGV) test. When sourcing HGV training, you can ask if an instructor holds a current National Register of LGV Instructors (NRI) or National Vocational Driving Instructor Register (NVDIR) registration.

You can confirm this registration by using the NRI website or by contacting the NRI office at

National Register of LGV Instructors (NRI)
Halesfield 17
Telford
TF7 4PW
Tel 01952 520210
lgvinstructorregister.com

or by contacting the National Vocational Driving Instructors Register

Email nationalvocationalregister@yahoo.co.uk
Tel 0330 053 9503
lgvregister.org.uk

Your supervising driver

Anyone training or supervising (accompanying) you as a learner must

- hold a full (that is **not** implied rights*) entitlement for the category of vehicle you're driving, and
- have held that entitlement for the relevant period of time – usually three years.

---

* Implied rights were granted to drivers who passed their car driving test before January 1997.
These drivers are permitted to drive small lorries (C1 and C1E), subject to certain restrictions.
Since April 2010, however, they are no longer permitted to supervise a learner C1 or C1E driver.

Applying for your licence

You should apply to the Driver and Vehicle Licensing Agency (DVLA) in Swansea (or the Driver and Vehicle Agency (DVA) if you live in Northern Ireland) for provisional entitlement to drive goods vehicles. An application form is available online from DVLA or DVA.

Your licence will be valid for a maximum of 5 years. You'll have to sign a medical declaration each time you renew your entitlement up to the age of 45. After the age of 45, you'll need to send a medical examination report to DVLA (DVA) each time you renew your entitlement.

Once you reach the age of 65, you will need to send a medical examination report to DVLA (DVA) every year.

For full details, visit **www.gov.uk** or **nidirect.gov.uk**

Licence restrictions

To drive a medium-sized goods vehicle (category C1), you must be at least 18. You can drive a medium-sized goods vehicle with a trailer (category C1E) at 18 as long as the maximum authorised mass (MAM) of the combination doesn't exceed 7.5 tonnes. If the MAM does exceed 7.5 tonnes, you can still drive a C1E combination at 18 if you hold a Driver Certificate of Professional Competence (Driver CPC). Otherwise, you must be at least 21.

For alternative fuel vehicles up to 4.25 tonnes, please contact DVSA technical support on 0115 936 6370.

The minimum age to drive a heavy goods vehicle (category C or, if driving with a trailer, CE) is normally 21, but you can also drive one if you're at least 18 and

- you hold a Driver CPC qualification authorising you to drive a motor vehicle of that class or
- the vehicle is being used during a driving lesson or driving test for the purpose of enabling you to obtain a driving licence or Driver CPC or
- you've been issued with a document authorising you to drive the relevant vehicle for a specified period of up to 12 months, while taking a vocational training course leading to a professional qualification relevant to the carriage of goods by road.

You'll also need to hold a full driving licence for a category B vehicle and a provisional driving licence for the category of goods vehicle that you wish to drive.

Automatic transmission

If your vehicle doesn't have a clutch pedal, it's classed as an automatic. If you already hold a driving licence for a vehicle with manual transmission in at least one of the categories B, C, CE, C1, C1E, D, DE, D1 or D1E, you will not be restricted to driving automatic vehicles if you take and pass your practical driving test in a category C, CE, C1, C1E, D, DE, D1 or D1E vehicle that has automatic transmission.

Some modern vehicles have transmission systems where sensors select the next gear without the driver using the clutch pedal. Although the vehicle is driven mainly as an automatic, it still has a clutch pedal and is therefore classed as a manual-transmission vehicle. The clutch is used for moving off and stopping, or for manoeuvring in a slow-speed situation – for example, while controlling the vehicle in a yard.

Articulated vehicles

If your provisional entitlement was issued on or after 15 November 2021, you will automatically have provisional entitlement to drive an articulated lorry (category CE).

This means you can take your test in a large articulated lorry without having to pass one in a large rigid lorry (category C) first.

> If your provisional entitlement to drive heavy goods vehicles was issued before 15 November 2021, you need to apply to DVLA to get the additional provisional entitlements added to your licence. See **www.gov.uk** for more information.

You can still learn to drive and take a driving test in a large rigid lorry (category C) if you do not want to drive anything larger.

If you pass your test in a large articulated lorry, you'll be allowed to drive

- a medium-sized lorry (C1)
- a medium-sized lorry towing a trailer (C1E)
- a large rigid lorry (C)
- a large articulated lorry (CE).

The same applies to medium-sized lorries towing a trailer (category C1E). This means you can learn to drive a medium-sized lorry towing a trailer (category C1E) and take your test in one, without having to pass a test in a medium-sized lorry (category C1) first.

⊕ The theory and practical tests

All new drivers wishing to drive HGVs have to pass a theory test before taking the practical driving tests. You can start your lessons before passing the theory test, but you must pass it before you can book your practical tests. The theory test pass certificate lasts for two years. If you don't pass your practical tests within that time, you'll have to retake the theory test.

Detailed information about the theory and practical tests can be found in sections 5 and 6 of this book.

When driving as a learner, you must

- be accompanied by a qualified driver over the age of 21 who has held a full licence for the category of vehicle being driven for at least three years
- display L plates (or D plates when driving in Wales, if you wish) to the front and rear of the vehicle.

⊙ Medical requirements

Eyesight

All drivers, regardless of vehicle category, **MUST** be able to read a car number plate made after 1 September 2001 from 20 metres, or from 20.5 metres if the number plate was made before that date. If you need glasses or contact lenses to do this, then you **MUST** wear them when driving.

In addition, applicants for a passenger-carrying vehicle (PCV) or HGV licence **MUST** have a visual acuity of at least 0.8 (6/7.5) in their better eye and at least 0.1 (6/60) in the other eye, measured on the Snellen scale (the chart shown on the right). Glasses or contact lenses may be used to reach this standard, provided that the glasses have a corrective power of not more than (+) 8 dioptres. There is no specific limit for the corrective power of contact lenses.

Applicants must also have a horizontal visual field of at least 160 degrees; the extension should be at least 70 degrees left and right, with 30 degrees up and down. No defects should be present within a radius of the central 30 degrees.

If you only have eyesight in one eye or any other eyesight problem, you must declare this. If you held your licence before 1 January 1997 but cannot meet these standards, you may still be able to renew your lorry or bus licence and should contact

Drivers Medical Group
DVLA
Swansea
SA99 1TU
Tel 0300 790 6807
Email eftd@dvla.gsi.gov.uk

If you need any further general or medical information, you should contact DVLA on **0300 790 6801** or visit **www.gov.uk**

For Northern Ireland, call DVA on **0300 200 7861** or visit **nidirect.gov.uk**

> **REMEMBER**, if you normally wear glasses or contact lenses, always wear them whenever you drive.

> Carry a second pair of glasses or contact lenses with you in case of damage or loss.

Medical examination and form D4 (DLM1 in NI)

Any driver of a goods vehicle must meet the required medical standards. Consult your doctor if you have any doubts about your fitness. In any case, if this is your first application for HGV entitlement, a medical report form must be completed by a doctor. You'll also need to send a medical report form with your application if you're renewing your HGV licence and you're aged 45 or over, unless you've already sent one to DVLA (or DVA) during the last 12 months.

You'll need to have a medical examination in order to complete form D4 (form DLM1 in Northern Ireland). Only complete the applicant details and declaration (section 8 on the forms) when you're with your doctor at the time of the examination. Your doctor will complete the other sections. The medical report will cover

- vision
- nervous system
- diabetes mellitus
- psychiatric illness
- general health
- cardiac health
- the doctor's details.

Your doctor will declare any reason why you wouldn't have full control of a large vehicle. There may be circumstances when adaptations to a vehicle may overcome a particular disability.

When using form D4, the explanatory leaflet (INF4D) will help you. It contains necessary information and useful notes that explain what needs to be done. You should keep this leaflet for future reference. Both form D4 and the leaflet can be found at post offices or downloaded from **www.gov.uk**

Form DLM1 (used in Northern Ireland) is available from DVA centres, local vehicle licensing offices and the post office. It contains some reference notes on pages 1 and 2, which include sections explaining what you and your doctor need to do. Send your application to DVA Licensing, Vocational Medical Records Section: the full address is given at the back of this book.

The medical examination isn't available for free under National Health Service (NHS) rules. Your doctor is entitled to charge the current fee for this medical examination, and you'll be responsible for paying it. The fee can't be recovered from DVLA or DVA, and it isn't refundable if your application is refused.

The completed form must be received by DVLA or DVA within four months of the date your doctor signed it.

Change in health

If you have, or develop, any serious illness or disability that's likely to last more than three months and which could affect your driving, you **must** immediately notify the Drivers Medical Group at DVLA, Swansea (DVA in Northern Ireland).

Medical conditions

You may be refused an HGV driving licence if you suffer from any of the following

- liability to epilepsy/seizure*
- diabetes requiring insulin (unless you held a licence on 1 April 1991 and the traffic commissioner who issued that licence had knowledge of your condition)
- eyesight defects (see the eyesight requirements earlier in this subsection)

* A driver who remains seizure-free for at least 10 years (without anticonvulsant treatment within that time) may be eligible for a licence but with restricted entitlement. Contact DVLA (DVA in Northern Ireland) for further information.

8

- a heart disorder
- persistent high blood pressure (see notes on form DLM1 in Northern Ireland, or on leaflet INF4D if using form D4)
- a stroke within the past year
- unconscious lapses within the past five years
- any disorder causing vertigo within the past year
- major brain surgery or severe head injury with serious continuing after-effects
- Parkinson's disease, multiple sclerosis or other chronic nervous disorder likely to affect the use of the limbs
- a mental disorder
- alcohol/drug problems
- serious difficulty in communicating by telephone in an emergency.

An applicant or licence holder failing to meet the epilepsy, diabetes or eyesight regulations must by law be refused a licence.

⊕ Professional standards

Driving a lorry requires skill, the right attitude and up-to-date knowledge of current driving techniques. To become a professional driver, you'll need

- a high level of driving skill
- a thorough knowledge of the regulations that apply to your work
- a comprehensive knowledge of The Highway Code, traffic signs and road markings – especially those that indicate restrictions for lorries
- the ability to plan well ahead.

You'll need to understand how driving an HGV differs from driving a smaller vehicle. It's also essential to understand the forces at work on your vehicle and its load.

As a professional driver, you have a responsibility to use your vehicle in a way that's sympathetic to the environment. For more information, see 'Helping the environment', in section 4 of this book.

One of the most important things to learn is that the way you drive matters. Drive responsibly and both you and the goods you're carrying will arrive safely at your destination.

The national standard for driving lorries sets out the knowledge, skills and understanding you need to be a safe and responsible driver of a category C vehicle. To read or download the national driving standards, visit **www.gov.uk**

⊛ Driver Certificate of Professional Competence

The training undertaken for this qualification has resulted in reduced fuel bills and lower insurance costs for operators. Drivers are adopting safe and fuel-efficient driving techniques, which reduce emissions and benefit the environment.

To get their Driver CPC, new drivers need to pass the 5 tests that make up Driver CPC. Then, they must keep their knowledge up to date with 35 hours of periodic training in each five-year period after passing the tests.

The tests

Driver CPC part 1: theory test

The test is made up of multiple choice questions and a hazard perception test. They can be taken one after the other on the same day or at different times.

The multiple choice part has 100 questions and the hazard perception part has 19 clips (with 20 scorable hazards). In total, the two parts take about 2 hours and 30 minutes.

To find out more about the theory test and where your nearest theory test centre is, visit **www.gov.uk**

Driver CPC part 2: case study test

Drivers who are working towards gaining their Driver CPC to drive professionally will also need to pass the case study test.

Each case study is based on a scenario that you may come across in your working life. Its aim is to check your knowledge and understanding, and also to test how you put this knowledge into practice.

After reading the case study, you'll be asked to answer questions based around the scenario. To answer, you'll select one or more answers from multiple-choice options, select an option based on an audio clip or click on an area of a photograph or image.

In part 2, you'll be given 7 case studies, each with between 6 and 8 associated questions. You'll need to answer a total of 50 questions and the test will take about 1 hour and 30 minutes.

Driver CPC part 3a: off-road exercises test

During this test, you'll demonstrate an 'S' shaped reverse into a bay. If you're taking the test with a trailer, you will also demonstrate the uncoupling and recoupling procedure.

Driver CPC part 3b: on-road driving test

This test includes vehicle safety questions and one hour of practical road driving. You'll be expected to show the examiner how you drive in various situations and on different types of road. You'll also be assessed on fuel-efficient driving.

Driver CPC part 4: practical demonstration test

This is also a practical test, but it's for new professional drivers only. It assesses your knowledge of, and abilities in, matters of safety and security. Examples include safe use of your vehicle, the security of your vehicle, preventing criminal acts, assessing emergencies and preventing risks. This test takes about 30 minutes.

Periodic training

Periodic training can be taken at any time within the five years, either as a single block or split into periods of at least seven hours at a time. It's recommended that you spread your periodic training by taking one course per year; that way, you'll be updating your knowledge on a more regular basis.

The syllabus for periodic training covers safe and fuel-efficient driving, legal requirements, health, safety, service and logistics. You can find full details at **www.gov.uk/government/publications/driver-cpc-syllabus**

DVSA suggests that drivers consider their own personal development needs when choosing their periodic training. For example, some drivers may benefit from training that focuses on advanced driving techniques, whereas others may benefit more from customer service training.

Drivers who regularly work in an urban environment or who regularly encounter vulnerable road users, such as cyclists or horse riders, should also undergo periodic training on a relevant subject. Examples include 'safe urban driving' and 'vulnerable road users'.

You can check your Driver CPC periodic training hours online at **www.gov.uk**

Driver Qualification Card

On completion of 35 hours of training, drivers who hold a GB photocard licence will automatically be sent a Driver Qualification Card (DQC, sometimes called a Driver CPC card) at no cost. The DQC will be sent to the address that's on your driving licence, so it's important that you tell DVLA (DVA in Northern Ireland) if you change address. Your DQC must be carried with you at all times when you're driving professionally.

Newly qualified drivers with a GB photocard licence will receive their DQC automatically when they've passed all 5 tests that make up Driver CPC.

If you're a driver who doesn't hold a full GB (or NI) photocard licence (or a driver who holds a licence from an EU member state), you may have to submit an application form to DVSA, and you may have to pay a fee for your Driver Qualification Card (DQC, sometimes called a Driver CPC card).

If you're a non-UK licence holder, you can get a DQC from DVSA if you live or work in the UK. For more information, visit

www.gov.uk/driver-cpc-training/if-you-have-a-licence-from-other-countries

It's illegal for an operator to cause, or allow, a driver who needs a DQC to drive without one. There are penalties for drivers and operators who do this. You're breaking the law if you're

- a driver and you knowingly drive a large vehicle without a DQC
- an operator and you cause a driver to drive a large vehicle without a DQC.

If they're found guilty of an offence, both the driver and the operator can be fined up to £1000.

Further information

You can get more information on Driver CPC at **www.gov.uk** or from the following

Great Britain
Driver and Vehicle Standards Agency
PO Box 280
Newcastle upon Tyne
NE99 1FP
Tel 0300 123 7721
Email CPCRE@dvsa.gov.uk
twitter.com/DVSAgovuk

Northern Ireland
CPC Section
Driver and Vehicle Agency
County Hall
Coleraine
BT51 3TD
Tel 0300 200 7861
Email dva@infrastructure-ni.gov.uk

⊙ Responsibility and attitude

As with any driving, being in charge of an HGV comes with a great deal of responsibility. A lorry is bigger and heavier than most other vehicles on the road, so it's especially important that you drive it safely.

Your vehicle will probably have the owner's name on display, and your driving will also be on display. So, make sure that your driving is of the highest standard and that your vehicle is always clean and well maintained. You'll have worked very hard to gain your HGV licence, and to keep it, so be a credit to yourself, your company and your profession by showing skill and courtesy towards other drivers.

You could also take further training in fuel-efficient driving. The skills you develop will improve your safety and that of your vehicle, load and other road users. They'll help you build confidence in vehicle control and driving techniques, as well as reducing your stress levels.

Operators are seeing reduced overall fuel costs as drivers raise their level of professionalism and their knowledge of fuel-efficient driving. These drivers are an asset to their employers.

Appropriate behaviour

As a professional driver, you should set a good example to others. You should always have an idea of how other road users may see you. Be aware that they might not understand why you take up certain positions to make turns or take longer to manoeuvre.

You'll spend a great deal of time at the wheel of your vehicle, so staying calm and treating other road users with respect will make your working day that much more pleasant. A good attitude will help you to enjoy your work and make it safer for others.

Many operators participate in the 'How's my driving?' scheme. Each vehicle in the scheme displays a freephone number on the rear, so that other road users can praise or complain about the driver's actions.

Mood and emotions

Drivers who are tired, stressed or emotional have an increased tendency to take risks. If you're feeling anxious, angry or fatigued before you drive, take some time to clear your mind and relax before you start your journey. This will help you to focus on driving safely.

If you experience something that makes you angry while you're driving, try to remind yourself that arriving at your destination safely is more important than responding aggressively to other drivers.

Remember, everyone makes mistakes or misjudgements at times, which may cause others to take avoiding action. This is especially true of learner drivers. How you react is important, as it will affect the safe control of your vehicle. Be particularly alert in areas where side roads or parked vehicles obstruct your view. If something happens that means you have to stop quickly, be tolerant, stay calm and learn from the experience. You must resist the temptation to retaliate.

Always drive

- courteously
- with anticipation
- calmly, allowing for other road users' mistakes
- with full control of your vehicle.

You can't act hastily without the possibility of serious loss of control when driving a goods vehicle.

Intimidation

Don't use the size, weight and power of your vehicle to intimidate other road users. Even the repeated hiss from air brakes being applied while your vehicle is stationary gives the impression of 'breathing down the neck' of the driver in front.

The sheer size, noise and appearance of a typical goods vehicle can be intimidating to a motorcyclist, cyclist or even the average car driver. Travelling dangerously close behind a smaller vehicle (tailgating) at speed can make the driver of that vehicle very nervous. When it appears that a large vehicle is being driven in an aggressive way, other road users often feel threatened.

Effects of your vehicle

As a good lorry driver, you must always be aware of the effect your vehicle and your driving have on other road users.

You need to recognise the effects of turbulence or buffeting caused by your vehicle, especially when passing

- pedestrians
- horse riders (on the road or grass verge)
- cyclists
- motorcyclists
- cars towing caravans
- other lorries and buses.

Take extra care when you need to drive close to the kerb on congested roads in built-up areas, particularly in shopping areas or when near ice-cream vans or mobile shops. Be aware of

- the possibility of a pedestrian stepping off the kerb (and under the wheels)
- your nearside mirror striking the head of a pedestrian standing at the edge of the kerb
- cyclists moving up on the nearside of your vehicle in slow-moving traffic.

On wet roads, slow down before you reach puddles and try to avoid splashing any pedestrians in the area.

Tailgating

As well as worrying other drivers, driving too close to the vehicle in front can severely restrict your view of the road ahead. You may not be able to see or plan for any hazards that might occur. The space in which you have to stop is also reduced – probably to less than the stopping distance for the speed at which you're travelling. This will greatly increase your risk of a collision.

Police forces around the UK are concerned about the number of incidents that are caused as a direct result of vehicles driving much too close to each other. Several of them have mounted campaigns to video and prosecute offenders.

In 2013, police officers were given new powers to stop drivers who are tailgating. They can issue these drivers an on-the-spot fine of £100 and three penalty points, or offer the alternative of attending a driver education course.

Tailgating can have commercial consequences for the business owner, as well as legal consequences for the driver. In an effort to improve the image of the transport industry, some large retail organisations are looking into whether distributors' vehicles have been seen repeatedly tailgating on motorways. This can affect a distributor's chances of winning a contract from that retailer.

Speed

You should always obey speed limits. Although distribution companies face greater pressure than ever to transport products to their destination quickly, don't allow your employer to set delivery targets that are unrealistic. You should never be under extreme pressure to meet deadlines.

You can't justify driving too fast simply because you need to reach a location by a specific time. A deadline is no defence in the event of an incident. Not only that, but your employer will be held liable for any death caused by dangerous driving if it's found that the company's regimes were behind the driver's behaviour on the road.

The horn

Goods vehicles are often equipped with powerful multi-tone air horns, but their use should be strictly confined to the guidance set out in The Highway Code – to warn other road users of your presence. Never use the horn

- aggressively
- between 11.30 pm and 7.00 am in a built-up area
- when stationary, unless a moving vehicle poses a danger.

See section 4 for more information about using the horn.

Headlights

To avoid dazzle, don't switch your headlights onto full beam when following another vehicle.

Don't

- switch on additional auxiliary lights that may be fitted to your vehicle unless the weather conditions make it necessary (they must be switched off when the weather improves)
- repeatedly flash your headlights while driving directly behind another vehicle.

Flashing your headlights lets other road users know that you're there. It doesn't mean that you wish to give or take priority. You may be misunderstood by others when using an unauthorised code of headlight flashing, and this could lead to a collision.

Never use the headlights or the horn(s) in anger or to intimidate another road user.

Driver distraction

In-cab technology can have a real effect on your ability to remain focused on your driving. Short tasks that require an easy response (such as changing a radio station) may not demand much of your concentration, but longer tasks (such as programming your sat-nav or answering a phone call) are very demanding and shouldn't be attempted on the move.

> **REMEMBER,** don't allow **any** distraction, large or small, to compromise your safety or that of other road users.
>
> You can find helpful advice about coping with distraction – and other human factors that can affect your driving, such as mood and emotions – in 'The Official DVSA Guide to Better Driving'.

Mobile phones

You **MUST NOT** use a hand-held mobile phone or similar device when driving, except to call 999 or 112 in a genuine emergency, when it's unsafe or impractical to stop.

Using any phone or microphone, even if it's hands-free, can take your attention off the road. It's far safer not to use any phone while driving.

Make sure that your mobile phone is switched off before you start to drive. Let your incoming calls go to voicemail, and stop in a safe place before checking your messages. Likewise, if you need to make a call, find a safe place to stop first.

If you're caught using your mobile phone while driving, you could have six points added to your licence or, if your case goes to court, you could be disqualified from driving. You may also receive a fine of up to £2,500.

For more information, visit

www.gov.uk/using-mobile-phones-when-driving-the-law

Cyclists

Over a quarter of cyclist deaths on UK roads are as a result of collisions with HGVs – and this figure rises to over half in London. Because cyclists are so vulnerable around lorries, you need to be very aware of the limited vision you have around your vehicle, due to its size and shape, and make every effort to overcome this limitation. Use your mirrors so that you have a constant picture of what's happening all around you. Always check any blind spots before you move away. Also remember that cyclists could be unbalanced by the buffeting effect of a large vehicle passing closely.

If you drive a lorry in or around London, you'll be expected to take part in the Safer Lorry Scheme. This scheme has been set up by Transport for London (TfL) to reduce the risk of vulnerable road users, such as cyclists, motorcyclists and pedestrians, being injured or killed by lorries on the capital's roads.

The scheme's measures include making sure that lorries have better mirrors (which have been designed to allow the driver to see cyclists more easily) and side guards to prevent cyclists from being dragged under the lorry.

Read more about the use of vehicle side guards in the DVSA guidance at **www.gov.uk**

⊙ Work organisation

Your route or delivery sequence may be set by your operator. Alternatively, it could be one of your duties to plan the most efficient route yourself, whether single or multiple drops are involved. Good scheduling and organisation are important in keeping down fuel costs and making sure that you have appropriate work/rest periods.

In many cases, you'll be the face-to-face contact with the customer on behalf of your operator. If you find you're going to be delayed while en route, it's important to let the customer know, so take any available contact details with you (but only make calls when it's safe to do so). The customer will appreciate being advised of any delay, and they'll be able to plan around your amended arrival time.

This is especially important if specific load/unload timeslots are necessary, due to space constraints at the customer's drop-off point. Any delays can also affect your working hours, rest periods and tachograph records, so keep track of where you are in your work/rest cycle. Remember that an apology, such as for a late delivery, can help to reduce a customer's anger or frustration. If goods are damaged, you should encourage the customer to describe the damage on the delivery note.

Delivery notes

Any delivery should have supporting paperwork that tallies with the load you're carrying. This will list the goods to be delivered, along with the customer's details. Always check the paperwork before you leave your base. There may be special instructions that need to be followed when you reach the customer's site.

On arrival at the delivery point, make sure that you have the paperwork to hand. The customer should check the goods against the delivery note during unloading. You'll also need the customer's signature and printed name (as some signatures are hard to read) on your paperwork. This is to confirm that the goods have arrived safely and to the customer's satisfaction.

Customer relations

Keeping the customer updated is also important from another point of view – it shows efficiency and customer care. This reflects well on both your operator and yourself, as you're seen to be taking an active role in helping the customer as much as possible.

Drivers become trusted company representatives and form a vital part of the customer service process. This can be especially important if there's a dispute of some sort; for example, faulty goods or a mix-up with the orders.

When dealing with 'just the driver, who only delivers the goods and knows nothing', the customer can become frustrated and angry. This could, in turn, affect customer–supplier relationships and result in lost business.

When dealing with 'the driver who's always helpful, courteous and can provide contact details when there's a problem', the customer sees efficiency and feels well looked-after. This develops good customer–supplier relationships and could result in further business.

Also important is the look of your vehicle – keeping it clean may help to improve the company's image. Remember that you're never 'just the driver'; as the person with customer contact, you have a responsibility to keep up the good image of the company. A helpful and courteous attitude is an important part of your work.

Telematics

Telematics is a system that collects performance information from a vehicle. An on-board computer can monitor such things as your driving style, vehicle efficiency, drivers' hours and load security. Global positioning systems (GPS) can also help with the general organisation of operations, allowing operators to track their fleets in real time.

The use of telematics is becoming more popular. It allows the operator to

- divert vehicles if a delivery point changes
- manage fuel consumption and costs
- pass up-to-date route information to the driver, helping them to avoid congestion and known trouble spots

- monitor the vehicle temperature
- monitor the safety and security of the vehicle and its load.

Telematics can also be used to identify driver habits that have an impact on vehicle running costs; for example

- unnecessarily changing gears in sequence
- using the accelerator when changing gear
- using the accelerator when starting the engine.

Freight transport modes

The different ways that goods and materials can be moved are known as 'transport modes'. Freight transport modes include road, rail, sea, air, inland waterway and pipeline. There are several factors to consider when choosing the most suitable mode of transport.

The shelf-life of a product may determine the best transport mode. For example, a consignment of expensive and perishable seafood, which landed this afternoon at a Scottish port and is needed by a customer in France tomorrow morning, may have to be sent by plane. In this example, distance, the product's short shelf-life and speed of delivery would all be taken into account.

Another example is the transportation of oil from the Middle East. Because of the enormous quantities to be moved around the world, the most practical and efficient mode of transport would be the use of pipelines and tanker ships.

Different modes of transport may be combined to reduce operational costs. For example, if a load needs to be delivered overseas, it may be cheaper and quicker to drive the load to a ferry port, then put it onto a container ship, rather than drive the vehicle itself onto a ferry. Also, there may be a choice of ways to move items – containers may also be transported as rail freight.

Supply chains and logistics

There are many types of supply chain; for example

- the food supply chain starts at the farm, where animals and crops are grown. It then moves on to food processing and packaging, before distribution to shops and supermarkets

- the petrochemical supply chain starts at the drilling rig, where oil is extracted. This oil is then sent for processing into products such as fuel and plastic goods, before distribution to retail outlets.

Supply chains depend on transport, and making sure the whole of the supply chain works efficiently is called logistics. In the UK, road freight is currently the most popular way of delivering goods to industrial, commercial and retail premises.

Therefore, the professional commercial vehicle driver plays a very important role in the operation of UK supply-chain logistics.

Types of operators

Haulage companies and owner–drivers who carry other people's goods for a living are known as hire-and-reward operators. These companies are also known as professional hauliers, distribution companies or third-party logistics suppliers. Such organisations can provide, for example, general haulage services or dedicated customer contracts including goods handling, warehousing and transport. Other operators include

- subcontractors – this is when a haulage company gives its customers' goods to other hauliers to deliver. Many owner–drivers make a living as subcontractors
- own-account operations – this is when manufacturers and service providers choose to deliver their own goods and materials, using their own drivers and vehicles
- freight forwarders – these companies, known as intermediaries, act on behalf of importers, exporters, or any other company or person. They organise the safe, efficient and cost-effective transportation of products. Many transport and logistics operators also offer freight-forwarding services.

Back-loading

Back-loading is when spare capacity in a lorry returning from a delivery is used to move loads to a destination along the route of the returning vehicle. These loads could be returns of your own goods, products from your customer or goods from a third party. Back-loading provides better use of fuel and maximum revenue by minimising empty running.

You'll need a national standard operating licence if you carry goods other than your own. The options for back-loads vary from forming a partnership or joining a supply-chain initiative, to contacting a return-load specialist. These organisations use the internet to match loads to available vehicles, and are also known as 'clearing houses'.

Before carrying any load, make sure it won't contaminate your vehicle or existing load. This may make it unsafe or dangerous to carry other goods. Be especially careful with vehicles that are used for foodstuffs. It's advisable **not** to carry any other types of products on vehicles that are normally used to carry foodstuffs, to avoid the danger of cross-contamination.

Some consignments have to be carried by specialised vehicles, such as in the chemical, fertiliser, cement and paper industries. However, specialised vehicles may find it harder to find a return load.

Specialised road-freight transport operations

Many products require specialist transport operators, with specially designed vehicles, to transport them.

Temperature-controlled goods

Frozen foods must be transported at temperatures below freezing point. It's essential that frozen food is delivered in refrigerated lorries and trailers if it's to arrive in good condition. Drivers should be trained in the operation of refrigeration units, as well as in correct hygiene procedures.

The same requirements apply to the movement of chilled and perishable goods. For example, fresh flowers are transported at controlled temperatures above freezing point.

Some highly dangerous chemicals also have to be transported at prescribed temperatures. Specially designed, temperature-controlled vehicles are normally used to carry these chemicals, and drivers must be fully trained in their use.

Road tankers and tank containers

Many customers want their goods delivered in large quantities, rather than in bags or drums, etc. Tankers and tank containers are an efficient way to do this. They also help to reduce packaging waste and product handling/storage costs.

On a road tanker, the tank (or shell, as it's often known) is permanently fixed to the lorry or trailer chassis. A tank container, on the other hand, is normally attached to the vehicle or trailer using twist-lock mechanisms. The advantage of this is that the container can be lifted onto or off the vehicle by crane or forklift. This means that the carrying lorry is freed up for other work while the tank container can continue its journey; for example, by ship or train.

Tankers and tank containers can be designed to carry solid materials (granules or powders), liquids or gases. Drivers must be properly trained in how to use the equipment and valves fitted to the vehicle.

There are many different types of tank and tank container; for example

- some need to be pressurised to assist in emptying (eg cement tanker)
- some empty themselves just by the effects of gravity (eg petrol tanker)
- some have to be raised like a tipper lorry to empty the contents. Drivers have to make sure this is done safely on level ground, using any fitted stabilisers so that the tank or tank container doesn't fall over.

You should never fill, transport or unload a tank or tank container unless you've been fully trained in the specific type of product and loading/unloading procedures. You must also understand the consequences of spillages and know what action to take. In such an event, human safety and the environment will be your top priorities.

REMEMBER, you should only use a vehicle that's been specifically designed to carry your load.

Bulk transport

Many types of bulk goods, such as solid coal, fertiliser, minerals, scrap and wastes, can't be transported in large quantities using tanks and tank containers. Instead, these are generally carried in tipper lorries or skips.

Like tankers and tank containers, bulk tippers and skips must be handled with skill and care. Open-top tippers and skips should be covered to prevent spillages that could cause environmental damage and other dangers to the public.

Intermediate bulk containers (IBCs) are an alternative form of bulk transport for liquids or granulated substances. IBCs are plastic or aluminium containers that usually hold 1000 litres of liquid.

Transport of livestock

In England, the principal legislation concerned with transporting animals is The Welfare of Animals (Transport) (England) Order 2006. There is parallel legislation in Scotland, Wales and Northern Ireland.

As a driver who may transport animals, you'll need to either

- receive specific training through your employer, or prove that you've already completed this training
- prove that you have relevant practical experience in caring for the animals.

Transporters on journeys of up to 65 km (40 miles) are not required to have vehicle authorisation or training and certificates of competence. However, they must comply with the technical rules on fitness to travel, means of transport and transport practices.

All animal transport vehicles are covered by general provisions on vehicle strength, size, ventilation, floor surface and roof suitability. For example, vehicles and trailers should have an anti-slip surface to prevent animals from falling. Livestock-carrying vehicles have movable panels that need to be adjusted to prevent animals from moving around freely. Loose animals are at greater risk of injury and would make the vehicle unstable.

More information can be found at
www.gov.uk/guidance/animal-welfare#animal-welfare-during-transport

As an experienced transporter of livestock, your operator should have the necessary information and guidance notes on all aspects of animal transport, such as

- authorisations required for the transport of animals
- relevant documentation (animal transport certificates and journey logs that need to accompany the animals)
- specific requirements for feeding, watering and rest periods for different animals
- cleaning and disinfection rules
- required driver training courses and competencies.

➡ Manual handling techniques

More than a quarter of all employee injuries reported each year are caused by manual handling – the moving or supporting of loads by hand or by bodily force.

To reduce the risk of an injury while manually handling loads

- follow appropriate systems of work (these are laid down for your safety)
- make proper use of any equipment provided
- inform the relevant person if you identify any hazardous handling activities
- make sure that your activities don't put others at risk.

Good techniques for lifting

Here are some practical points to remember when lifting a load.

Think before lifting/handling Plan the lift. Can handling aids be used? Where's the load going to be placed? Will help be needed with the load? Remove any obstruction beforehand. For a long lift, consider resting the load midway to change grip.

Adopt a stable position

Start in a good posture

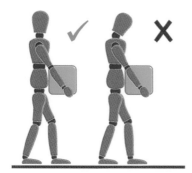

Keep your head up

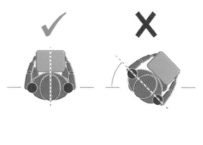

Avoid twisting or leaning sideways

Keep the load close to your waist Keep the load close to your body for as long as possible while lifting. Keep the heaviest side of the load next to your body. If a close approach to the load isn't possible, try to slide it towards your body before attempting to lift it.

Adopt a stable position Your feet should be apart, with one leg slightly forward to help keep your balance (alongside the load, if it's on the ground). Be prepared to move your feet during the lift to keep stable. Avoid wearing tight clothing or unsuitable footwear, which may make this difficult.

Start in a good posture When you're lifting something off the ground, always bend at the knees, not the waist. Your leg and stomach muscles are stronger than your back muscles and are more able to take the weight.

Get a good hold Where possible, the load should be hugged closely to your body. This may be better than gripping it tightly with hands only. Avoid twisting or leaning sideways, especially while your back is bent. Shoulders should be kept level and facing in the same direction as your hips. Turning by moving your feet is better than twisting and lifting at the same time.

Keep your head up Look ahead, not down at the load, once it's held securely.

Move smoothly The load shouldn't be jerked or snatched, as this can make it harder to keep control and can increase the risk of injury.

Don't lift or handle more than can be easily managed There's a difference between what people can lift and what they can lift safely. If in doubt, seek advice or get help.

Put down, then adjust If precise positioning of the load is necessary, put it down first, then slide it into position.

Good techniques for pushing and pulling

Follow these tips when pushing or pulling a load.

Handling devices The handle height of a barrow or trolley should be somewhere between your shoulder and waist. Try to push, rather than pull, when moving a load with a trolley. Make sure you can see over the load and can control steering and stopping.

Slopes Ask another person to help if you have to go up a slope or ramp, as the forces involved when pushing or pulling on a slope can be very high.

Uneven surfaces Moving an object over soft or uneven surfaces is also more difficult. Using a trolley with larger wheels could make things easier.

Stance and pace To make it easier to push or pull, keep your feet well away from the load and go no faster than walking speed.

Before using any specialist equipment (eg forklift trucks or overhead cranes), you must be fully trained in its operation. You should also keep any licences or certificates of competence relevant to such equipment up to date.

Ergonomic considerations

'Ergonomics' is the science of designing work equipment and furniture to suit the people who'll be using it. This includes how your driving seat is adjusted, how you hold the steering wheel, etc.

You may spend considerable time in the same position while driving your lorry, and what's comfortable for five minutes may feel very different after 90 minutes. You should make any necessary adjustments before you start your journey, especially if you're driving an unfamiliar vehicle for the first time.

Never adjust your seat while the vehicle is moving. Before starting the vehicle, you should check carefully that

- the seat position feels comfortable for you, and is locked in position
- the angle of the seat back provides suitable support for good posture
- the head restraint is in the correct position for your safety and comfort
- you can reach all the controls without straining or overreaching in any way
- you can see the road ahead clearly – it may also be possible to adjust the seat or steering wheel for height or angle
- the mirrors are correctly adjusted
- the seat belt is comfortable and in the right position across your body.

If you find any of the above can't be adjusted to meet your needs, you should ask your operator or the company health-and-safety representative for advice.

⮕ Diet and driving ability

Medical standards are higher for goods vehicle and bus/coach drivers than they are for car drivers. This is because people who drive for a living generally spend longer at the wheel than the average car driver. A lorry or bus would also do more damage to others if the driver became ill and lost control. So, it's important that you look after your health.

Your health and eating habits

Many common conditions, such as heart disease and diabetes, are linked to poor eating habits. Other factors, such as smoking and lack of exercise, increase the risks. These serious diseases can take many years to develop, and your dietary habits throughout your life will affect your chances of contracting them.

A sensible approach to food, fluid and caffeine intake can benefit your driving performance and safety in the short term and improve your health in the longer term. This will help to extend your career as a driver and reduce the risk of disability, early death or withdrawal of your driving licence on medical grounds.

The main ways in which your diet can contribute to future serious ill-health are

- excessive calorie intake, especially from sugars and fat – this can lead to obesity, which not only impairs your physical performance but is also linked to increased risk of late-onset diabetes, high blood pressure and heart disease
- intake of saturated fats – these are usually the hard fats (eg butter and lard), rather than oils (eg sunflower and olive oil). You can usually find information about levels of saturated fat on food packaging. High intake is associated with increased risk of arterial disease, leading to heart attack and stroke
- salt – while your body needs salt in small amounts, most western diets contain far more than is necessary. High salt intake can lead to high blood pressure and increased risk of heart disease and stroke.

It isn't always easy to know how much sugar, fat and salt is in our food. Pies and other processed foods may be very high in both salt and saturated fat, but these are hidden by the food's taste and texture. Cakes may contain large amounts of both fat and sugar. Even savoury foods often contain sugar.

Soft drinks, when they don't use non-sugar sweeteners, often contain very large amounts of sugar. This can be hidden by the acidity of other ingredients. Look at the label on the food or drink to see what ingredients it contains. You can then decide whether it's a healthy option.

A well balanced diet is essential to long-term good health. A moderate amount of protein is essential to your diet, but large quantities can add unnecessary fat and salt, and increase your cholesterol levels. So, include foods such as meat, cheese and eggs in your healthy eating plan, but keep them to a minimum.

Recommended protein portion sizes vary according to sources, but a general approximation of a single portion would be any one of the following

- 4 ounces (113 g) of meat, fish or poultry
- 1 ounce (28 g) of hard cheese or nuts
- two whole eggs.

Many traditional ways of serving proteins, such as frying, battering and in pies and puddings, can add unnecessary calories. Added fats should be limited to unsaturated ones such as sunflower or olive oil, or spreads made from these oils.

Fibre in fruit, vegetables and unrefined cereals makes you feel fuller for longer and may protect you against certain illnesses. It's recommended that you eat five portions of fruit/vegetables/salad each day as part of a healthy, balanced diet.

Diet and performance while driving

Your concentration can be improved by eating regular, light, balanced meals, timed to fit into your rest breaks, rather than snacking while on the move. Taking regular meals is also preferable to snacking when you're trying to control your diet. This is because, with the exception of fruit, most snack foods are high in sugar, fat or salt.

Meals containing proteins (such as meat, fish, eggs, cheese, peas or beans) and slowly digested foods (such as bread, rice, pasta and vegetables) will keep you satisfied for longer than those high in sugar, which give an immediate energy boost.

When driving through the night or on late-evening or early-morning shifts, it's very important to consider the timing and quality of your meals. Plan your meals to help you stay alert at work and to relax/sleep when you need to rest.

- Regular light meals are less likely to affect alertness or cause drowsiness than a single heavy meal.
- Choose foods that are easy to digest, such as pasta, rice, bread, salad, fruit, vegetables and milk products.
- Avoid fatty, spicy and/or heavy meals, as these are more difficult to digest. They can make you feel drowsy when you need to be alert. They may also disturb sleep when you need to rest.
- Avoid sugary foods, such as chocolate – they provide a short-term energy boost, followed by a dip in energy levels.
- Fruit and vegetables are good snacks, as their sugar is converted into energy relatively slowly and they also provide vitamins, minerals and fibre.

(Taken from the Health and Safety Executive website: **hse.gov.uk**)

Fluid intake

The amount you'll need to drink will depend, in part, on the temperature of your cab and the physical demands of loading and unloading. You should carry water in case of delays on the journey, especially in summer.

Water is the ideal drink: it quenches thirst for longer than drinks such as tea and coffee, which increase urine production. The only advantage of bottled waters over tap water in developed countries is their convenience.

The amount of caffeine in hot drinks can vary, depending on where you buy them. Caffeine from coffee, and to a lesser extent from tea, doesn't reduce sleepiness; it masks sleepiness and can keep you awake for an hour or so, but an increase in tiredness usually follows. Tea and coffee without sugar provide fluid and caffeine with few calories, but large amounts of caffeine can cause jitteriness and anxiety.

Branded soft drinks may contain caffeine and often contain a lot of sugar, so go for sugar-free or artificially sweetened options if you can.

> **REMEMBER**, if you're feeling sleepy, stop driving and sleep. Don't rely on caffeine, energy drinks or tablets.

Alcohol and drugs

Never drink alcohol and drive, because it will seriously affect your judgement and ability. There are strict alcohol limits for drivers and severe penalties for anyone found exceeding them.

It's also illegal to drive if you

- have illegal drugs in your blood
- are unfit to do so because you've taken either legal or illegal drugs.

For more information on drugs and alcohol, see section 3.

Section two

⊙ Understanding heavy goods vehicles

This section covers

- Understanding HGVs
- Forces affecting your vehicle
- Vehicle characteristics
- Vehicle limits
- Vehicle systems and maintenance
- Loads and load restraint

⊙ Understanding HGVs

You'll need to study and understand the information given in this book before you can consider driving a heavy goods vehicle (HGV). You'll also need to understand the characteristics of different types of HGV in order to drive them safely.

First, you must appreciate the main differences between small and heavy goods vehicles. These are

- weight
- width
- length
- height
- distance needed to pull up
- distance needed to overtake
- control needed when going downhill
- power needed to climb uphill
- the need to avoid any sudden changes of speed or direction.

Some of these differences will be obvious from the moment you start to drive an HGV. Others will only become apparent after you've gained experience. The essential thing to recognise is that much more forward planning and anticipation is needed to drive an HGV safely.

Whether a goods vehicle is laden or unladen, rigid, towing a drawbar trailer or articulated, it's most stable when travelling in a straight line under gentle acceleration.

Sudden or violent

- steering
- acceleration
- braking

can cause severe loss of control. All braking should be carried out smoothly and in good time.

Laden articulated trailer

Drawbar trailer

Articulated refrigerated trailer

Box van

Vehicles carrying loads

Harsh acceleration might cause an insecure load to fall off the back of a vehicle. If the brakes are used harshly

- the load will continue moving forward unless something stops it; the forces acting on any restraints will be increased
- the tyres may lose their grip on the road surface, causing the vehicle to skid
- the weight of the vehicle will be transferred forwards, causing the front of the vehicle to dip.

Any sudden steering movement may also cause the load to move. This is likely to make the vehicle unstable.

Jack-knifing

In the case of an articulated vehicle, severe braking can result in jack-knifing as the tractor unit is pushed by the semi-trailer pivoting around the coupling (fifth wheel). This is even more likely if the vehicle isn't travelling in a straight line when the brakes are applied.

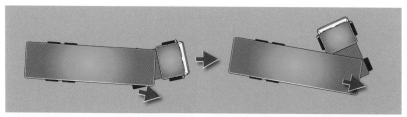

Jack-knifing

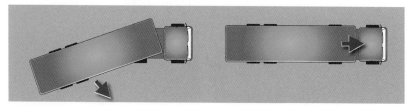

Trailer swing

Similar results will occur with a drawbar trailer, where there may be two pivoting points: at the coupling pin and at the turntable of the front wheels of a trailer with two or more axles.

Changing to a lower gear when travelling too fast or releasing the clutch suddenly can produce much the same effect, as braking is only applied to the driven wheels.

For some years now, systems have been available that reduce the risk of jack-knifing on articulated vehicles.

Trailer swing

Trailer swing can occur on a drawbar combination (or occasionally on an articulated unit) when

- sharp braking is applied on a bend
- excessive steering takes place at speed
- the brakes on either the tractor unit or the trailer aren't properly adjusted.

It follows that all braking, gear changes, steering and acceleration should be smooth and under full control.

⊕ Forces affecting your vehicle

Friction

The grip that rubber tyres have on a road surface is a result of friction between the two surfaces. This friction enables a vehicle to

- move away or accelerate
- turn/change direction
- brake/slow down.

The amount of friction determines the amount of tractive force that can exist between the tyre and the road surface. This will depend on

- the weight of the vehicle
- the vehicle's speed
- the condition of the tyre tread
- the tyre pressure
- the type and condition of the road surface
  - anti-skid
  - loose
  - smooth
- weather conditions
- any other material present on the road
  - mud
  - wet leaves
  - diesel spillage
  - other slippery spillages
  - inset metal rail lines
- the rate of change of speed or direction (sudden steering/braking)

- the condition of mechanical components
  - steering alignment
  - suspension.

You can ask too much of your tyres if you turn and brake at the same time, especially at higher speeds. Once any or all of the tyres lift or slide (that is, lose traction), you're no longer in control of the vehicle. What happens next will depend on the particular forces that are acting on the vehicle.

Sudden acceleration or deceleration can also reduce the grip your vehicle has on the road. Under these conditions, the vehicle may

- lose traction (wheelspin)
- break away on a turn (skid)
- not stop safely (skid)
- overturn.

Gravity

When a vehicle is stationary on level ground, the only force generally acting upon it (ignoring wind forces, etc) is the downward pull of gravity.

On an uphill gradient, gravity will affect a moving vehicle and its load so that

- more power is needed from the engine to move the vehicle and its load forward and upward
- less braking effort is needed and the vehicle will pull up in a shorter distance.

On a downhill gradient, the effect of gravity will tend to

- make the vehicle's speed increase
- require more braking effort to slow down or stop
- increase stopping distances.

A vehicle's centre of gravity is the point around which all of its weight is balanced. To keep the vehicle and its load stable, this should be arranged to be

- as low as possible
- along a line running centrally down the length of the goods vehicle.

The higher this centre of gravity occurs, the less stable a vehicle and/or its load will be. As a result, the vehicle and its load will more easily be affected by

- braking
- steering
- the slope (camber) of a road
- the vehicle tilting, resulting in either the load moving and possibly tilting or falling, or, in severe cases, the vehicle overturning.

End-tipper vehicles

When a loaded tipper-vehicle body (whether a tanker, bulk carrier or high-sided open body) is raised to discharge a load, the centre of gravity is raised to a critical position. It's vital to ensure that the vehicle is on a level, solid surface before engaging the hoist mechanism. Don't stand behind a tipper door, even if it appears to be closed.

Make sure that there are no overhead power lines in the vicinity. Keep clear of scaffolding or any other obstructions.

Side-tipper vehicles

Always select the firmest level site available before tilting the vehicle body. Until the load is discharged, all the weight will be transferred to one side. Unless the vehicle is on firm, level ground, there's a risk of it overturning.

Always take the time to check the ground before tipping. Get out and check all around the vehicle. Make sure that it's safe before you tip.

Safety issues

There should be on-site warnings for tipper drivers, alerting them to overhead cables and pipework. These can be in the form of goal posts, height gauge posts or barriers. However, it's always up to the driver to check before tilting the body.

Tipper vehicles may have extra safety features, such as audible movement alarms and inclinometers. These can warn the driver and others in the vicinity of potential load instability.

It's important for drivers of vehicles with forklifts, crane mounts and overhead lifting devices to check the area where the jib will lift and swing, especially when lifting loads in residential areas. You should avoid swinging the lifting device too quickly, as this will cause instability and may cause the vehicle to tip over.

These lifting devices are becoming more common because they reduce loading and unloading time. This leaves the driver less tired from the exertion of loading and unloading, and in better physical condition to drive the vehicle.

Articulated tipper vehicles help to reduce fuel costs because they can carry a larger load, reducing the number of journeys that have to be made. As the load is spread over more axles, they also cause less damage to roads.

Kinetic energy

Kinetic energy is the energy held by a moving vehicle. The amount depends on the

- mass (weight) of the vehicle plus its load
- speed of the vehicle.

Kinetic energy must be reduced by the brakes in order to stop a vehicle. The kinetic energy of a stationary vehicle is zero.

Momentum

Momentum is the tendency for a vehicle and/or its load to continue in a straight line. It depends on the

- mass (weight) of the vehicle plus its load
- speed of the vehicle.

The higher the speed, the greater the momentum and the greater the effort required to stop or change direction.

Cornering force

When a vehicle takes a curved path at a bend, the forces acting on it tend to cause it to continue on the original, straight course. This is known as cornering force.

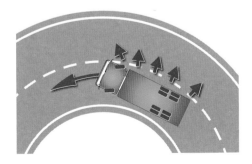

If a goods vehicle takes a bend too fast, cornering force will cause the load to be thrown towards the outside of the bend. If the load isn't properly secured, it may move and can even fall from the vehicle. The vehicle may also skid, especially if the road surface is at all slippery.

Forces on the load

If the forces acting on a load cause it to become detached from the vehicle, the load will move in the direction of the force.

While

- accelerating, it will fall off the back
- braking, it will continue moving forward
- tilting, it will topple over
- turning, it will continue on the original path and fall off the side.

There are significant weight and handling differences between a loaded vehicle and an unloaded vehicle. The factors affected include the

- handling
- road holding
- acceleration
- braking
- fuel consumption.

Stay aware of the feel and handling of your vehicle at all times. If you're on a multi-drop delivery, things might change dramatically as goods are delivered and the load distribution changes.

Shedding loads

When any change is made to a vehicle's motion or direction, the same forces will act on any load being carried. The load needs to be secured to the vehicle so that it can't move.

The following are common causes of shedding of a load (this list isn't definitive)

- driver error
  - sudden change of speed or direction
  - driving too fast

- instability of load
  - unsuitable vehicle
  - badly stowed load
  - movement in load
  - failed restraints
  - unsuitable type of restraint
- mechanical failure
  - suspension failure
  - tyre failure
  - trailer disengaged
  - wheel loss
- collision
  - another vehicle
  - a bridge, etc
  - lampposts
  - signs
  - signals
  - bollards.

Most of these situations are preventable. You should know the handling characteristics of the vehicle you're driving and drive in a manner that takes account of the forces affecting both your vehicle and its load.

Maintaining control

You can't alter the severity of a bend or change the weight of a load. However, you do have control over the speed and braking of your vehicle.

Reduce speed in good time, by braking if necessary, before negotiating

- bends
- roundabouts
- corners.

To keep control, you should ensure that all braking is

- controlled
- in good time
- applied when travelling in a straight line wherever possible.

Avoid braking and turning at the same time (unless manoeuvring at low speed). Look well ahead to assess and plan.

When turning a long vehicle, it's often necessary to straddle lanes in order to avoid mounting the kerb. Use all your mirrors to check all around your vehicle. Other vehicles might try to move up into the gap you've left, and vulnerable road users such as cyclists may be difficult to see, so make sure this area is clear before you start your turn.

Take up your position in good time and signal your intentions clearly. If you do hit the kerb at speed, check your vehicle as soon as possible for any damage to the steering or tyres.

(➡) Vehicle characteristics

You'll need to adjust the way you drive depending on the type of HGV you're driving. This subsection describes the key characteristics of each category of vehicle.

Short-wheelbase vehicles

These

- will bounce more noticeably than some long-wheelbase vehicles when empty. (This can affect braking efficiency and all-round control)
- shouldn't be pushed into bends or corners at high speeds simply because the vehicle appears to be easier to drive.

Long-wheelbase rigid vehicles

These require additional room to manoeuvre, especially when

- turning left or right
- negotiating roundabouts
- entering or leaving premises.

Typical examples of this type of vehicle are

- removal vans
- brick carriers
- bulk carriers (for aggregates, etc)
- eight-wheeler tankers.

Box vans

In addition to the extra space needed when turning, the box type of body, when lightly loaded or empty, is very susceptible to side winds on exposed stretches of road. Failure to heed adverse weather warnings may result in the vehicle being blown over. For this reason, high-sided vehicles are often banned from using certain roads and  bridges where these problems are known to occur.

It's essential to observe any temporary speed limits imposed during poor weather conditions.

Refuse collection vehicles

These vehicles are fitted with hoists to lift, empty and lower a 'wheelie'-type bin. Drivers need to take special care, as refuse collection often takes place in narrow or congested areas and can pose a danger to both operatives and members of the public.

Operatives should be fully trained in safe operating procedures. These include manual handling, safe standing positions, and the ability to recognise a risk when using the hoist equipment – for example, if a bin is overflowing or has unacceptable content.

In addition to the normal walkaround checks, any refuse collection vehicle with specialist equipment should be routinely checked for faults. This will help to

- keep the vehicle free from any residual waste build-up
- allow reporting and repair of faults before an injury occurs
- identify areas of misuse
- identify incompatibilities between equipment and job.

Your employer should have carried out risk assessments on the tasks associated with the use of refuse collection vehicles. You should have received appropriate training that takes the results of these assessments into account.

When driving your vehicle, you should always be certain that you've assessed all the dangers before manoeuvring. Never allow any operatives to ride on the outside of the vehicle, even for short distances. A fall from a moving vehicle is classed as a 'significant cause of injury', so reasonable steps must be taken to prevent this from happening.

Further advice on this subject can be found in the Waste Industry Safety and Health (WISH) Forum publication *Safe use of refuse collection vehicle hoists and bins*, which is available online at
wishforum.org.uk/wp-content/uploads/2019/06/WASTE-05.pdf

Articulated vehicles

Drivers of these vehicles should be especially vigilant before turning corners or negotiating roundabouts, because failure to plan ahead and choose the right course might result in the rear wheels cutting in. This could cause your vehicle to

- clip the kerb
- collide with street furniture.

It could also endanger

- pedestrians
- cyclists and motorcyclists
- other vehicles.

You should avoid overshooting left or right turns, because the stability of the vehicle is at risk if an excessive steering lock is applied in order to make a swan-neck turn.

Take care when moving out to take a bend – be sure there's no oncoming traffic. Signal in good time and watch for traffic behind that may try to come up on your left.

Articulated tankers

Roll-over

When an articulated tanker is driven on a curved path, the wheels on the inside of the curve may start to lift if the

* centre of gravity is high enough
* speed is high enough.

In many cases, this is followed seconds later by roll-over. The problem frequently involves tanker vehicles carrying fluids in bulk. It appears most likely to occur when modern, heavier and more powerful vehicles (and, in the majority of cases, those equipped with power steering) reach a critical situation.

It's important to remember that roll-over can also occur at really low speeds. As an example, the forces acting on a typical loaded articulated tanker negotiating a roundabout at a speed of about 25 mph (40 km/h) will cause it to overturn if only a further quarter turn is applied to the steering wheel.

You must be fully alert to the possibility of this happening. Adjust the speed of your vehicle to avoid wheel-lift and roll-over.

The driver training schemes for large petrochemical companies include specialised training to help prevent such incidents.

Vehicle design

The type of suspension fitted to a vehicle will influence its resistance to roll-over.

Modern tri-axle semi-trailers fitted with single wheels on each side have greater available tracking width than twin-wheeled units, and hence have improved resistance to roll-over.

Although vehicles equipped with air suspension systems are often considered to have better anti-roll stability than those with traditional steel-leaf spring suspension, tests have shown that their levels of stability are similar.

The wave effect

If drivers of certain tanker vehicles relax the footbrake when braking to a stop, there's a danger that the motion in the fluid load could force their vehicles forward. This is due to the wave effect created in the tank contents, especially where baffle plates are omitted from the tank design. Such tanks are sometimes found on vehicles carrying foodstuffs. Having baffle plates would help to reduce the wave effect but would make it difficult to clean the tanks.

Using walkways

Drivers of tanker vehicles must exercise special care when climbing onto walkways to gain access to tank hatches – not only to avoid injury as a result of slipping off, but also to avoid the danger of overhead cables, pipeways, etc.

Venting

All tanks must be vented according to instructions. This will avoid serious damage to the tanker body as the external air pressure becomes greater than the pressure within the tank.

Articulated car transporters

These vehicles have unique characteristics and require a high standard of driving.

The overhang created by the top deck swings through a greater arc than the cab of the tractor unit, particularly when negotiating turns. This means that there's a risk of collision with

- traffic signals
- lampposts on central refuges
- traffic signs
- walls and buildings.

Items such as mirror projections can also come into contact with

- pedestrians
- street furniture
- other vehicles.

You should plan ahead and take an appropriate avoiding line on the approach to turns when driving these vehicles. Before driving any large vehicle, you should identify specific overhangs and projections, and make sure that you use good all-round observation at all times. You should also check for any rear-end sweep.

The stability of these vehicles also needs to be considered. It's a case of 'last on, first off', so the lower deck may be emptied while there are still several vehicles on top. In such cases, the transporter's centre of gravity is shifted substantially.

You should be aware of the height of your vehicle at all times, especially if you're carrying vans.

Demountable bodies

This type of vehicle is similar to a container, except that the body is fitted with legs that can be lowered to enable the carrier vehicle to drive under or out.

Care needs to be taken to ensure that the

- legs are secured in the 'down' position before the carrier vehicle is driven out
- legs are secured in the 'up' position before the connected vehicle moves off
- height is correct and the body is stable before driving the carrier vehicle underneath
- surface is firm and level before demounting the body.

The legs are usually secured with a locking pin and safety clip or similar device. If the legs or securing devices are damaged in any way, leave the box on the vehicle chassis and report the defect.

Another type (often an open, bulk, high-sided body) is fitted with skids and is winched onto the carrying vehicle. Apart from the dangers of overloading, care must be taken when operating such winches.

The construction of these vehicles often means that the centre of gravity can be higher than normal when conveying a loaded skip. Take this into account, especially when cornering.

Double-decked bodies

These vehicles are constructed to give increased carrying capacity to box-van or curtain-sided bodies. They're only suitable for certain load types, but they help keep distribution costs down by making more efficient use of the available space.

Care must be taken to ensure that, when the vehicle is in transit, the lower deck isn't left empty while a load remains on the upper deck. Such a shift in the centre of gravity will result in the high-sided vehicle being even more vulnerable in high winds and, therefore, more likely to overturn.

Refrigerated vehicles

When driving refrigerated or 'reefer' vehicles carrying suspended meat carcasses, care must be taken to avoid the pendulum effect (where weight swings to one side of the vehicle) when cornering. Always reduce speed in good time.

The internal temperature of the van or trailer should be checked periodically to ensure it's correct. When the fridge fuel tank is independent of the main tank, make sure it contains enough fuel for the journey.

If the fridge unit fails, make sure that you have details of who to contact. Depending on how many drops/deliveries you have left, you may need to decide whether it's better to make your drops and get the fridge fixed later.

After loading or unloading a refrigerated vehicle, make sure that the doors are properly closed. Leaving them open will increase the temperature in the vehicle.

Also take care when working inside the body, as the floor may be wet, icy or slippery.

Light rail (or rapid) transit systems

Trams, light rail (or rapid) transit systems (LRTs) or 'metros' are being introduced in large towns and cities to provide a more efficient, environmentally friendly public transport system. They run on electricity, and reduce town traffic and noise pollution.

As a lorry driver, you probably won't drive these vehicles, but you still need to be aware of their limits and how to act in the areas where they operate.

Trams are sometimes completely segregated from other traffic, but they may also run on roads that are open to other traffic. As trams run on rails, their routes are fixed and they can't manoeuvre around other vehicles or pedestrians. They may run singly or as multiple units, and they may be up to 60 metres (about 200 feet) long.

The area occupied by a tram is marked by paving or markings on the road surface. This 'swept path' must always be kept clear. Other road users must avoid blocking tram routes. Be aware of the following

- In some towns and cities, certain roads are restricted to buses and trams only.
- Tram drivers and vehicles are subject to all the normal rules of the road, as well as specific rules on tram operation.

When a tram approaches, other vehicles (and pedestrians) must

- keep away from the swept path
- obey box-junction rules and not block junctions
- anticipate well ahead and never stop on or across the tracks
- obey all traffic-light signals and never jump lights that show the tram has priority.

Take care when driving under overhead LRT power-supply lines, especially when your vehicle has overhead lifting devices or crane mounts. Know the height of your vehicle and don't take chances. Also, whenever possible, you should avoid driving directly along metal rails, especially in wet weather, to prevent skidding.

Be cautious when you first encounter trams until you're accustomed to dealing with the different traffic system. Take extra care when

- tracks run close to the kerb to pick up or set down passengers
- lines move from one side of the road to the other.

Crossing points
Deal with these in exactly the same way as normal railway crossings. Bear in mind the speed and silent approach of trams.

Reserved area
Drivers mustn't enter the reserved areas for trams. This is marked with white line markings, or a different type of surface, or both.

Tram stops

Where a tram stops at a platform, either in the middle or at the side of the road, follow the route shown by road signs and markings. At stops without platforms, don't drive between a tram and the left-hand kerb when the tram has stopped to pick up or set down passengers.

Warning signs and signals

Obey all warning signs and signals controlling traffic. Diamond-shaped signs give instructions to tram drivers only. Where there are no signals, always give way to trams.

Do

- watch out for additional pedestrian crossings where passengers will be getting on and off trams. You **MUST** stop for them
- make allowances for other road users who may not be familiar with tram systems
- be especially aware of the problems of cyclists and motorcyclists. Their narrow tyres can put them at risk when they come into contact with slippery rails.

Don't

- try to pass a tram where the road space is insufficient for both vehicles side by side. Remember that the ends of the vehicle sweep out on bends
- overtake trams at tram stops in the street
- drive between platforms at tram stations. Follow the direction signs
- park so that your vehicle obstructs trams or would force other drivers to do so.

Examples of relevant signage are shown below.

⊙ Vehicle limits

The transport industry is subject to an extremely large number of regulations and requirements relating to

- drivers
- operators
- companies
- vehicles
- goods.

It's essential that you keep up to date with all the changes in road transport legislation that affect you.

The first thing you'll need to know about is your vehicle. The various aspects to consider are its

- weight (restrictions)
- height (clearances, restrictions, etc)
- width (restrictions)
- length (clearances, restrictions)
- ground clearance (low-loader or dual-purpose trailers only).

You'll also need to know the speed limits that apply to your vehicle and the speed at which it will normally travel.

Before moving any large vehicle, you should familiarise yourself with its limits, restrictions and clearances. Also be aware of any overhangs or mirror projections that may come into contact with street furniture, pedestrians or other vehicles. Use good all-round observation at all times.

Weight

It's essential that you're aware of, and understand, the weight limits relating to any vehicle that you drive. In many cases, these refer to the gross vehicle weight (GVW) or the maximum authorised mass (MAM) – see section 7 for definitions of these and other terms. Don't exceed either the vehicle's maximum weight or individual axle weights. The plate showing the MAM and individual axle weights of a vehicle could be located in the vehicle cabin, under the body panel or on the trailer chassis.

All limits must be complied with in order to avoid overloading and possible prosecution. Overloading your vehicle past its weight limits is not only dangerous but also means that the engine needs to work harder and, as a result, will use more fuel.

Roadside checks by the Driver and Vehicle Standards Agency (DVSA), the police and local authorities frequently reveal contraventions of weight-limit regulations. Both the driver and the operator are liable to prosecution if a vehicle is found to be overloaded on a public road.

Before you begin your journey, you should make sure that your vehicle hasn't been overloaded. Visual checks that you can carry out include

- a check of the vehicle suspension
- a check for any excessive leaning of the vehicle body
- checks for tyres touching/rubbing together or spray-suppression equipment touching the ground.

If you notice problems with any of these, or are in any doubt whatsoever, you should take your vehicle to the nearest weighbridge for confirmation before beginning your deliveries. Drivers are allowed to do this. They're then allowed to drive to a place where they can remove some of the load if the vehicle is found to be overloaded.

Loads must also be correctly distributed and secured to prevent movement while in transit. (See section 3 for more information about the safety of loads on vehicles.) Heavy items should be placed at the bottom of the load, with lighter items on top. In addition, heavy items should be distributed evenly along the length of the vehicle, so that individual axles aren't overloaded (see 'Calculation of payload', later in this section, for more details).

Articulated units and part-loads

To increase stability and reduce the risk of the trailer wheels lifting when turning, it's preferable to have part-loads (such as an empty single International Standards Organisation (ISO) container) located over the rear axle(s).

Recovery vehicles

Always make sure that axle loading limits aren't exceeded when a recovery vehicle removes another HGV by means of a suspended tow. This is sometimes overlooked.

Height

You must know the travelling height of your vehicle before setting off. If the overall travelling height of the vehicle, its equipment and load (including any trailer) is more than 3 metres (9 feet 10 inches), you as the driver must ensure that

- the overall travelling height is conspicuously marked in figures not less than 40 mm high in such a manner that it can be read in the cab, by you, from your driving position. It should be marked in feet and inches, or in feet and inches and in metres
- any height indicated isn't less than the overall travelling height of the vehicle.

A height notice isn't required on a particular journey if you're carrying sufficient documentation about the route or choice of routes. This should include the height of bridges and other overhead structures to allow you to complete your journey without any risk of collision with such structures. You must then travel on the route described in these documents.

When en route, remember that your vehicle height can change for a variety of reasons (adjustment of the fifth wheel; trailer loaded, unloaded or reloaded; diminishing load, etc). Avoid shortcuts to save time, as this could lead you to a low bridge. Stop and seek advice on an alternative route if you

- are diverted from your planned route
- realise that your route is obstructed by a bridge lower than the height of your vehicle.

For information on emergency diversion routes, see section 4.

Road traffic signs

If your vehicle exceeds the height shown on a circular road sign, you're legally required to stop and not pass the sign. You **MUST** find an alternative route to avoid the height restriction.

Maps are available that show signed height limits on public roads. Similarly, satellite navigation systems are available that can determine a route to avoid these signed restrictions, depending on your vehicle's height. However, you shouldn't rely on such systems or maps exclusively, as the information can become outdated at any time.

If your vehicle exceeds the height shown on a triangular road sign warning drivers of a height restriction ahead, you shouldn't pass the sign unless you know that you'll be turning off the road before you reach the restriction.

Overhead clearances

Drivers of any vehicle exceeding 3 metres (9 feet 10 inches) in height should exercise care when entering roofed premises such as

- loading bays
- depots
- dock areas
- freight terminals
- service-station forecourts
- any premises that have overhanging canopies when passing underneath
- bridges
- overhead cables
- overhead pipelines
- overhead walkways
- road tunnels

or when negotiating level crossings on lines with overhead electrification.

Electric cables

Height restrictions under overhead electrified cables may be temporary or permanent, and signs may warn of a permanent restriction in advance of railway level crossings.

Overhead electricity lines crossing public roads will normally be clear for a vehicle of 5 metres (16 feet 6 inches) in height – or 6.1 metres (20 feet) on routes designated by the Department for Transport (DfT) as high-vehicle routes. As high-voltage electricity can 'jump' across a gap, the wire will be positioned higher than this to allow for safe electrical clearance. This clearance must not be compromised.

The power-supply conductors for railways and tramways on public roads will normally allow clearance for a vehicle of 5 metres (16 feet 6 inches) in height unless signage on the approach indicates otherwise. At level crossings where the safe height is less than 5 metres (16 feet 6 inches), a height barrier will be provided in the form of a wire supporting bells. If your vehicle won't pass under this barrier, it's not safe to pass under the electrical line.

You **MUST** obey the safe-height-warning road signs and you **MUST NOT** continue forward if your vehicle touches any height barrier or bells.

When transporting a high load, contact the local electricity company to ask how much advance notice needs to be given to the electricity authorities concerned (at least 19 days). You should inform them of the load, routes, etc. See your local telephone directory for details or visit **nationalgrid.com**

Telephone wires
If your load exceeds 5.25 metres (17 feet 6 inches) in height, the telephone companies **MUST** be notified.

Street furniture
The local highways authority will need to be contacted where overhead gantry traffic signs or suspended traffic lights are likely to be affected by vehicles/loads over 5 metres (16 feet 6 inches) in height.

Low bridges
Every year, there are a significant number of incidents that involve vehicles or their loads hitting railway or motorway bridges. Bridge strikes happen for various reasons, such as

- drivers being unaware of their vehicle's height
- drivers not reading or obeying road traffic signs
- drivers relying totally on satellite navigation systems that don't include the locations of low bridges
- load movement

- drivers not positioning their vehicle in the centre of the road on the approach to an arch
- distractions
- poor lighting or poor traffic signage
- a lifting arm being left in a raised position.

Height guide	
Metres	Feet/inches
5.0	16 6
4.8	16
4.5	15
4.2	14
3.9	13
3.6	12
3.3	11
3.0	9 10
2.7	9

The headroom under bridges in the UK is at least 5 metres (16 feet 6 inches) unless marked otherwise. Signs showing height restrictions are generally provided at and in advance of bridges over public roads with less than this clearance height.

Where the overhead clearance is arched, the indicated height normally applies only between the limits marked and will reduce towards each kerb, so you may need to use the centre of the road when passing under the arch. Oncoming traffic may restrict the road width available, so give way until there's space for you to use the centre of the road in order to pass under the bridge. You mustn't swerve to avoid an oncoming vehicle when under the arch, as you'll strike the bridge. Stop and, unless you can reverse, wait for the other vehicle to reverse.

Bridge strikes

If your vehicle collides with a bridge, you **MUST** report the collision to the police. If a railway bridge is involved, report it to the railway authority as well by calling the number shown on the bridge identification plate or, if no plate is provided, call **999**. Do this immediately to avoid the possibility of a serious collision or loss of life.

THIS IS BRIDGE EGM1/001

Saughton Road

between Haymarket and Edinburgh Park

In the event of any road vehicles striking this bridge please phone

THE RAILWAY AUTHORITY on
0141 335 3399

as quickly as possible. The safety of trains may be affected.

Give your name and telephone number, as well as information about

- the road name, identification number and bridge location
- the damage and when it occurred
- whether the vehicle is wedged under the bridge and if persons are trapped or if you're carrying any hazardous or dangerous goods
- the vehicle registration number and owner's name
- your insurance details as the driver.

Failure to notify the police is an offence. If there's no plate at the bridge giving a telephone number, the police will advise the railway authority. The railway authority will take action, depending on the bridge, to protect the safety of the railway, so it needs to be able to identify the bridge involved.

Arrangements will also be made for the bridge to be examined to establish the damage caused and the requirements for repair.

You must inform your employers about the incident, as they must report to the traffic commissioners any incident in which road traffic offences have been committed.

Effects of a bridge strike

Striking bridges is potentially dangerous and expensive. You could

- be killed or seriously injured
- cause death or serious injury to another road user
- lose your job
- suffer serious economic loss
- cause serious disruption to the community.

Your company may lose its operator's licence and it will also be liable for the costs of bridge examination and repair.

Don't take chances. If you aren't sure of the safe height, stop and call the authorities. Always

- plan your route
- slow down when approaching bridges
- know the overall vehicle/load height
- keep to the centre of arched bridges
- wait for a safe gap if there's oncoming traffic.

Width

As the driver of a goods vehicle, you must be aware of the road space that your vehicle occupies. This is particularly important where width is restricted because of parked or oncoming vehicles. Look out for signs showing restrictions.

The width limit for vehicles and trailers is 2.55 metres (8 feet 4 inches). This is increased to 2.6 metres (8 feet 5 inches) for refrigerated vehicles or trailers, to allow for the extra thickness of the insulation. The exception to this limit is for locomotives, which have a width limit of 2.75 metres (9 feet 4 inches).

Traffic-calming measures are becoming much more common. Don't get into a situation where you're forced to reverse or turn.

Wide loads

Loads projecting over 305 mm (12 inches) beyond the width of the vehicle or those over 2.9 metres (9 feet 5 inches) but less than 3.5 metres (11 feet 5 inches) require side markers and notification to the police.

Wide loads that are over 3.5 metres (11 feet 5 inches) but less than 4.3 metres (14 feet 1 inch) require side markers, police notification and an attendant.

Wide loads that are 4.3 metres (14 feet 1 inch) to 5 metres (16 feet 6 inches) are also subject to the following speed limits

- 40 mph (64 km/h) on motorways

- 35 mph (56 km/h) on dual carriageways

- 30 mph (48 km/h) on all other roads.

Wide loads between 5 metres (16 feet 6 inches) and 6.1 metres (20 feet) require

- side markers
- police notification
- an attendant
- Department for Transport approval

and are subject to the above speed limits. Side marker boards must comply with regulations so that they show clearly on either side of the projection to the front and to the rear. All marker boards must be independently lit at night.

Length

Locations where length restrictions apply are comparatively few but they include

- road tunnels
- level crossings
- ferries
- certain areas in cities.

Drivers of long rigid vehicles (either with or without drawbar trailers) or articulated goods vehicles must be aware of the length of their vehicle, especially when

- turning left or right
- negotiating level crossings
- negotiating roundabouts or mini-roundabouts
- emerging from premises or exits
- overtaking
- parking, especially in lay-bys
- driving on narrow roads where there are passing places.

You must be particularly aware of the risk of grounding – for example, on a hump bridge. This will be indicated by appropriate traffic warning signs.

Maximum length limits		
Metres	**Feet/inches**	**Type of vehicle**
12	39 4	Rigid vehicles
16.5	54	Articulated vehicles*
18.75	61 6	Vehicle and trailer combinations**
18	59	Articulated vehicles with low-loader semi-trailer manufactured after 1 April 1991 (not including step-frame low-loaders)
Car transporter semi-trailers		
12.5	41	Kingpin to the rear
4.19	13 8	Kingpin to any point at the front
Other semi-trailers		
12	39 4	Kingpin to the rear
2.04	6 7	Kingpin to any point at the front
14.04	46	Composite trailer
12	36 4	Drawbar trailer with four or more wheels, and drawing vehicle is more than 3500 kg maximum gross weight
7	23	Other drawbar trailers

* Maximum length limit for vehicles designed to carry exceptionally long indivisible loads is 27.4 metres (89 feet 9 inches)

** See *Construction and Use Regulations* (The Stationery Office)

Level crossings

There's a risk of grounding long, low vehicles at some railway level crossings. A warning sign is displayed, with instructions to contact the railway controller. The vehicle must be stopped where indicated, and a phone call made to the number displayed or by using the dedicated telephone provided.

The driver must follow the instructions of the railway controller, and call back once the vehicle is safely clear of the crossing.

Large or slow vehicles

At some railway level crossings, drivers of large or slow vehicles, which might take an abnormally long time to cross, must contact the railway controller before crossing. The contact with the railway controller is the same as for long, low vehicles.

⊙ Vehicle systems and maintenance

Preventative maintenance

Carrying out daily walkaround checks (see section 3) will enable you to find any defects that could become a problem and cause the vehicle to break down or be illegal. The time taken to complete a thorough check will be less than that required to organise a repair or replacement while out on the road.

Brakes, steering and lubricants must be checked regularly. Having your vehicle serviced when recommended will help to prevent breakdowns and also helps the engine to work more efficiently, thereby saving fuel and reducing the effects on the environment. Follow the manufacturer's guidelines for service intervals.

Causing excessive exhaust emissions is an offence, and it also contributes to the possibility of a collision. If you notice thick black smoke coming from the exhaust, stop in a safe place and get help.

Technical support

Traffic commissioners and DVSA provide advice to operators on safety inspection intervals. DVSA offers a brake performance check, headlight alignment and an emissions check at all of its full-time HGV testing stations.

You can contact your local trading standards officer for a list of weighbridges currently in calibration.

Construction and functioning of the internal combustion engine

There are two main types of internal combustion engine

- spark ignition (petrol) – the fuel-and-air mixture is ignited by a spark

- compression ignition (diesel) – the rise in temperature and pressure during compression causes spontaneous ignition of the fuel-and-air mixture.

Both types of engine can be designed to operate using a two-stroke or four-stroke principle. Almost all modern goods vehicles use the diesel four-stroke principle.

The four-stroke operating cycle

Induction stroke

The open inlet valve allows the piston to draw in a charge of air when travelling down the cylinder. In spark-ignition engines, the fuel is usually pre-mixed with air.

Compression stroke

Both inlet and exhaust valves close and the piston travels up the cylinder. As the piston approaches the top, ignition occurs. Compression-ignition engines have the fuel injected towards the end of the compression stroke.

Expansion or power stroke

Combustion created throughout the charge raises the pressure and temperature and forces the piston down. At the end of the power stroke, the exhaust valve opens.

Exhaust stroke

The exhaust valve remains open. The piston then travels up the cylinder and the remaining gases are expelled. When the valve closes, the residual exhaust gases dilute the next charge.

Diesel fuel system

In compression-ignition (diesel) engines, the fuel-injection system, operated by the accelerator pedal, controls the engine speed by delivering a precisely measured amount of fuel at high pressure, in a fine spray.

Air is drawn into the combustion chamber, or more usually forced in under pressure by a turbocharger or supercharger. A turbocharger is an exhaust-gas-driven turbine, while a supercharger is a mechanically driven turbine. Both systems improve the engine's performance by increasing and maintaining power and torque over a wider range of engine speeds than in a normally aspirated engine.

Never use poor-quality diesel fuel. This may lead to increased wear of the injection pump and early blockage of fuel-injector nozzles.

In winter, cold temperatures can lead to 'waxing' or partial solidifying of diesel fuel. If this happens, the engine may not start or, if it does, it may run unevenly or stop. To combat this problem, diesel fuel is mixed with additives to lower the temperature at which waxing occurs. Winter-grade fuels should be perfectly satisfactory in all but very severe conditions. Electrically powered fuel-line heating systems are often fitted.

You should open the water drain valve, usually fitted to the base of the fuel filter, at least as frequently as the vehicle manufacturer recommends.

Bleeding of fuel systems

It may be necessary to 'bleed' the fuel system to remove any trapped air if

- the engine is new or has been renovated
- the fuel system has been cleaned or the filter changed
- the engine hasn't been run for a long time
- the vehicle has been driven until the fuel tank is empty.

Engine lubrication system

Friction reduces the performance and life expectancy of an engine. This friction increases when there's direct metal-to-metal contact between sliding parts. The engine lubrication system helps to reduce friction and wear by applying a film of lubricant (oil) to the various surfaces in the engine. This oil prevents corrosion of the engine's internal components, and removes the heat generated in the bearings or caused by combustion and absorbed by metal parts. It also seals piston rings and grooves against combustion leakage.

The engine uses a pressure-fed, full-flow, wet-sump lubrication system. The oil filter, which is normally disposable, contains a bypass valve that operates if the filter becomes blocked. The oil pump is driven directly from the engine. A pressure-relief valve in the oil-pump housing controls the oil pressure.

Oil is drawn from the sump to the oil pump via a wire-mesh pre-filter. From the pump, the oil circulates through the main filter, which collects sediment. The oil then passes to the engine bearings and other moving parts before draining back into the sump to complete its circle.

Always use the type and viscosity of oil suggested by the manufacturer. The oil should also be changed at the recommended intervals.

Checking oil levels

You should check the oil level frequently. Make sure the vehicle is parked on a level area, not on a slope, and check the oil while the engine is cold for a more accurate result. If your vehicle is fitted with automatic transmission, there may be an additional dipstick to check the level of transmission oil.

You shouldn't run the engine when the oil level is below the minimum mark on the dipstick. Don't add so much oil that the level goes above the maximum mark: this creates excess pressure that could damage the engine seals and gaskets and cause oil leaks. Moving internal parts can hit the surface of the oil in an overfull engine, causing possible damage and loss of power.

If the oil-pressure warning light on your instrument panel comes on when you're driving, stop and check the oil level as soon as it's safe to do so. If the level is satisfactory, there may be a more serious problem, such as failure of the oil pump, which would lead to severe engine damage.

Gearbox oil

Most vehicles have a separate supply of lubricating oil for the gearbox. This oil is specially formulated for gearbox use. Follow the instructions in the vehicle handbook.

Engine coolant

Liquid coolant is used to remove heat from the engine and transfer it, via the radiator, to the air outside the vehicle. It's generally recognised that mixing water with an approved coolant solution containing an anti-freeze additive will give your engine the best protection throughout the year. These solutions protect the cooling system from freezing in cold weather. They also contain a corrosion inhibitor that reduces oxidation and corrosion of the cooling system, prolonging its life.

Check the coolant level frequently; if you need to top it up regularly, this might indicate a leak or other fault in the cooling system. Never remove the cap on the radiator or expansion tank to refill the system when the engine is hot, because hot coolant or steam could be forced out at high pressure. Always allow the engine to cool before adding further coolant. Don't overfill the system, as the excess will be expelled as soon as the engine warms up.

Transmission system

Goods vehicles are fitted with either manual or increasingly, automatic transmission systems. A manual transmission system is made up of the clutch, gearbox and driveshafts. These components transmit the torque (turning force) from a vehicle's engine to the road wheels.

All transmission systems are vehicle-specific, so you should check the vehicle handbook for information about your system. However, to help you drive in the most efficient way, the rev counter (sometimes called the tachometer) on most vehicles is colour-coded. This gives an easy guide to optimum use.

The colours may vary, depending on the manufacturer, but as a general guide the bands and their meanings are

- **green** – normal use: adequate power and optimum fuel efficiency
- **amber** – occasional use when accelerating firmly
- **blue** – optimum use of engine braking
- **red** – driving within this section could damage the engine.

You should normally keep the rev counter within the green band when driving.

If the fuel is regulated by an engine management system, as it is on most modern vehicles, you don't need to press the accelerator to give additional revs when starting the engine. This causes excessive fuel injection and will waste fuel.

The clutch

The clutch temporarily disconnects/connects the drive between the engine and the gearbox. It enables the drive to be taken up gradually.

The normal type of clutch is a friction clutch. Its three main components are the driven plate (sometimes referred to as the clutch plate or friction plate), the pressure plate and the release bearing. The driven plate is clamped between the pressure plate and the engine flywheel by spring pressure.

The engine creates torque, which is transmitted from the crankshaft to the flywheel. The driveshaft, attached to the friction plate, transmits the torque to the gearbox. Depressing the clutch pedal operates the release bearing to relieve the spring clamping pressure and free the driven plate.

The life of a clutch can be prolonged by careful use and avoidance of 'slipping' or 'riding' the clutch. (Slipping the clutch means repeatedly applying and releasing the clutch; for example, to keep a vehicle stationary on a slope. Riding the clutch means keeping your foot on the clutch pedal as you drive along.)

Replacement of the clutch should be carried out before the driven plate becomes too worn, as further use could cause the flywheel to become scored.

The gearbox

The purpose of the gearbox is to

- control the torque being transmitted by the engine
- provide a means of reversing the vehicle
- disconnect the engine from the road wheels.

The gears in the gearbox allow the driver to vary the speed of the road wheels corresponding to any particular engine speed. This also varies the tractive effort applied through the tyres to the road to overcome the resistance to movement of the vehicle when moving off from rest, accelerating and hill climbing.

It's common for multiple gear ratios to be used in the gearboxes of HGVs and there's widespread use of semi-automatic and automatic gearbox systems to assist the driver and improve vehicle performance. In many systems, there's no need for a normal clutch pedal and vehicle movement from rest is achieved in response to movement of the accelerator pedal. Gear changing may be controlled by the driver (semi-automatic), hydraulically or, increasingly, through the use of electronic systems that change gear according to the requirements of the situation.

All manufacturers now use range changers and splitter boxes to change between the high- and low-range ratios. These use either the single-H layout (also referred to as four-over-four) or the double-H layout (also referred to as four-beside-four). The gear layout may vary according to the make of vehicle, so you should consult the vehicle handbook for guidance.

Older vehicles were fitted with gearboxes that required a driver to double-declutch when changing gear (see the glossary in section 7 for an explanation of this term). On modern vehicles fitted with synchromesh transmission, there's no need to double-declutch. Doing so can waste fuel and cause unnecessary extra wear.

When the vehicle is cold, you may have difficulty selecting a gear in a synchromesh gearbox. However, once the gearbox has had a chance to warm up, gear changing will be easier.

Types of gearbox
Splitter box
The splitter box is operated electrically but the gears are split in the gearbox rather than at the rear drive axle. A switch is fitted to the gear lever, allowing the driver to select a gear that's half a ratio higher or lower.

Range changer
The range changer is generally air-operated and the gears are split in the gearbox. Effectively, you can change through the gears twice: once in the low range, then again in the high range.

Unlike the splitter box, the gears may not be independently split. When reversing with this type of gearbox, it must be in the low range.

Electronic power shift
There are several similar systems that use a semi-automatic gearbox. They're simple to use and the gearshift lever is very small, with a splitter switch and a function button. The shift control is pushed forward to change up a gear, pulled back to change down a gear, and pushed left for neutral. An alarm will sound if an attempt is made to change down when the engine speed is too high.

Electrical system

Much progress has been made in the systems within vehicles, and most mechanical units are now controlled by electricity. In some vehicles, the wiring requirements are so extensive that a system called 'multiplexing' is used. This system is computer-controlled and uses a cable carrying electronic messages to switch equipment on or off. A power cable carries the main electric current to operate the equipment.

HGVs commonly use 24-volt lead/acid batteries to provide the power to start the vehicle. Once the engine is running, the alternator takes over and provides the electrical power needed for the vehicle's systems while also recharging the battery. The alternator is usually driven directly by the engine, via a belt.

Fuses of various ratings, depending on the equipment's power consumption, protect the electrical circuits within the vehicle. They prevent excess current from overloading the system and potentially causing an electrical fire. It's advisable to carry spare fuses, but make sure that you use a fuse of the correct rating and find out why the original fuse blew before replacing it.

Care should be taken when checking batteries, as explosive gases can build up and the dilute sulphuric acid used as an electrolyte will burn skin. Always follow the manufacturer's recommendations when dealing with batteries.

Braking system

Braking technology used on large vehicles

Most modern large vehicles are fitted with a full air-brake system or air-assisted brakes (a hydraulic system with air assistance). Smaller vehicles have vacuum-assisted hydraulic braking systems (sometimes called a hydraulic vacuum servobrake circuit).

Hydraulic brakes

Vehicles fitted with air-assisted hydraulic brakes use a compressor to provide high-pressure air. This air is used to assist the hydraulic system.

Vehicles fitted with vacuum-assisted brakes use either a vacuum pump or rely on the intake manifold depression to provide the force to assist the hydraulic system.

With either system, you should check

- the brake-fluid level as part of your daily walkaround check
- that no braking-system warning lights are illuminated.

Before you move off, you should press the brake pedal to get a feel for it. If it's too hard, this suggests a loss of vacuum or that the air compressor isn't working. If the brake pedal gives too little resistance and goes down too far, this suggests a loss of fluid or that the brakes are badly out of adjustment. If there are any problems, you should have the system checked by a qualified mechanic before moving off.

In addition, you should test the brakes every day as you set out. Choose a safe place to do this. If you hear any strange noises or the vehicle pulls to one side, consult a qualified mechanic immediately.

Air brakes

Air brakes use air, compressed by the vehicle's compressor, to enable great braking force to be applied at the wheels with little effort from the driver.

Air-brake systems draw their air from the atmosphere. This air contains moisture, which condenses in the air reservoirs and can be transmitted around a vehicle's braking system. In cold weather, this can lead to ice forming in valves and pipes and may result in air-pressure loss and/or system failure. Some air-brake systems have automatic drain valves to remove this

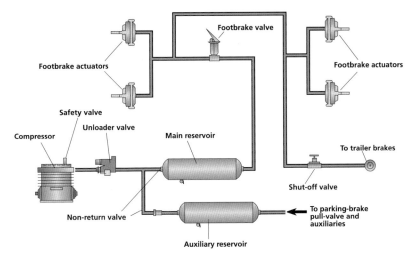

An air-brake system

moisture, while others require daily manual draining. You should establish whether your vehicle's system reservoirs require manual draining and, if so, whose responsibility it is to make sure this is done.

You should also make a physical check of the air system, ensuring the air lines are serviceable, and listen for leaks while the engine is switched off. You could also empty the air tanks by pumping the footbrake, then restart the engine and recharge the system. If you suspect a problem, seek expert help and don't start your journey.

Applying the brakes

It takes much more time and distance to stop a fully laden goods vehicle travelling at 56 mph (90 km/h) than it does to stop an ordinary motor car travelling at the same speed. You'll need to allow extra time and space to stop an HGV safely, so plan your braking and anticipate hazards. Don't follow other vehicles too closely – always leave a safe separation distance.

Harsh or heavy braking should be avoided when driving any HGV, especially when it's fully laden. Brake smoothly, in good time and while travelling in a straight line. Harsh braking can result in a vehicle's wheels locking, leading to a loss of control, particularly on slippery surfaces (for example, wet, icy or snow-covered roads). It also increases the vehicle's fuel consumption and the likelihood of its load shifting.

In an emergency, you may be forced to brake heavily. If your vehicle is equipped with an anti-lock braking system (ABS)* and you're unlikely to be able to stop the vehicle before reaching an obstruction, apply maximum force to the brake pedal, maintaining this force. You shouldn't pump the brake pedal, as this will reduce the effectiveness of the ABS system.

If your vehicle doesn't have ABS, wheel lock can be controlled during heavy deceleration by cadence braking (rapid pumping of the brake pedal).

Types of braking system

Three types of braking system are fitted to HGVs

- the service brake
- the secondary brake
- the parking brake.

The service brake is the principal braking system and is operated by a foot control. It's used to control the speed of the vehicle and bring it safely to a halt. It may incorporate an anti-lock braking system.

The secondary brake may be combined with the footbrake or the parking brake. It's provided for use in the event of the service brake failing. The secondary brake normally operates on fewer wheels than the service brake and therefore has a reduced level of performance.

You must always set the parking brake (handbrake) when

- the vehicle is parked
- you leave your vehicle unattended
- during the loading/unloading of goods or passengers.

A parking brake must be mechanical and is usually a hand control. The parking brake may also be your secondary brake but unless your service brake isn't working you should only use this when your vehicle is stationary.

Other types of braking systems such as hill assist, park assist and halt brake, are not substitutes for the parking brake.

HGVs are also frequently equipped with endurance braking systems (commonly called retarders) – see later in this subsection for more information.

* ABS is the registered trade mark of Bosch (Germany) for Antiblockiersystem.

Anti-lock braking systems

ABS is only a driver aid. It doesn't remove the need for good driving practices, such as anticipating events and assessing the road and weather conditions. You still need to plan well ahead and brake smoothly and progressively.

ABS systems employ wheel-speed sensors to anticipate when a wheel is about to lock. Just before the wheels lock, the system releases the brake and then rapidly reapplies it. This may happen many times a second to help maintain braking performance and prevent the wheels from locking. This allows you to continue to steer the vehicle during braking.

ABS is in common use on HGVs and is required by law on some. You'll need to know which vehicle combinations are required to have ABS fitted by law. Care needs to be taken to ensure that the braking system on the tractor unit or rigid towing vehicle is compatible with the braking system on the semi-trailer or trailer.

Electronic braking systems

Electronic braking systems (EBS) combine the operation of ABS and a load-sensing system, and offer a superior reaction time. The purpose of these systems is to improve vehicle control, reaction and stability during braking, over and above what is currently possible from a conventional pneumatic system. This is achieved by using electrical signals to operate pneumatic valves. A back-up system is usually retained in case of electrical failure.

If a vehicle with EBS is towing an EBS-equipped trailer, the two systems can communicate via a data bus. This offers improved tractor/trailer compatibility. On motor vehicles, EBS can also provide anti-slip regulation (ASR).

Checking ABS

It's important to ensure that the ABS is functioning before setting off on a journey. Driving with a defective ABS system may constitute an offence.

Modern ABS and EBS systems require electrical power for their operation. Multipin connectors carry the electrical supply to the trailer brakes. The satisfactory operation of the system can be checked from a warning light on the dashboard.

The way the warning light operates varies between manufacturers, but all types should light up when the ignition is switched on and go out when the vehicle has reached a speed of about 10 km/h (6 mph). On some vehicles, the braking-system warning lights aren't operated by the ignition switch. If this is the case, look for a 'check' switch on the dashboard.

Endurance braking systems

As the brakes reduce the speed of a vehicle, kinetic energy is converted into heat. Continuous use of the brakes can cause them to overheat and lose their effectiveness, especially on long downhill gradients. This is known as 'brake fade'.

Endurance braking systems, commonly referred to as retarders, provide a way of controlling a vehicle's speed without using the wheel-mounted brakes. This is particularly useful when descending long or steep hills. Using this system instead of the footbrake also extends the life of the vehicle's brake linings.

Retarders operate by applying resistance, via the transmission, to the rotation of the vehicle's drive wheels. This may be achieved by

- increased engine braking
- exhaust braking
- transmission-mounted electromagnetic or hydraulic devices.

Using an exhaust brake is beneficial to fuel economy. When the exhaust brake is applied, fuel delivery to the combustion chamber is halted. The vehicle is driven forward by its own momentum, so there's no need for fuel to be burnt. In addition, by making the engine work as a compressor, the combustion chamber is hotter than it would be if the driver were simply to take their foot off the accelerator and press the footbrake. As a result, when fuel is injected back into the combustion chamber, it will atomise more efficiently than in a cooler chamber.

Retarders may be operated with the same foot pedal as the service brake (an integrated system) or by using a separate hand or foot control (an independent system). They normally have several stages of effectiveness, depending on the braking requirement. With independent systems, the driver has to select the level of performance required.

While retarders generally apply the brakes in a more progressive way, you need to be aware that the wheels could still lock under certain conditions – for example, when driving on slippery surfaces. Some retarders are under the management of the ABS system to help avoid this problem.

Connecting brake lines

It's vital that you understand the rules that apply to connecting and disconnecting the brake lines on either an articulated vehicle or a rigid vehicle and trailer combination. You'll be asked to demonstrate this during your practical driving test.

There are two brake configurations that you may encounter: the three-line system and the two-line system. A three-line system comprises

- emergency line – **red**
- auxiliary line – **blue**
- service line – **yellow**.

A two-line system has only an emergency line and a service line.

Two-line vehicles and two-line trailers are obviously compatible, as are three-line vehicles and three-line trailers. A two-line vehicle can be connected to a three-line trailer (the trailer auxiliary line being left unconnected).

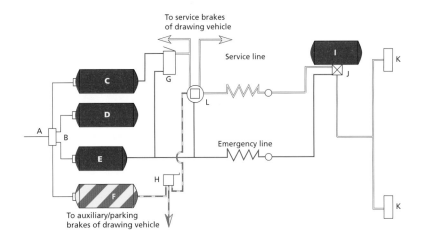

A – Supply from compressor	**E** – Service reservoir (trailer)	**I** – Trailer reservoir
B – Multi-protection valve	**F** – Parking/auxiliary reservoir	**J** – Relay emergency valve
C – Service reservoir (front)	**G** – Dual foot valve	**K** – Single diaphragm actuators
D – Service reservoir (rear)	**H** – Hand control valve	**L** – Trailer control valve (or triple relay valve)

Example of an acceptable two-line connection: two-line vehicle drawing a two-line trailer

When connecting a three-line vehicle to a two-line trailer, it's important that you follow the vehicle manufacturer's advice as to what to do with the auxiliary (blue) line. Failure to follow the manufacturer's instructions could render the combination dangerous.

When coupling a modern vehicle that's fitted with automatic sealing valves in the 'suzie' lines (see glossary in section 7), make sure that the trailer is equipped to activate them. Some older vehicles may be equipped with taps, or hand-operated valves. If these are fitted, you must ensure that they're opened after coupling the 'suzies' and closed before uncoupling them.

A number of fatal incidents have been caused by trailer brakes releasing as the air lines were connected. It's a mistake to believe that disconnecting the air lines engages the trailer parking brake; on some systems only the emergency brake is applied, and this will release as soon as the air line is reconnected – or over time, as air pressure is lost from the system. **Before connecting or disconnecting any brake line, make sure that the trailer parking brake has been correctly applied.**

Safety

Air-brake systems are fitted with warning devices that are activated when air pressure drops below a predetermined level. In some circumstances, there may be sufficient pressure to release the parking brake even though the warning is showing. In these cases, the service brake may be ineffective. You should never release the parking brake when the brake-pressure warning device is operating.

Towing vehicles are equipped with braking lines for attachment to a trailer. On modern vehicles, these lines are fitted with automatic sealing valves rather than manual taps. When a trailer is coupled to a towing vehicle, it's important to check that the brakes of the trailer function correctly. If they don't, remedial action must be taken **before** the vehicle is driven. Failure to do so could result in the loss of braking effectiveness on the whole combination.

Inspection and maintenance

You aren't expected to be a mechanic. However, there are some braking-system checks that **are** your responsibility.

Before each journey, make sure that all warning systems are working. Brake-pressure warning signals may be activated automatically when the ignition is turned on (as for ABS) or may require that you use a 'check' switch on the driving controls.

Never start a journey with a defective warning device or when the warning is showing. If the warning operates while you're travelling, stop as soon as you can do so safely and seek expert help. Driving with a warning device operating may be very dangerous and is an offence.

Action in the event of brake failure

If air pressure drops when driving a vehicle fitted with either full air brakes or air-assisted hydraulic brakes, there will be a warning light and/or buzzer to alert you. The warning will show while there are still sufficient reserves of air pressure to allow you to pull up safely.

In the event of total loss of air pressure on a full air-brake system, the brakes could be locked on. You may find yourself stuck in a position that causes an obstruction to other traffic. The brakes will only be released when air pressure is restored.

Some steep hills have an escape lane for traffic – particularly larger vehicles – travelling downhill. These lanes are most commonly situated on long downhill stretches of road and are for use in the event of brake failure. They're designed to safely slow or stop the vehicle through the use of an uphill gradient and/or gravel-filled arrester bed, either alongside or adjacent to the carriageway. These areas are not to be used for ordinary parking.

Emergency areas are different from escape lanes and are more commonly found on motorways. They're defined as a 'place or facility where drivers can stop in an emergency'. Again, these areas are not to be used for ordinary parking.

Tyres

All the tyres on your vehicle and any trailer must be in good condition. They need to be checked weekly for damage or wear, and they must be at the correct pressure. Follow the manufacturer's recommendations for the pressure required, and check the pressure when the tyres are cold (that is, before the vehicle is used).

The life of a tyre will depend on the load, the inflation pressure and the speed at which the vehicle is driven. Under-inflating a tyre will increase the wear on the outer edge of the tread area. Over-inflating a tyre will distort the tread and increase wear in the centre of the tread area. Keeping tyres correctly inflated will help to prevent failure and will also improve fuel consumption.

Check the tread depth carefully. Your tyres must have a minimum of 1 mm of tread in a continuous band throughout three-quarters of their width, all the way around their circumference. Also check regularly for any damage to the tyres. Any serious fault, such as a lump or bulge in the tyre wall, exposed ply or cord, or a deep cut more than 1 inch (25 mm) long, will make that tyre illegal for a large vehicle.

Driving at higher speeds for long distances (for example, on motorways) can cause tyres to overheat. A bulge in the tyre wall could mean that, at speed, the tyre may burst. This can scatter debris over a wide area, creating a serious hazard for other road users.

Check wheels and tyres for balance to avoid uneven wear. When a wheel and tyre rotate, they're subject to centrifugal forces. If the mass of the wheel and tyre is dispersed uniformly, then the wheel is balanced. Balance weights are used to rectify any imbalance.

When leaving building sites or other areas with loose debris, check between the tyres for bricks or other large objects that could damage your tyres or following traffic should they fall out.

Types of tyre

Radial-ply tyres have textile cords, arranged radially across the tyre almost at right angles to the width of the tread. The tyre walls are quite supple and a rubber-covered steel-mesh belt, which runs around the tyre underneath the tread rubber, braces the tread area. The belt keeps the tread in flat contact with the road to improve traction and grip.

Energy-saving tyres have reduced rolling resistance, so they contribute to better fuel economy.

Commercial vehicles with tubeless tyres use metal valve stems fitted to the wheel rim. Either an O-ring or a flat-flanged rubber washer makes the sealing airtight. Vehicles fitted with tubed tyres have an adaptor that's moulded to a rubber patch and vulcanised to the inner tube. The valve-stem casing is then screwed onto the tube adaptor.

Make sure that all tyres are suitable for the loads being carried. Tyres for HGVs and passenger-carrying vehicles (PCVs) have codes on their side walls, indicating the maximum load and speed capability. These must be appropriate for the vehicle's particular conditions of use.

Fitting a new tyre

Great care must be taken when changing the tyre of a large vehicle; you would normally call out a professional tyre fitter. However, it's still useful for you to be aware of the procedure involved.

- Select a firm, flat surface.
- Check that the parking brake is applied.
- Make sure that passengers or other personnel are clear of the area in which you're working.
- Check that the wheel isn't damaged and that another tyre can be fitted to it.
- Deflate the tyre before attempting to remove the wheel.

- Don't loosen or unscrew the clamping nuts if they're connected to divided wheel rims.
- Take care not to damage the flanges and locking rings when taking the tyre off.

Having checked the condition of the wheel, you should

- renew the complete valve whenever a tubeless tyre is being replaced
- fit the wheel to the tyre while the wheel is lying flat on the ground. This will enable the tyre to fit the rim and obtain a good airtight seal
- inflate commercial tyres in a cage or similar safety cell
- inflate the tyre to 1 bar level with the valve core removed
- insert a valve core
- inflate the tyre to the manufacturer's recommendation.

Changing a wheel

As a driver, you're unlikely to have to change a wheel. Many companies will only allow specialist fitters and breakdown organisations to change wheels. However, the following information may be useful.

- Where possible get someone to assist you. Never attempt to change a wheel by yourself on a motorway or dual carriageway, or in a busy location.
- Be aware of the danger from other traffic.
- Make sure the vehicle is parked on firm, level ground, with the parking brake on. Also use chocks if they're available.
- The jack or lifting device should be suitable for the height and weight of the vehicle.
- When refitting the wheel, fully tighten the wheel nuts to the torque recommended by the manufacturer, using a calibrated torque wrench. Tighten the wheel fixings gradually and alternately, moving from one to another diagonally across the wheel.

The wheel nuts should be checked shortly after any wheel change. This check should take place after 30 minutes if the vehicle has remained stationary or after about 40–80 km (25–50 miles) of driving.

Tyre management system

Professional vehicle operators should have a tyre management system in place. It should be used throughout the fleet and make sure that

- tyres in service are appropriate for the vehicle and operating conditions

- tyre age is monitored. Tyres over 10 years old **MUST NOT** be used on the front steering axle or axles of goods vehicles with a maximum gross weight of more than 3.5 tonnes. A tyre's age is proved by the manufacture date printed on the tyre. This date must always be legible. It's an offence to use a tyre where the date marking is damaged or defaced

- tyre pressures are maintained and monitored

- vehicle tyres are regularly examined with clear guidance on how to deal with any problems

- staff dealing with tyre management are trained and authorised to take action

- technicians dealing with tyre inspections or repairs are trained and qualified

- on-site tyres are properly stored

- drivers are trained and equipped to recognise and report tyre issues.

More information

Further information is given in the British Standard *Code of practice for the selection and care of tyres and wheels for commercial vehicles.* This has been developed with the support and involvement of the major transport operators' associations. The reference number is BS AU 50-2.7b: 2017, and copies are available from

British Standards Institution
389 Chiswick High Road
London
W4 4AL
Tel 020 8996 9001
Website bsigroup.com/en-GB/

Axles

Lifting axles

The more tyres a vehicle has in contact with the road, the greater the friction (rolling resistance) between vehicle and road. Using a lifting axle where appropriate can reduce rolling resistance and help to save fuel.

However, you need to make sure that the weight limits on the remaining axles aren't exceeded. You should lower the lifting axle when your vehicle is laden (assuming it doesn't deploy automatically).

Self-steering axles

These are fitted on the rear of trailer bogies or multi-axle vehicles and follow a similar course to the front steering axle. The rear axle is therefore able to follow the curve of the road as the front of the vehicle turns.

Some are free to move independently, while others have hydraulic assistance. They can reduce tyre scrub, increase tyre life and improve fuel consumption. There must be some method of locking them when the vehicle is reversing.

Coupling system

The coupling system, often referred to as the fifth wheel, is a device used to connect the tractor unit to a trailer. It permits articulation between the units. Guidance on the safe and correct way to uncouple or recouple a unit can be found in section 5.

Maintenance

The fifth wheel must be maintained properly to ensure safety. Inspection and lubrication should be carried out every 10 000 km (or every month). To do this, uncouple the tractor and clean the fifth-wheel mechanism, rubbing the plate and kingpin. Inspect the fifth wheel for damage and defects. Re-grease with clean, heavy-duty grease with a lithium or calcium base.

On a drawbar (also known as wagon and drag) unit, you should check the eyelet couplings regularly for wear or damage. Use heavy-duty grease to lubricate the couplings.

⊙ Loads and load restraint

When securing a load, you need to take into account

- the nature of the load
- the suitability of the vehicle
- the stability of the load
- the type of restraint
- protection from weather
- prevention of theft
- prevention of damage to the load
- ease of delivery.

You also need to consider how the weight of the load could affect the handling of the vehicle during transportation. The object is to ensure a secure load and a stable vehicle when braking and steering even in emergency situations.

Tyre failure on the vehicle or trailer shouldn't cause the load to become insecure. This is particularly important when stowing loads such as wooden pallets, hay, etc, which are usually stacked high on flat-bed vehicles.

Any load must be carried so that it doesn't endanger other road users at any time. It should be

- securely stowed, with the load centre of gravity as low as possible
- evenly distributed, so that excessive stress isn't applied to the restraints
- within the weight limits permitted for your vehicle
- within the size limits for the vehicle (unless clearly marked or proceeding under a special movement order under escort).

You should ensure that all devices for securing the load are effective: in other words, that all

- ropes, chains and straps are secure
- sheets are fastened down
- nets are securely fastened
- container locking handles are secured
- doors, drop sides and tailgates are fastened

- doors and curtains are secure and unable to blow about, whether open or closed
- hatches on tank vehicles are closed to prevent spillage.

You should also prevent

- material falling from bulk cement vehicles
- any nets covering skip loads being lost.

You should make sure that other road users are aware of the length of your vehicle, particularly if the load you're carrying overhangs the vehicle. You must use triangular projection markers if the load overhangs by more than 2 metres (6 feet 6 inches).

Types of load

A load may be large and heavy, but that doesn't mean it will stay in place throughout a journey. Fatalities have occurred as a result of such items falling from a vehicle or shifting under braking or cornering. Loads should always be secured firmly and carefully.

When making a decision about the type of restraints to use, consider what might happen if you have to brake hard and swerve to avoid an incident. Your vehicle might have to negotiate

- roadworks
- a construction site
- a lorry park

where uneven surfaces may cause it to tilt.

Large plant and machinery

Carrying large machinery and plant, excavators, diggers, etc requires specialist knowledge and, usually, specially adapted vehicles. General rules and safety precautions include

- stowing equipment to give the lowest overall height

- butting the wheels or tracks against chocks and/or front and rear bulkheads (chains are the preferred type of lashing)
- preventing forward, rearward and sideways movement
- securing buckets and arms to prevent independent movement
- relieving hydraulic pressure by operating all controls with the engine switched off.

When loading a digger or other machine onto a low-loader trailer, you need to ensure that the weight of the main part of the machine is distributed evenly between the axles. On a digger, the arm should be kept as low as possible, with the bucket folded underneath and secured to prevent movement. The load should be restrained against forward, backward and sideways movement using chain or webbing lashings. All lashings should have some form of tensioning device.

Metal loads

Metal loads can take various forms, but they can be broadly divided into nine categories:

- long sections
- flat sheets
- large units and castings
- coils
- scrap vehicles
- scrap metal
- machinery and tools
- steel for concrete reinforcement
- combination of the above, ie mixed load.

All types of metal load should be handled with care and should have sufficient lashings in firm contact with the top surface of the load. If the load is stacked, it should be kept as low as possible, with heavier items at the bottom. No layer should be larger than the one below.

In general, small heavy items (for example, small castings) should be securely restrained and carried on vehicles with sides that are higher than the load and strong enough to withstand the forces generated by motion. Loads such as heavy steel sections or scrap metal should be secured to the vehicle by chains. Care should be taken to ensure that chain links don't damage the load, and that any lashings aren't damaged by sharp edges on the load. Corner protectors and sleeves should be used as necessary.

Some items, such as coils of wire, may come ready strapped to a pallet, but remember that such strapping is only sufficient to secure the coil to the pallet. It will be necessary to further secure the entire unit to the vehicle – securing just the pallet won't be sufficient.

Scrap metal can be a very diverse load. Loose items of scrap can be carried in sided vehicles with no additional means of restraint, provided that the headboard, sideboards and tailboards are higher than the load. Scrap vehicles can be difficult to transport because of the way that movement, caused by their own tyres and suspension, can affect stability. Chain or webbing lashings with tensioning devices should be used to secure them.

When transporting machinery and tools, larger pieces of equipment should be placed in contact with the headboard. Smaller items and tools should be boxed and secured to the vehicle body with anchored restraints. Excavators, plant and other types of heavy machinery should be secured using suitable chocks, straps and chains as appropriate. Don't rely on the weight of the machine alone.

Bundles of concrete-reinforcing mesh should have the lashings carefully located between the cross-wires, so there's no danger of damage to the lashing from the ends of the cross-wires. Bundles with smaller cross-sectional areas should be on top of the load, and placed so there's no overhang. Bundles of reinforcing bars must be secured in a manner suited to their individual shape and size, and the load planned to avoid any instability.

The restraints may need reconfiguration after delivery of a part-load. While it's essential to take into account any loading/unloading patterns when configuring a load, it's also vital that every part of a mixed load is suitably restrained.

Timber loads

Timber is a 'live' commodity that may swell, shrink or warp. This can lead to independent movement of part of a load if it's inadequately restrained. Any load should be placed against the headboard where possible. Bulk-packaged sheets are usually strapped or wired at each end; these straps should be checked for security, and further restraints used if any damage or insecurity is noted.

Loose timber, generally made up into standard sets, should be loaded to a uniform height. Light loads (for example, for retail deliveries) can be carried on sided vehicles, but the load height shouldn't exceed the height of the headboard, sides or tailboard. If it does, additional lashing must be used. In general, chain or webbing lashings are recommended, and these should be placed at points where the load is rigid. Large, heavy packs of timber should be secured by ratchet straps.

Timber can settle on a vehicle, so all types of restraint should be checked regularly and retightened as necessary. Any loose ends of timber at the rear of the vehicle should be secured with rope or webbing to minimise the 'whip' effect caused by excessive movement.

Round timber should be stacked along the length of the vehicle. Shorter logs should be positioned in the middle to ensure maximum safety. The outer logs must extend past the ends of the securing uprights by at least 300 mm (12 inches) and there shouldn't be any gaps between the logs and the uprights. Logs should be laid top to tail for even balance, with each pile lashed together. The lashing should be secured by a suitable device. Staples can be used in conjunction with chains.

Some rounded timber loads, particularly logs or trees, can spread sideways. It's important that vehicles are fitted with side stanchions that reach the height of the load, and which are capable of resisting any outward movement of the load. The top middle log should be the highest point of the load. This should prevent movement and limit the effect the load has on the vehicle's handling.

Loose bulk loads

Loose bulk loads are those that don't lend themselves readily to any form of packaging: sand, ballast, etc. These are usually carried in open-bodied vehicles.

This category also includes loads such as waste skips. Before lifting a full skip, a sheet or net should be secured over the contents to prevent items falling off.

Particular care should be taken with granular or flaked materials. There can be a danger of small quantities of material being blown from the top of the load compartment or falling through gaps in the bodywork. The load compartment should be covered if there's a risk of this happening. The type of cover to be used will depend on the nature of the load.

Dry sand, ash and metal-turning swarf are especially susceptible to being blown away, and should be covered by suitable sheeting. Mesh netting is suitable for loads such as builders' waste. With loaded skips, the driver can't control what's placed inside but is responsible for ensuring safe carriage of the skip and its contents.

When it's raining or snowing, certain loads can get wet and become very heavy. This is most likely to happen with open tipper lorries and sheeted or netted loads. Examples of the loads affected include sand and ballast, but other types of load can also be affected.

Loose loads within a container should be checked periodically, as these can move within the container while the vehicle is travelling up and down steep gradients, potentially overloading one of the axles.

Palletised loads

Palletised loads have two main problems to be considered: the stability of the load on its pallet and the securing of the pallet to the transporting vehicle. The strapping used to secure the load to the pallet is intended merely to keep load and pallet together. It isn't sufficient to restrain the load during transit. Both load and pallet must be secured to the vehicle.

Before loading, pallets should be examined for any damage or weakness. They shouldn't be used if there's any doubt that they're strong enough to withstand the load. Pallets should be positioned so that the load is balanced across the vehicle. If load space isn't fully utilised, pallets should be placed along the centre line of the vehicle, front to back, and closed up to one another to further restrict any movement.

The best way to secure palletised loads is to use nets and straps. However, the chosen method will depend on the vehicle type and size, relevant anchorage points, and load size and weight. Whatever method is used, lashings should be positioned to prevent movement of the pallets in any direction. Vertical and tipping motions can be prevented by a lashing placed across the top of the pallet load. Empty pallets should still be restrained and secured, as wind can easily blow them from a vehicle.

High loads

When transporting high loads, it's important to consider the danger from bridges or other structures across the road. Any vehicle fitted with equipment capable of exceeding a height of 3 metres (9 feet 10 inches) must be fitted with a visual warning device that tells the driver if the equipment has been left in an extended position.

Other loads

There are other types of load with special requirements for transport. For example, plate glass is often carried on vehicles with side frames attached, so the glass can stand up against the side of the vehicle within the frame.

Ultimately, the most important thing to remember about any load is that you, as the driver, are responsible for ensuring that the load is suitably and safely restrained throughout its journey. Follow any instructions provided by your operator and make sure your vehicle is adequate for the task, with sufficient and appropriate restraints available to secure the load you're required to carry.

Dangerous loads

Vehicles carrying certain dangerous goods, and other materials that may pose a hazard, are subject to detailed emergency procedures.

Drivers of these vehicles must possess (and carry with them at all times when driving the vehicle) an ADR vocational training certificate issued under appropriate UK regulations. This shows that they're licensed to carry dangerous goods by road. For more details, see section 3.

Compressed gases

Drivers of vehicles carrying compressed gases, especially at low temperatures (for example, liquid nitrogen, oxygen, etc), must comply with the regulations relating to the transport of such materials.

Plates and markings

Vehicles carrying dangerous or hazardous goods must have markings that clearly identify the load. This will help the emergency services to deal with any incident quickly and safely. The symbols on the back or sides of a vehicle should relate to the type of material that the vehicle is (or will normally be) carrying.

As the driver, you must make sure the correct symbol or mark is clearly visible on your vehicle. You should be aware of what each symbol means. (Some examples are shown in section 7.)

More information on the limits and regulations relating to the carriage of dangerous goods can be found in section 3.

Classifications

Dangerous or hazardous goods are divided into nine classes, as follows

- Class 1   Explosive
- Class 2.1–2.3   Compressed gases
- Class 3   Flammable liquids
- Class 4.1   Flammable solids
- Class 4.2   Spontaneously combustible
- Class 4.3   Dangerous when wet
- Class 5.1   Oxidising agents
- Class 5.2   Organic peroxides
- Class 6.1   Toxic
- Class 6.2   Infectious
- Class 7   Radioactive
- Class 8   Corrosive
- Class 9   Miscellaneous.

There are also a number of other products that are classified as obnoxious but aren't included in the list above. These include animal waste, hospital waste, refuse, pressurised gases or liquids, and asbestos.

When driving a vehicle carrying hazardous or dangerous goods, make sure you have with you all the necessary protective clothing, safety equipment and any documentation relevant to the class of goods being carried.

Always follow all safety instructions, procedures and training provided by your operator. If you're in any doubt, check with your operator to be sure you've had the most appropriate training and that your certificate is up to date. (Also see section 4 for information on carrying dangerous goods through tunnels.)

Fire or explosion

Where there's a risk of fire or explosion, it's especially important that all safety precautions are strictly followed.

The electrical systems of vehicles carrying petrochemicals and other highly inflammable materials are modified to meet stringent safety requirements. No unauthorised additions or alterations must be made to such vehicles. Any defects must be reported immediately.

Appropriate fire-fighting equipment must be available and drivers must be trained in its use.

Loading methods

It isn't possible to suggest loading methods for all types of load, in view of the diversity involved. However, the following paragraphs give some brief general advice. Whenever loading or unloading, the engine should be switched off in order to save fuel and in the interests of safety.

Rolls, drums and cylindrical loads

These should be placed with the axis across the vehicle if possible, so that the rolling tendency will be to the front or rear. Lashings should be used over each layer (plus sheeting to provide extra downforce on lighter loads; for example, cardboard tubes) and chocks provided to prevent backward movement.

There are alternative loading procedures. For example, if the length of the cylinders is less than twice their diameter, they can be placed on end. However, lashings must be used to prevent sideways movement, in addition to the usual cross-lashings. If drums need to be kept upright, it's best to secure them with straps. Tubular steel would be best restrained using chains or webbing straps with tensioning devices.

Boxes

Boxes should be tightly placed so they're prevented from moving in any direction, interlocking if possible and loaded to a uniform height. There should be at least one lashing for each row of boxes.

Sealed sacks

Sealed sacks should be laid on their backs, with alternate layers at 90 degrees (right angles) to one another. The load should be of uniform height, with at least one cross-lashing for each sack length. Loads of sacks should be sheeted if possible.

Material packed in plastic sacks and loaded onto pallets may be liable to slip unless shrink-wrapped or secured by banding. However, material in canvas sacks may well remain totally stable.

Open sacks

Open sacks (for example, those used for coal delivery) should be loaded to uniform height, with cross-lashings for each layer, and the overall load should be sheeted to prevent loose materials being lost from the vehicle.

Empty sacks

These can be hazardous if they fall from a vehicle in motion. They should be securely restrained to the vehicle platform.

Loose bricks

Both bulk mass and individual items should be restrained, and the load height shouldn't exceed the height of the surrounding body. This type of load may require purpose-made restraint systems.

Metal cages

Metal cages often have wheels or castors, which may not always have immobilisers. Cages should be restrained using a load-restraining bar to immobilise them in transit. Load-restraining bars can also be used as a safety measure to immobilise other types of part-load if necessary.

Mixed loads

Each part of the load should be secured by cross-lashings in a manner suitable for that type of load. Longitudinal (lengthwise) lashings must be adequate for the total load weight and separators must be used so that no part of the load can move forward independently.

For maximum stability, the load should be placed to keep the centre of gravity as low and as near to the vehicle's centre line as possible, along both the vehicle's length and width. Also, the load should be spread to give an even weight distribution over the whole floor area.

- Heavy articles should form the base and central part of the load.
- Light, crushable articles should form the top and sides of the load.
- Different-sized containers should be loaded with the smaller items placed centrally, and the larger items forming the outer walls of the load. Avoid projections beyond the vehicle's sides.
- Irregular shapes should be kept to the upper part of the load if it isn't possible to place them centrally.
- Dangerous substances that may interact should be segregated. Protect them from rain, and handle and stow them carefully to reduce the risk of damage to vulnerable containers. Load them so that the labels can be easily read. Make sure that you've gained the necessary vocational training certificate if you're going to handle hazardous substances.

Plastic containers

Plastic containers can become slippery if damp, so care must be taken when loading, securing and sheeting them – especially if dangerous substances are involved.

Glass

Fragile loads such as glass need extra care during loading and handling, and they must be secured with the most appropriate form of restraint. The most suitable vehicles for transporting glass are those with road-friendly suspension (see section 3). Large glass panels are often carried in specially constructed frame restraints mounted on the offside of vehicles involved in the glazing industry.

Bales

One suggested loading pattern for bales (for example, hay or cloth) is as follows

- The first two tiers should be loaded crosswise and the centre five bales secured to the vehicle.
- The third tier should be loaded lengthwise and each bale secured individually to the vehicle.
- If a fourth tier is necessary, it should be no more than two rows of bales, loaded lengthwise, with the front and rear bales secured to the vehicle.
- The whole load should be covered with sheeting if appropriate.

Dual-purpose trailers

Dual-purpose trailers have been developed incorporating

- a belly tank installed along the centre of the trailer for transporting fluids
- a flat-bed deck above the tank for the conventional carriage of goods.

In such instances, care must be taken not to rupture the tank below.

Load shift

During a journey, loads may shift – you may notice leaking liquid or hear noises that could indicate cargo moving inside your vehicle. If you suspect a problem, pull up at the nearest safe and suitable place to inspect the load.

Be very careful when opening doors or curtains. Stay aware of your own safety at all times, and follow any specific safety instructions given by your operator. The problem may be a minor one that you can easily and safely rectify yourself before continuing your journey. However, in more serious situations, seek advice and/or assistance. Don't resume your journey until the problem has been addressed.

Anchorage points

It's common practice to use the rope hooks that are bolted or welded to the underside of side rails/outriggers on most platform vehicles as the anchor points for the load-restraint system. However, rope hooks aren't subject to constructional standards, so they vary in strength, size and material content. They shouldn't be used to anchor loads, as they're rarely designed to withstand forces exceeding 1–1.5 tonnes. Many are so weak that they can be distorted by use of the ratchet buckle that tightens webbing straps.

Load anchorage points should be rated at capacities of 0.5 tonne, 1.0 tonne or 2.0 tonnes and beyond, and the capacity of each point should be indicated on the vehicle. Depending on the size of the vehicle and its load capacity, sufficient load anchorage points should be provided (with a minimum of three on each side) so that the sum of the capacity of the anchorage points on both sides of the vehicle isn't less than the maximum rated load of the vehicle.

Vehicles being carried piggyback must always have some form of chock applied to their wheels, in addition to a restraint. Never rely merely on a parking brake holding them in place. Each individual trailer should be secured to the one on which it rests and should also be secured independently to the carrying vehicle.

Headboards and front bulkheads

In most circumstances, a headboard, when present, can be treated as part of the load-restraint system. It should be capable of withstanding a horizontal force, uniformly distributed over its vertical area, that's equal to at least half the vehicle payload. It should be no less than the width of the cab, and equal to the width of the loading platform. The height should be sufficient to obstruct forward movement of the load the vehicle is designed to carry, unless adequate load restraint is provided by other means.

For loads such as metal bars, beams or sheet metal, the headboard must be adequately reinforced to resist damage from individual load elements.

Tubular loads such as scaffolding poles, lamp standards, extrusions, girders, etc may move forward with some force if emergency braking occurs. In such cases, the headboard on the vehicle or semi-trailer can be demolished, with fatal results. The load being carried should always be in contact with the headboard, for maximum benefit and for reasons of safety.

Calculation of payload

The payload is the maximum load you can carry and is equal to the maximum authorised mass (MAM) of the vehicle minus the kerbside weight, the weight of the crew and the weight of any driver's equipment.

For example, on a vehicle with a MAM of 40 tonnes and where the kerbside weight plus the weight of the crew and any extra equipment totals 10 tonnes, the maximum payload able to be carried would be 30 tonnes.

For definitions of weights, refer to the glossary in section 7.

Always remember that the kerbside weight doesn't take into account the weight of the crew and extra equipment, such as fridge and televisions. When loading the vehicle to (or close to) its capacity, the vehicle may need to be weighed with crew and extras to ensure it isn't overloaded.

Calculation of axle load

Maximum permitted gross axle weights are determined by axle spacing and tyre equipment. The formula for calculating axle loads is

$$\frac{P \times D}{W} = FAL$$

where

P = payload

D = distance from centre of load to rear axle

W = wheelbase

FAL = front axle load

In the image that follows, these figures are relevant

- the payload carried is 10 tonnes
- the distance from the centre of the load to the rear axle is 2 metres
- the wheelbase is 5 metres.

The calculation is $\frac{10 \times 2}{5} = 4$ tonnes

This means that 4 tonnes of the 10-tonne payload are being imposed on the road through the front axle. The balance of the payload (6 tonnes) is therefore being imposed on the road through the rear axle.

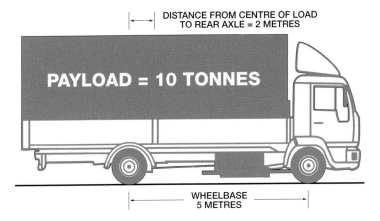

These figures only reveal how much of the payload is being imposed on the road. The operator must add axle kerb weights (the empty vehicle weight) to those figures to get the total weight being imposed on the road by the entire loaded vehicle.

If you suspect that your vehicle is overloaded, take it to the nearest weighbridge to check. Also see section 2 for more information on vehicle weight.

Axle weight limit

Permitted individual axle weights are shown on the vehicle plate. Operators have a responsibility to ensure that vehicles are operated safely and legally, and that the maximum weights shown on the plates aren't exceeded.

Using lifting axles

If your vehicle has a lifting axle, you should lower it when the vehicle is laden (assuming it doesn't deploy automatically). This is to avoid exceeding the weight limits on the remaining axles.

Diminishing payload

An area of concern is the diminishing load on a payload comprising two or more deliveries. The key point is that any loads put on a vehicle where the centre of the load is behind the rear axle will act as a counterweight to the front axle.

For example, two or three sections of a load could be placed on a vehicle in such a manner as to cause the front axle to be overloaded. A fourth section could then be placed on the vehicle with the centre of the load behind the rear axle. This could result in the front axle load being temporarily within the axle plated weight. When the fourth section was offloaded, however, the front axle would revert to being overloaded.

In this example, although the total weight of the load decreases, the remaining weight isn't spread evenly over the axles: unloading from the back increases the weight on the front axle. Therefore, care should be taken to redistribute part-loads during multi-drop journeys.

Consequences of overloading an axle

In addition to damaging the road surface, too much weight over the axle could lead to

- reduced braking power and, therefore, an increase in stopping distance

- increased likelihood of brake fade
- less vehicle stability
- steering becoming heavy, if the affected axle is a steering axle
- tyres overheating and failing
- legal consequences and possible prosecution.

If an enforcement officer finds that a vehicle is overloaded, this can result in a prohibition notice. This notice will prevent the driver from continuing their journey until the weight is corrected. Correcting the problem may involve the goods being redistributed (in axle overload cases) or unloaded to bring the weight down.

The driver will then be issued with a 'removal of prohibition' notice to allow them to continue their journey. In some cases, the driver may be issued with a 'direction to drive' notice, which allows them to travel to a specified place to off-load.

Legislation imposes an unlimited fine for each offence, ie each overloaded axle plus any overloading on the total weight. If the vehicle is dangerously overloaded, the driver could face a charge of dangerous driving, with a maximum penalty of two years in prison.

Other offences that carry an unlimited fine include

- refusal to allow a vehicle to be weighed
- obstruction of an officer.

If an overloaded vehicle results in someone being killed, both the driver and the operator could face a prison sentence for manslaughter or death by dangerous driving.

Use of gearbox ratios

Your use of the gears should depend on the load being carried and the profile of the road. For example

- when driving a fully laden vehicle, you may need to use all the gears (for example, when going uphill), as this requires more power. Using most or all of the gears will make optimum use of the available power
- when driving an empty or partially loaded vehicle, less power is required from the engine, so it may be possible to miss out some gears
- when driving downhill, it may be necessary to hold a lower gear to increase the engine braking. This reduces the need to use the brakes, and so reduces the likelihood of brake fade.

Safety factors relating to vehicle loads

Drivers should wear suitable personal protective equipment, which employers are required to provide where there's a risk to health and safety. This should be worn whenever necessary during loading, carriage or delivery of goods.

Regulations require drivers of

- tankers carrying dangerous goods
- tanker container vehicles
- vehicles carrying dangerous goods in packages

to hold a vocational training certificate issued by DVLA. They must carry this certificate whenever they drive the relevant vehicle. To obtain a certificate, you must attend and pass an approved course set by City and Guilds. The certificate is valid for five years before needing to be renewed by attending a refresher course.

Hydraulic lorry loaders and cranes have helped to reduce the number of incidents during loading or unloading of vehicles. This machinery saves loading and unloading time, and also helps drivers by reducing fatigue, so they're better prepared to drive the vehicle. When using a lorry-mounted crane or forklift truck to load and unload, be aware of any overhead obstructions.

Two codes of practice cover the use of lorry loaders as cranes

1. *Code of Practice for Safe Use of Cranes. Lorry Loaders* (BS 7121-4: 2010) – this is published by the British Standards Institution and is available from

British Standards Institution
389 Chiswick High Road
London
W4 4AL
Tel 020 8996 9001
Fax 020 8996 7001
Email cservices@bsigroup.com
Website bsigroup.com/en-GB/

2. *Safe Use of Lorry Loaders: CPA/ALLMI best practice guide* – this is published by the Construction Plant-hire Association (CPA) and the Association of Lorry Loader Manufacturers and Importers (ALLMI) and is available from

ALLMI
Unit 7b, Prince Maurice House
Cavalier Court
Bumpers Farm
Chippenham
SN14 6LH
Tel 0844 858 4334
Fax 0844 858 4332
Website allmi.com

Weather conditions

Rain can increase the weight of certain loads and could take the vehicle over its legal weight. Handling, stability and braking could be dangerously affected. This is most likely to occur with open tippers or flat-bed vehicles. The loads that are most at risk include

- sand
- rubble
- hay bales.

Types of restraint

It's important that the correct anchoring points are used, irrespective of the type of restraint chosen. Remember that the hooks fitted under some decks are only intended for fastening sheeting ropes.

Straps

These are generally made of webbing and are used to secure many types of load. Make sure that all straps, tensioners, etc are kept in serviceable condition. If a load has sharp edges, straps with suitable sleeves and corner protectors can be used.

Battens and chocks

Large, heavy objects such as metal ingots, castings, fabrications, etc should be chocked by nailing battens to the vehicle or trailer deck.

Chains

If there's any danger of either the weight of the load being too great for ropes or straps, or the load having sharp edges that would shear ropes or straps, then chains and compatible tensioning devices must be used. Chains are the best method of securing scrap metal to vehicles/trailers, or a scissor lift to a flat-bed vehicle.

Chains provide added security when tree trunks or logs are being carried. Don't rely solely on vertical stanchions to hold the load. However, chains of the split-link type, or those made of iron or other unsuitable materials, shouldn't be used, as they're less reliable than solid-link or steel chains.

Ropes

Traditionally, ropes have been the most common method of securing both a load and sheets. Ropes may be made of fibre or modern man-made materials, such as nylon, polypropylene, etc.

When using ropes, the ends should be spliced or otherwise treated to prevent fraying. The rope should be of at least three-strand construction, with a minimum normal diameter of 10 mm. There should be an attached label or sleeve, on which the manufacturer should have indicated the maximum rated load for the rope. Knots and sharp bends will reduce the effective strength, and ropes made of sisal or manila can be further affected by water saturation. Wet ropes should always be allowed to dry naturally.

Whatever type of rope is used, you should gain experience in the correct methods of securing the load. The knots used are known in the trade as 'dolly knots' (see illustration in section 7). These can only be released when required (and not otherwise). Additionally, you should ensure that the proper tension is applied and that the correct securing points are used.

Ropes are totally unsuitable for some loads, such as steel plates, scrap metal, etc.

When using wire ropes, it's recommended that the diameter shouldn't be less than 8 mm and the rope should be completely rust-free. If there are any broken wires or strands, **don't use the rope.**

Nets

Nets are sometimes used around loads as an additional means of containing items. They should be fastened securely to avoid the possibility of them coming loose and creating a potential danger.

Sheeting

If sheeting is used (whether tarpaulin, plastic, nylon or any other material), it must be secured in such a way that it can't become loose and create a hazard to other road users.

When covering a load with more than one sheet, you should start with the rear-most sheet and work forward. This type of overlap will reduce the possibility of wind or rain being forced under the sheeting as the vehicle travels along. This protection is especially important in bad weather conditions, and when carrying loose sand, etc, to prevent the load from being blown away. The same principle should be applied to folds in the sheeting at the front or sides of the vehicle, so that wind pressure will close any gaps, rather than open them.

To secure the sheets onto a load, you'll need to use the same type of knots used when restraining loads (dolly knots). These remain taut in transit but can be released with a minimum of effort.

All spare sheets and ropes must be tied down securely when not in use, so that they don't fall into the road and potentially cause damage to other vehicles or injury to other road users. When travelling with an empty vehicle, **all** restraints should be stowed securely.

You should check your load and securing devices periodically to ensure nothing has moved or become loose. A loose load could make your vehicle unstable and this could be dangerous for other road users.

> **REMEMBER,** take extra care when you're securing a sheet or net, as this can involve working at height.

Hanging loads

Hanging loads will move in response to vehicle momentum and change of direction. Fixed, hinged stops can help to restrict movement of a load such as hanging meat carcasses when in transit.

Curtain sides

The manufacturers of vehicles fitted with curtain-sided bodies may be satisfied that a high degree of protection is given by the material used in their construction. This doesn't, however, relieve the driver of the responsibility for ensuring that a load is properly stowed and secured so that it won't move while in transit. This is particularly important in the case of a multi-drop load of various materials, some of which may be classified as hazardous. Unless the curtains are specifically designed for that purpose, they must **not** be used for load restraint, only containment. Curtains mainly protect against the weather and provide a level of security.

Any rips or tears in a curtain should be repaired immediately. The torn material can flap about, thereby

- creating wind resistance (drag)
- increasing fuel consumption.

Take notice of weather warnings on the television, radio or online, especially if your vehicle is empty. Under such conditions, it's often safer to secure both curtain sides at one end of the vehicle, cutting down the wind resistance and removing the likelihood of being blown over or off the road. Make sure the curtains are tied securely so they don't come loose and flap around during high winds, as this could be a hazard to other road users. When the vehicle is fully loaded, keeping the curtains tightly closed reduces wind resistance and helps to save fuel.

Irrespective of vehicle type, once on the road, it's your responsibility as the driver to ensure that the load remains secure. In the case of curtain-sided vehicles, this would normally be confined to a periodic visual inspection of the curtains and a check of the tensioning straps.

If you notice that one side of the curtain is bulging, you must stop as quickly and safely as possible. The curtain might be the only support to a slipped load, so don't open it before checking. Enter the compartment by the rear door (or by carefully opening the opposite curtain if it shows no sign of bulging). Be aware of your own safety at all times.

Once the situation has been assessed, a judgement can then be made to either continue the journey if only a minor bulge is evident or, in the event of a more serious situation, to seek advice and/or assistance.

Container lorries

International Standards Organisation (ISO) cargo containers should only be carried on vehicles or trailers equipped with the appropriate securing points, which are designed to lock into the container body.

Such vehicles may be intended for carrying

* a single 12-metre (40-foot) or 13.7-metre (45-foot) container
* one or two 6-metre (20-foot) containers
* larger numbers of smaller, specially designed units.

Whatever type of container is carried, all locking levers (twistlocks) must be in the secured position during transit. When emptying a container, you should be aware that some of the load may have moved during transit and may be resting against the rear doors. Take great care when opening the doors, for your own safety.

Steel ISO containers shouldn't be carried on flat-bed vehicles that don't have any means of locking the container in position. Never rely on the weight of the container and its contents to hold it in place on a flat deck.

Ropes are totally inadequate to hold a typical seagoing steel container in place. Skeletal vehicles or trailers that have a main chassis frame with outrigger supports, into which the ISO container can be locked, are safer and more secure.

Ferry operations

When a vehicle is carried on a ship, the vehicle and load will be subject to forces due to the rolling and pitching motions of the vessel. It's important to note that a restraint system suitable for road use may be inadequate at sea.

The securing of the vehicle to the ship is also important. Vehicles should be fitted with lashing points that are of adequate strength to withstand the forces likely to be encountered at sea. These lashing points should be easily accessible to deck crews.

More information can be found in the Maritime and Coastguard Agency's *Roll-on/Roll-off Ships – Stowage and Securing of Vehicles: Code of Practice*, which gives guidance on securing vehicles on ships and an indication of the forces likely to be encountered at sea.

Unloading

If your vehicle is fitted with equipment for lifting and/or removing heavy loads, one of your main responsibilities prior to lifting is to ensure the vehicle is parked on firm, level ground. This will help to eliminate any possibility of the load becoming unstable during lifting.

Certain vehicles are fitted with stabilisers; for example

- those with a hydraulic lifting arm for moving skip containers
- those with crane mounts for delivering bagged or strapped loads such as sand or bricks
- recovery trucks that have hoists for lifting and moving other vehicles.

If your vehicle is fitted with stabilisers, you should make sure that all of them are in contact with firm, level ground and locked in position. The safety and stability of the load itself should then be checked before any unloading begins.

Take care when using lifting gear, especially where there are overhead cables and pipework in the area – see 'Forces affecting your vehicle', earlier in this section, for more advice.

For more guidance on the topics in this chapter, visit

www.gov.uk/government/publications/load-securing-vehicle-operator-guidance

Section three

⊙ Limits and regulations

This section covers

- Environmental impact
- Drivers' hours and records
- Operator licensing and the driver's responsibilities
- Driving in Europe
- Your health and conduct
- Your vehicle
- Your driving

⊙ Environmental impact

Transport is an essential part of modern life, but we can't ignore its environmental consequences – local, regional and global. Motor vehicles account for most of the movement of people and goods, and the increase in the number of vehicles on the roads has resulted in

- changes to the landscape
- air pollution, causing
    - human health problems (in particular, respiratory disease)
    - damage to vegetation
- building deterioration
- bridge weakening
- changes to communities
- the using up of natural resources
- disruption of wildlife.

There's increasing public concern for the protection of our environment. As a result, many motor vehicle manufacturers are devoting more time, effort and resources to the development of environmentally friendly vehicles.

When planning your route and delivery schedule, remember that local authorities can impose delivery restrictions to improve the local environment and quality of life. For example, this could mean preventing deliveries from being accepted or despatched during the night or early hours of the morning, to reduce noise disturbance to nearby residents. A local traffic authority can also make Traffic Regulation Orders (TROs) to restrict rights to use a public highway.

Exhaust emissions

Fuel combustion produces carbon dioxide, a major greenhouse gas. Transport accounts for about one-fifth of the carbon dioxide we produce in the UK.

MOT tests now include a strict exhaust emissions test to ensure that all vehicles are operating efficiently. If you drive a vehicle that's emitting lots of exhaust smoke, you're breaking the law and you risk being reported. If you become aware of excessive exhaust smoke from your vehicle, you should take steps to have the problem dealt with as soon as possible.

Diesel engines

Diesel engines are more fuel-efficient than petrol engines. Although they produce higher levels of some pollutants (nitrogen oxides and particulates), they produce less carbon dioxide (a global warming gas). They also emit less carbon monoxide and fewer hydrocarbons.

To improve exhaust emissions even further, ultra-low-sulphur diesel (or city diesel) can be used. Sulphur is the main cause of particulates in exhaust emissions, and it also produces acid gases. The lower the sulphur content in fuel, the less damage is done to the environment.

Alternative fuels

Compressed natural gas

Compressed natural gas (CNG) offers improvements in the quality of exhaust emissions produced.

Electricity

Trials have been taking place with electric vehicles for a number of years, but it's only recently that advances have been made in overcoming the problems of battery size and capacity.

Fuel cells

A fuel cell is a device that converts the chemical energy from a fuel into electricity through a chemical reaction of positively charged hydrogen ions with oxygen or another oxidising agent. Fuel cells operate like rechargeable batteries and produce few or no pollutants, but they have a greater range and better performance than most battery electric vehicles.

Hybrid vehicles

These offer the advantages of electricity without the need for large batteries. The combination of an electric motor and battery with an internal combustion engine gives increased fuel efficiency and greatly reduced emissions.

Liquefied petroleum gas

Liquefied petroleum gas (LPG) consists mainly of methane, produced during petrol refining. Vehicles can run on LPG alone or on both LPG and petrol (known as dual fuel). Benefits include low fuel costs, lower emissions and reduced wear to engine and exhaust systems. Disadvantages include cold-start problems and valve-seat wear.

Solar power

Needing only daylight to function, solar vehicles are small, light and silent, and they produce no emissions at all. However, they're slow and very expensive as yet, and improvements are needed so they can store energy for use in the dark.

Diesel spillages

Diesel fuel is extremely slippery, so care must be taken at all times to avoid spillages. Not only is diesel fuel dangerous to anyone stepping on it (especially when getting down from a vehicle cab), but it also creates a serious risk for other road users – particularly motorcyclists.

Take care when refuelling and ensure that all filler caps and tank hatches are properly closed and secure at all times. If you notice your fuel filler cap is missing, you **MUST** replace it before continuing your journey.

Don't be tempted to overfill your fuel tank, as this can contribute to fuel leaks. For more advice, see 'Helping the environment' in section 4.

Road-friendly suspension

Road-friendly suspension is required to be fitted to vehicles that are intended to carry increased weight. By replacing springs with some form of compressible material (usually air), the vibration caused by the impact of heavy goods vehicle (HGV) wheels on road surfaces is reduced. This, in turn, reduces the damage to

- the road surface
- adjacent structures
- under-road services (gas, water, etc)
- bridges.

It also has the benefit of reducing damage to goods in transit.

Specialised semi-trailers have been developed to carry fragile goods. When loading takes place

- the hollow trailer body is positioned to surround the racks holding a fragile load (eg glass)
- the body is lowered into place
- the load is secured
- the body is raised into the travelling position.

The whole process is carried out by controlling the sophisticated road-friendly suspension system on each trailer wheel assembly.

In some instances, road-friendly suspension can be retrofitted to vehicles. However, the vehicle will usually have to be equipped with additional compressed-air storage tanks, creating some additional weight.

Audible warning systems

As a goods vehicle driver, it's up to you to recognise the effects your vehicle, and the way in which it's driven, can have on the environment around you.

Reversing your vehicle can create a hazardous situation. There may be pedestrians in the area that you'll need to warn. There are various types of audible warning device that give a signal to others around the vehicle that it's reversing, such as a

- bleeper
- horn
- recorded verbal message.

These **MUST NOT** be allowed to operate on a road subject to a 30 mph (48 km/h) speed limit between 11.30 pm and 7.00 am.

Also take care when setting any vehicle security alarm. You only want such an alarm to sound when it's necessary – not by mistake.

> **REMEMBER,** using an audible warning device doesn't take away the need to practise good all-round observation. If you aren't sure whether it's safe to reverse, ask for a banksman to help you.

Dangerous goods

All hauliers transporting dangerous goods must now comply with international standards. The rules for vehicles, operators and drivers are set out in the Carriage of Dangerous Goods and Use of Transportable Pressure Equipment Regulations 2009, otherwise referred to as the ADR regulations.

Any quantity of dangerous goods transported in a tank or tank container must adhere to the ADR regulations. The rules for packaged dangerous goods depend on the category of goods, the size of the containers and the total load carried. More information on the different classes of dangerous goods can be found under 'Dangerous loads', in section 2.

Rules also relate to the safe parking of vehicles carrying dangerous substances: make sure that you're aware of them if you're driving these types of vehicles.

Equipment

All vehicles transporting dangerous goods must carry, as a minimum

- a wheel chock
- two warning signs or lights
- fire extinguishers
- high-visibility jackets and torches for the crew.

Operators will need to demonstrate the availability of this equipment at roadside checks, although it isn't part of the ADR annual vehicle inspection.

Annual vehicle inspection

Vehicles used to transport dangerous or hazardous goods must undergo annual checks to certify that they're roadworthy.

Certain dangerous-goods vehicles must have an extra test and certificate over and above the normal HGV roadworthiness test. This is known informally as an 'ADR test'. It ensures that vehicles comply with Part 9 of the European Agreement Concerning the International Carriage of Dangerous Goods by Road. Vehicle requirements vary according to the nature of the goods being carried.

Documentation and signage

The main requirements you should be aware of when transporting dangerous goods by road are that

- the sender of the goods must provide the vehicle operator with written information about the load, in the form of a declaration confirming the goods are in a fit condition for carriage
- the vehicle operator must provide the driver with documents containing details about the goods prior to loading. The details must include emergency information.

These documents must be kept in the cab during transportation of the goods.

You should always comply with any loading, stowing or unloading instructions. Certain dangerous goods may have to be segregated or aren't permitted on the same vehicle.

Keep all warning plates on your vehicle clearly visible; they should be covered up or removed if no dangerous goods are being carried.

Driver qualifications

The driver of any vehicle carrying dangerous goods should ensure they have adequate training or instruction to understand the requirements associated with transporting this type of load.

The following groups of drivers must have a vocational training certificate showing that they're licensed by DVLA to carry dangerous goods by road

- drivers of road tankers with a capacity of more than 1000 litres
- drivers of vehicles carrying tank containers with a total capacity exceeding 3000 litres
- drivers of all vehicles carrying explosives (subject to limited exemptions)
- drivers of all vehicles that are subject to the Carriage of Dangerous Goods and Use of Transportable Pressure Equipment Regulations 2009.

DVLA will only issue the certificate upon receipt of proof that the driver has attended a course at an approved training establishment and passed examinations set by the Scottish Qualifications Authority (which is the examining body for the whole of the UK). The certificate is valid for five years.

Enquiries about courses and certificates should be directed to the Scottish Qualifications Authority (see section 7 for contact details).

As well as having a vocational training certificate, drivers of vehicles carrying dangerous goods must have the correct driving licence entitlement for the vehicle they're driving.

What you can do to help

You have a part to play in reducing the impact that road transport has on the environment.

You should

- plan routes to avoid busy times and congestion
- anticipate well ahead
- cover bulky loads with sheets to reduce wind resistance
- switch off the engine when stationary in a queue for a long time
- drive sensibly and always keep within the speed limit (good driving habits save fuel)
- use the appropriate gear and avoid overrevving in low gears
- avoid rapid acceleration or heavy braking, as this leads to greater fuel consumption and more pollution (driving smoothly can reduce fuel consumption by about 15%, as well as reducing wear and tear on your vehicle)
- check your fuel consumption regularly
- use air conditioning sparingly – running air conditioning continuously increases fuel consumption.

You can find further information about environmentally friendly driving in section 4.

Your vehicle

Fuel consumption is influenced by the design of your vehicle.

- Cab-mounted wind deflectors, together with lower side-panel skirts, can lower the wind resistance created by large box bodies.
- Tipper bodies with prominent strengthening ribs on the outside can be plated over to give improved performance.
- A flysheet tightly fastened over the top of a tipper body (especially when it's empty) can reduce the drag effect.

You should also

- have your vehicle serviced as recommended by the manufacturer. This will help to prevent unnecessary breakdowns. The cost of a service may well be less than the cost of running a badly maintained vehicle. Make sure that your garage includes an emissions check in the service

- make sure that the engine is operating efficiently. Badly adjusted engines use more fuel and emit more exhaust fumes

- make sure that filters are changed regularly

- make sure that your tyres are properly inflated. Under-inflated tyres increase fuel consumption and can be dangerous. Over-inflated tyres tend to wear unevenly and so need to be replaced more frequently

- make sure that brakes are correctly adjusted

- make sure that diesel injectors are operating efficiently

- if you do any of your own maintenance, make sure that you send oil, old batteries and used tyres to a garage or a local-authority site for recycling or safe disposal. Don't pour oil down the drain: it's illegal, harmful to the environment and could lead to prosecution

- consider buying energy-saving tyres with reduced rolling resistance. These increase your vehicle's fuel efficiency and also improve its grip on the road.

Further information and publications can be found at **energysavingtrust.org.uk**

Traffic management

Traffic flow

Strict parking rules have been introduced in major cities and towns to help the traffic flow. Red Routes (see later in this section) are an example of this type of scheme. The rules have reduced journey times considerably.

Speed reduction

Traffic-calming measures, including road humps and chicanes, help to keep vehicle speeds low in sensitive areas. There are an increasing number of areas where a 20 mph (32 km/h) speed limit is in force.

Parking

Large vehicles have many blind spots, resulting in very limited vision when reversing. It's preferable to choose a parking space that you can drive into forwards and then drive out forwards, without having to use reverse gear. If this isn't possible, it's better to reverse into the parking space and drive out forwards.

Don't park your large vehicle where it could cause an obstruction; for example, on or near a zebra crossing. This will restrict the view of other road users and pedestrians, and it could easily result in someone being injured.

Verges

Vehicles with a maximum laden weight of more than 7.5 tonnes **MUST NOT** be parked on a verge, pavement or any land situated between carriageways without police permission. The only exception is when parking is essential for loading and unloading, in which case the vehicle **MUST NOT** be left unattended.

Whenever possible, it's best to avoid parking your vehicle on a grass verge. The weight will cause damage to the verge, which may even collapse under the vehicle's weight. Your vehicle might become stuck or even roll over. Also, as you drive away, mud and other debris may be deposited on the road surface.

For more information about environmental issues, visit

www.gov.uk/defra

⊕ Drivers' hours and records

Goods vehicle drivers' hours of work are controlled in the interests of road safety, drivers' working conditions and fair competition. A European regulation sets maximum limits on driving time and minimum requirements for breaks and rest periods. These are known as the EU rules. Drivers who break the rules are subject to heavy fines and could lose their licence to drive goods vehicles.

Altering drivers' hours records with intent to deceive, or tampering with tachographs, can lead to a prison sentence. Similar penalties apply to those who permit such offences.

EU rules

Keep up to date

The rules about drivers' hours are changing now that the UK has left the EU. The rules were still being confirmed at the time of print, so some of the information below may have changed.

You can find the most up-to-date information about drivers' hours on **www.gov.uk**. You should check back regularly to make sure you are following the latest rules. See **www.gov.uk/guidance/drivers-hours-goods-vehicles**

The rules

The EU rules apply to vehicles used for the carriage of goods, where the maximum permissible weight (MPW) of the vehicle – including any trailer or semi-trailer – exceeds 3.5 tonnes. They apply to national and international journeys throughout the European Union (EU), and are consistent with the rules adopted by many countries beyond the EU. Tachographs must be used under the EU rules.

Drivers of light goods vehicles with an MPW of 3.5 tonnes or less aren't required to keep daily records but must comply with the legal limits on daily driving time and daily duty time under the UK domestic drivers' hours rules (see later in this section).

Where a light goods vehicle of 3.5 tonnes or less has a trailer attached, increasing the combined MPW to more than 3.5 tonnes, then the EU rules will apply. Exceptions may arise due to the nature of the operations on which the vehicle is engaged. However, if none of the exemptions apply, then a tachograph must be fitted and used to monitor the hours worked under the EU rules.

Exemptions

The following are exempt from EU drivers' hours and tachograph rules. In most of these cases, the domestic rules apply

* vehicles with a maximum authorised speed not exceeding 40 km/h (just under 25 mph)
* vehicles owned or hired, without a driver, by the armed services, civil defence services, fire services and forces responsible for maintaining public order, when the carriage is undertaken as a consequence of the tasks assigned to these services and is under their control
* vehicles used in emergencies or rescue operations, including vehicles used in the non-commercial transport of humanitarian aid
* specialised vehicles used for medical purposes
* specialised breakdown vehicles operating within a 100 km radius of their base
* vehicles undergoing road tests for technical development, repair or maintenance purposes, and new or rebuilt vehicles that haven't yet been put into service
* vehicles or combinations of vehicles with an MPW not exceeding 7.5 tonnes, used for the non-commercial carriage of goods
* commercial vehicles which have a historic status according to the legislation of the member state in which they're being driven and which are used for the non-commercial carriage of passengers or goods.

In addition to the exemptions above, which apply to all EU member states, the following derogations have been implemented in the UK

* vehicles used or hired, without a driver, by agricultural, horticultural, forestry, farming or fishery undertakings for carrying goods as part of their own entrepreneurial activity within a radius of up to 100 km from the base of the undertaking

- vehicles owned or hired, without a driver, by public authorities to undertake carriage by road and which don't compete with private transport undertakings
- agricultural tractors and forestry tractors used for agricultural or forestry activities within a radius of up to 100 km from the base of the undertaking that owns, hires or leases the vehicle
- vehicles or combinations of vehicles with an MPW not exceeding 7.5 tonnes, used
  - by universal service providers as defined in Article 2(13) of Directive 97/67/EC of the European Parliament and of the Council of 15 December 1997 on common rules for the development of the internal market of community postal services and the improvement of quality of service to deliver items as part of the universal service, or
  - for carrying materials, equipment or machinery for the driver's use in the course of his/her work within a 100 km radius from the base of the undertaking, and on condition that driving the vehicles doesn't constitute the driver's main activity
- vehicles operating exclusively on islands not exceeding 2300 sq km in area, which aren't linked to the rest of the national territory by a bridge, ford or tunnel open for use by motor vehicles
- vehicles used for the carriage of goods within a 100 km radius from the base of the undertaking and propelled by means of natural or liquefied gas or electricity, the MPW of which – including the mass of a trailer or semi-trailer – doesn't exceed 7.5 tonnes
- vehicles used for driving instruction and examination with a view to obtaining a driving licence or a Driver Certificate of Professional Competence, provided that they aren't being used for the commercial carriage of goods or passengers
- vehicles used in connection with sewerage, flood protection, water, gas and electricity maintenance services, road maintenance and control, door-to-door household refuse collection and disposal, telegraph and telephone services, radio and television broadcasting, and the detection of radio or television transmitters or receivers
- specialised vehicles transporting circus and funfair equipment
- specially fitted mobile project vehicles, the primary purpose of which is use as an educational facility when stationary

- vehicles used for milk collection from farms and the return to farms of milk containers or milk products intended for animal feed
- vehicles used for carrying animal waste or carcasses which aren't intended for human consumption
- vehicles used exclusively on roads inside hub facilities such as ports, interports and railway terminals
- vehicles used for the carriage of live animals from farms to local markets and vice versa, or from markets to local slaughterhouses, within a radius of up to 100 km
- vehicles operated by the Royal National Lifeboat Institution (RNLI)
- vehicles manufactured before 1 January 1947
- vehicles propelled by steam
- vehicles used for the provision of ambulance services by, or at the request of, a National Health Service (NHS) body
- vehicles used to transport organs, blood, equipment, medical supplies or personnel by, or at the request of, an NHS body
- vehicles used by a local authority to provide services for old persons or for mentally or physically handicapped persons
- vehicles used by HM Coastguard and lighthouse services
- vehicles used for maintaining railways by the railway authority or by any holder of a network licence which is a company wholly owned by the Crown, Transport for London (or a wholly owned subsidiary), a Passenger Transport Executive or a local authority
- vehicles used by the British Waterways Board when engaged in maintaining navigable waterways.

Additionally, drivers who are members of the Territorial Army or Cadet Corps instructors have limited exemption from daily and weekly rest requirements in certain circumstances. Further information can be obtained from the Driver and Vehicle Standards Agency (DVSA – see section 7 for contact details).

Analogue tachographs

When driving under the EU rules, drivers' hours and rest periods are monitored by means of a tachograph. A tachograph is a device that records the time spent on driving, other work, breaks and rest periods. It can also record the distance covered and the speed at which the vehicle travels.

135

In the case of analogue tachographs, this information is recorded on a paper chart that's inserted into the tachograph.

The tachograph must be properly calibrated and sealed by an approved vehicle manufacturer or calibration centre. It must be checked every two years, at a calibration centre approved by the Department for Transport (DfT) or the Driver and Vehicle Agency (DVA) in Northern Ireland, and recalibrated every six years. A plaque either on or near the tachograph will say when the checks were last carried out.

If there's anything wrong with the tachograph, it should be replaced or repaired by a DfT/DVA-approved centre as soon as possible. If the vehicle can't return to base within seven days of failure of the tachograph or the discovery of its defective operation, the repair must be carried out during the journey. While it's broken, you must keep a written manual record either on the charts or on a temporary chart to be attached to the charts.

Charts

You must carry enough charts with you for the whole of your journey. You'll need one for every 24 hours. You should also carry some spares in case the charts become dirty or damaged, or in case your chart is retained by an authorised inspecting officer. Your employer is responsible for giving you enough clean charts, of an approved type, for the tachograph installed in the vehicle.

You, the driver, must ensure that the correct information is recorded on the charts. You must enter on the chart

- your surname and first name (you should do this before departure)
- the date and the place where use of the chart begins (before departure) and ends (after arrival)
- the registration number(s) of the vehicle(s) driven during the use of the chart (this should be entered before departing in a different vehicle)
- the odometer reading at the start of the first journey and at the end of the last journey shown on the chart (and the readings at the time of any change of vehicle)
- the time of any change of vehicle.

Recording information

The tachograph will start recording onto the chart as soon as it's inserted.

You must make sure that the time recorded on the chart is the official time of the vehicle's country of registration and that the mode switch is in the appropriate position. The modes are shown as symbols.

⊘	Driving (this is automatically recorded on some tachographs)
✕	Other work
▱	Periods of availability (POA) (only when length is known in advance)
⊢⌐	Break or rest

Under 'other work', you should include time spent on daily vehicle walkaround checks, attending training courses, loading and unloading, and travelling (when requested by the employer) to join or leave the vehicle.

If you drive more than one vehicle in one day, you must take your chart with you and use it in the next vehicle. If for some reason the equipment in the other vehicle isn't compatible, you should use another chart.

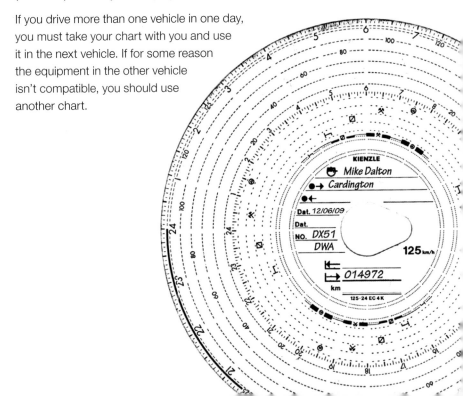

If you're working away from the vehicle and can't leave a chart in the tachograph (for example, because the vehicle is likely to be used by someone else), or if you've left a chart in the tachograph but have changed work mode while away from the vehicle, you must make a manual entry on the reverse of the chart; for example, OW 09.15–10.20. If your chart is dirty or damaged, you should start another and then attach it to the damaged one.

Make sure that all the information for the day is entered on your chart(s). The obligation to record the information correctly falls on you, the driver, as well as on the operator. Heavy fines are imposed for the misuse or falsification of charts.

Chart inspections

Your tachograph records must be available for inspection at the roadside by the enforcement authorities. You must carry the record sheet (and printouts) for the current day and for the previous 28 days. (Note: you should also carry and be able to produce your digital tachograph driver card if one has been issued to you. You'll be committing an offence if you don't, even if you're pulled over while driving a vehicle equipped with an analogue tachograph.)

If your records are kept by an enforcement officer, you should ask the officer to endorse the replacement chart with their name and telephone number. The officer should also state the number of charts retained. Alternatively, they may provide you with a receipt.

To ensure that all records are kept up to date and available for inspection by enforcement staff, you must give the completed charts to your employer within 42 days. This requirement must be complied with even when a driver changes employer. If you're working for more than one employer, you must provide each with sufficient information to ensure the rules are being met.

The law says that employers must keep tachograph records and printouts (where applicable) in chronological order and in a legible form for at least one year from the date of their use. The records must be submitted to enforcement officers as required. Also, if a driver requests it, employers must provide copies of the records and, if requested, copies of downloaded data from the driver card.

There are various methods of storing the charts (on pegs, in envelopes, in folders, etc, and either under vehicle registration number or under each driver's name).

Working time records

The law says that employers must keep a record of the hours worked by all employees, including mobile workers (see glossary in section 7). This can be in a very simple form, such as through the normal payroll system. These records should be stored/filed for at least two years after the end of the period covered. Employers must be able to give employed drivers and other workers copies of the records of hours worked if requested.

Digital tachographs

Digital tachographs became mandatory on all new goods vehicles 'in scope' of the EU rules on 1 May 2006. This type of tachograph doesn't use paper charts but instead stores encrypted electronic data both in the vehicle unit and on a **digital driver tachograph card**. The vehicle unit records the movement of the vehicle, as well as details of the drivers and crew who use the vehicle. The driver card records the driver's activities and details of the vehicles that they drive.

A digital tachograph must be calibrated when first installed and at least every two years after that. It must also be recalibrated after any repair and if the vehicle's tyre sizes are changed. A plaque either on or near the tachograph will say when the last calibration was carried out.

Unlike an analogue tachograph, which only records activity on a paper chart, a digital tachograph records the date, time and duration of all driving activity, irrespective of whether a driver card has been inserted. This information can be printed off and produced if requested by an enforcement officer. The printout can be manually corrected if the card or equipment malfunctions, or if the rules are breached due to an unforeseen event.

The tachograph also records within its own memory a record of events and faults, such as driving without a driver card inserted, speeding, power disconnections, attempts to breach security, etc, as well as a detailed speed trace for the last 24 hours of driving.

Downloading and storing of data should be carried out frequently enough for the operator to be able to monitor the driver's hours and record-keeping, and at least as frequently as regulations require.

As with analogue tachographs, if a digital tachograph becomes faulty, drivers may continue to use the vehicle but must make a manual temporary record on the printout (or the paper roll if a printout is unavailable). This should contain data enabling the driver to be identified (name, driver card number or driving licence number, and signature), plus all information for the periods of time that can't be recorded or printed out correctly by the recording equipment.

If it's impossible to use a driver card (for example, if the card has been lost, stolen or damaged, or is malfunctioning), a driver may drive without the card for a maximum of 15 calendar days (or longer if this is necessary for the vehicle to be returned to its premises), provided that he or she produces two printouts – one at the start of the journey and another at the end. Both printouts must be marked with

- the driver's name, and their driver card number or driving licence number, so the driver can be identified
- any manual entries needed to show periods of other work, availability, and rest or break
- the driver's signature.

Recording time with a digital tachograph

The internal clock of a digital tachograph is set to Coordinated Universal Time (UTC). The display can be set to any time zone the driver chooses, but all data recorded to the tachograph or card will be in UTC.

UTC is effectively the same as Greenwich Mean Time (GMT), so it must be remembered that, during British Summer Time (BST), UTC will be one hour behind BST. Any manual inputs for activities not recorded on a driver card must take account of the one-hour time difference during BST.

Digital driver tachograph cards

These are a 'must have': a driver can't legally drive a vehicle that's in scope of the EU rules and equipped with a digital tachograph unless he or she is first issued with a driver card. Driver cards for digital tachographs are issued by DVLA (in Swansea) and DVA (in Northern Ireland). You can apply for a card at **www.gov.uk**

The card, like a driving licence, belongs to the Secretary of State for Transport. Cards are personalised to the driver and include

- identification information
- expiry date
- driving licence number
- photograph of the driver
- copy of the driver's signature
- unique issue number of the card.

Information is held electronically on the card chip, as well as being printed on the card. If you report for work, intending to drive a vehicle equipped with a digital tachograph, and find that you've left your card at home, you should return home to collect it.

Drivers aren't allowed to have more than one valid driver card issued to them. Cards are valid for a maximum period of five years. You should receive a reminder about three months before the expiry date. However, it's your responsibility to make sure that you apply for a new card at least 15 days before the old one expires.

The card should be inserted into the digital tachograph whenever the driver takes charge of a vehicle equipped with one. The tachograph will then prompt the driver to manually enter a record of any work activities undertaken since the card was last removed from a digital tachograph. Where the driver conducts both 'in-scope' and 'out-of-scope' driving, this can also be recorded by a manual entry.

The card normally allows for a record of driving and other activities spanning a period of 28 days. It will start to overwrite the earliest records once full, so it's a legal requirement that data is downloaded from driver cards and stored before this occurs.

While in charge of a vehicle, drivers are required to be able to provide records of their activities on the current day and the previous 28 days (ie their driver card and any analogue tachograph charts they may have used). If a driver has been issued with a digital tachograph card, they must carry the card at all times when driving professionally, irrespective of whether they've driven a vehicle equipped with a digital tachograph during this period. This is to enable inspection and checking of the data record by DVSA (DVA in Northern Ireland) or the police.

Lost or stolen cards

As a professional driver, you have a responsibility to report any loss or theft of your digital driver tachograph card to DVLA. This must be done within seven days. (In Northern Ireland, report the loss to DVA.) You can apply for a replacement card by telephone if none of the details on the card have changed. There will be a fee to pay.

If your card is lost, stolen or faulty, you must take a printout at the start and end of each working day, showing your start and end times. On both printouts, you need to make manual entries showing periods of driving, rest, breaks, other work and availability. You also need to add your

- name
- driving licence number or driver card number
- signature.

You can do this for a maximum of 15 calendar days (unless you're returning a vehicle and you can prove that it's impossible to produce or use the card during this period). If you don't have a replacement card by then, you must cease driving vehicles equipped with digital tachographs.

Company cards

Company cards are used as 'keys' by vehicle operators, to lock in data recorded when the vehicle is being used by their drivers. Doing so enables them to readily identify their own data and prevents unauthorised persons from seeing or downloading their data. The card also enables them to download data from the tachograph. Without a company card and suitable equipment and/or access to support services, an operator won't be able to manage tachograph data properly.

Workshop cards

A workshop card is issued only to qualified fitters who have successfully completed a training course approved by DVSA. It should be used in the same way as a driver card, during digital-tachograph-related road tests, to enable these to be recorded together with the calibration or check. This will then form a complete record of the activities relating to a vehicle, which can be downloaded at a later time.

Because of the security implications, the loss or malfunction of a card must be notified to DVSA immediately. A replacement card will be issued through a DVSA office.

A workshop card mustn't be used as a company card. Since this would be recorded by the vehicle unit, any such abuse or any other illegal use would probably lead to the card being withdrawn. Workshop cards are issued to holders of company cards only under the strictest conditions, with the consequences of illegal use fully explained.

Control cards

Control cards are used by DVSA (DVA in Northern Ireland) enforcement officers or the police. You must stop when requested to do so by such officers. An enforcement officer or vehicle examiner can use a control card to download information from a digital tachograph.

Any person who fails to comply with, or obstructs, a vehicle examiner during the course of their duties can be fined an unlimited amount.

Tampering

Drivers who are convicted of forging, using or altering in any way the seal of a tachograph with intent to deceive can be fined an unlimited amount or imprisoned for a term not exceeding two years.

The penalty for tampering with tachographs/data or falsifying record sheets/driver cards is two years' imprisonment or an unlimited fine, or both.

EU drivers' hours

This section summarises the EU rules on drivers' hours of work. For more information, visit **www.gov.uk**

Daily driving

'Driving' means being at the controls of a vehicle for the purposes of controlling its movement, whether the vehicle is moving or stationary with its engine running.

A day is defined as any period of 24 hours beginning when you start other work or driving after the last daily or weekly rest period. You may drive a maximum of nine hours in a day. This can be increased to 10 hours twice a week.

The daily driving period must be between two daily rest periods, or between a daily rest period and a weekly rest period.

daily rest period	4.5 hours driving	45 mins break	4.5 hours driving	45 mins break	1 hr driving	daily rest period

Breaks

You must make sure that you take an uninterrupted break of 45 minutes immediately after four-and-a-half hours of driving.

daily rest period	4.5 hours driving	45 mins break	4.5 hours driving	daily rest period

This break may be split into a break of at least 15 minutes followed by a break of at least 30 minutes, each distributed over the driving period. To comply with the EU rules, a break must be at least 15 minutes and the second break must be at least 30 minutes. A 45-minute break (or split breaks totalling 45 minutes) is required before you get back behind the wheel. You mustn't drive or undertake any other work during any break. For example:

daily rest period	2 hours driving	15 mins break	2.5 hrs driving	30 mins break	4.5 hours driving	daily rest period

If the authorities find that any scheduled breaks have been missed, immediate prohibition and possible prosecution could result.

Unforeseen events

If there are unforeseen events, a departure from the rules may be permitted, provided that road safety isn't compromised. Examples of such events are

- delays caused by severe weather
- road traffic incidents
- mechanical breakdowns

- interruption of ferry services
- any event that's likely to cause, or is already causing, danger to people or animals.

This concession is only to enable drivers to reach a suitable stopping place, not necessarily to complete their planned journey. The stopping place should be chosen to ensure the immediate safety of persons, the vehicle and its load. The reasons for exceeding driving hours must be recorded while at this stopping place, either on the back of an analogue tachograph chart or on a printout or temporary sheet if the vehicle has a digital tachograph. Drivers and operators would be expected to reschedule any disrupted work to remain in compliance with the EU rules.

Repeated and regular occurrences could indicate that employers aren't scheduling work correctly. Planned breaches of the driver's hours aren't permitted.

During a journey on which the vehicle has been driven on a public road, any driving off the public roads now counts as driving time and should be recorded as such. However, if no driving has been carried out on a public road, then it counts as other duty and should be recorded as other work.

To avoid exceeding drivers' hours when experiencing traffic delays on a motorway, exit at the next junction and find a suitable place to take a break.

Daily rest periods

A regular daily rest period means any period of rest of at least 11 hours.

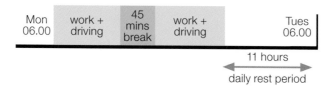

Alternatively, this rest may be taken in two periods, the first of which must be an uninterrupted period of at least three hours and the second an uninterrupted period of at least nine hours.

A reduced daily rest period is any period of rest of at least nine hours but less than 11 hours. This reduced daily rest period can't be taken more than three times between any two weekly rest periods.

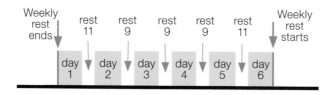

If you take your rest period when accompanying a vehicle on a ferry or train, your regular daily rest period may be interrupted up to twice by other activities, which mustn't exceed one hour in total. However, you must have access to a bunk or couchette during that rest period.

Weekly driving

A week means the period of time from 00.00 on Monday to 24.00 on the
following Sunday.

There's a weekly driving limit of 56 hours and you mustn't exceed 90 hours in
any two consecutive weeks.

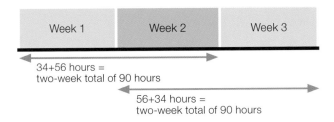

Weekly rest periods

A regular weekly rest period is any period of rest of at least 45 hours. In any
two consecutive weeks, you must take either two regular weekly rest periods
or one regular weekly rest period and one reduced weekly rest period of at
least 24 hours.

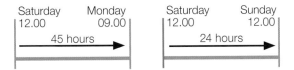

If you take a reduced rest, you must add the period of time by which it was
reduced to a daily or weekly rest period of at least nine hours before the end of
the third week following the week in question. Rest taken as compensation for
the reduction of a weekly rest period must be taken in one continuous block.

Any period of compensatory rest taken away from base can be taken in a
stationary vehicle as long as the vehicle has suitable sleeping facilities for
each driver.

Weekly rest
33 hours

Sunday
24.00

| Week 1 | Week 2 | Week 3 | Week 4 |

Compensation of 12 hours must be paid back by 24.00 on the Sunday of the third week following the week of reduced rest

A weekly rest period that begins in one week and continues into the following week may be added to either of these weeks.

Saturday
08.00

Sunday
24.00

Monday
05.00

—— 45 hours ——

Two or more drivers (multi-manning)

If a vehicle is used by two drivers at the same time (multi-manning), each driver should make sure their card is inserted into the correct slot on the digital tachograph. The person who is currently driving the vehicle needs to insert their card into slot 1, while the second person's card goes into slot 2. When the drivers change seats, the cards are swapped over.

By selecting the 'crew' option, the tachograph will recognise that the vehicle is being used in a multi-manning capacity. The system records availability and time for the driver in the passenger seat who isn't currently driving.

Multi-manning enables drivers' duties to be spread over 21 hours, so their duty time can be extended. During each period of 30 hours, each driver must have a rest period of not less than nine consecutive hours. There must always be two or more drivers travelling with the vehicle for this rule to apply. A driver may take a break while another driver is driving, but not a daily rest period.

Domestic drivers' hours

The domestic rules apply to most goods vehicles that are exempt from EU rules.

Driving limits

You mustn't drive for more than 10 hours in any one day. This limit applies to the time actually spent driving.

Daily duty

You mustn't be on duty for more than 11 hours in any working day. You're exempt from the daily duty limit on any working day when you don't drive. You'll also be exempt from this limit if you don't drive for more than four hours on each day of the week.

Exemptions

Exemptions apply to

- drivers of vehicles used by the armed forces, the police and fire brigades, and drivers of vehicles used for flood protection
- drivers who always drive off the public road system
- private driving.

Goods vehicles, including dual-purpose vehicles and those not exceeding 3.5 tonnes MPW, are exempt from the duty limit but not the driving limit when they're used by

- doctors
- dentists
- nurses
- midwives
- vets.

Vehicles used for any inspection, cleaning, maintenance, repair, installation or fitting

- by a commercial traveller
- by the AA, RAC or RSAC
- for cinematograph or radio and television broadcasting

are also included among the exemptions.

The domestic rules further allow for events needing immediate action to avoid danger to the life or health of people or animals, and for the prevention of serious disruption to essential services or danger to property.

Keeping records

If the vehicle isn't subject to operator licensing, then no records are required to be kept. If the vehicle is subject to operator licensing, isn't being driven for more than four hours a day and remains within a 50 km radius of its base/operating centre, then no records are required to be kept.

In other cases, you must keep a written record of your hours of work on a weekly record sheet, which is available from commercial printers. If you drive a vehicle in excess of 3.5 tonnes MPW that carries parcels on postal services, you must use a tachograph.

Mixed EU and domestic driving

It's possible to drive under both EU rules and domestic rules during a week or even during a single day. If you wish, you can choose to drive under EU rules for the whole of the time. If you use a combination of both sets of rules, you must make sure that EU limits aren't exceeded when driving vehicles on EU work.

You can't use the time spent driving under EU rules as off-duty time under the domestic rules: driving under EU rules counts towards the driving and duty limits under the domestic rules. Similarly, you can't claim driving and other work under the domestic rules as rest time for EU rules.

> **REMEMBER,** if you do any driving under EU rules during a week, you must take daily and weekly rest periods.

Rules on working time

Drivers who are subject to the UK domestic drivers' hours rules are affected by four provisions under the Horizontal Amending Directive (HAD), introduced on 1 August 2003. These are

- a requirement to limit working time to no more than 48 hours per week, on average (although individuals are allowed to opt out of this requirement if they want to)
- an entitlement to four weeks' paid annual leave
- health checks for night workers
- an entitlement to adequate rest.

The reference period for calculating the 48-hour average working week is normally a rolling 17-week period. However, this reference period can be extended to 26 weeks if representatives from both sides of the industry agree to do so.

Self-employed drivers aren't subject to the HAD, but they are now subject to the Road Transport Directive.

Drivers who are subject to EU drivers' hours and tachograph rules are required to adhere to separate working-time provisions under the Road Transport (Working Time) Regulations, which came into force in March 2005. The following are the main provisions of the UK's implementing regulations.

Weekly working time
Weekly working time mustn't exceed an average of 48 hours per week. The reference period for these calculations is usually 17 weeks, but it can be extended to 26 weeks with appropriate agreement. A maximum of 60 hours can be worked in any single week, provided that the average 48-hour limit isn't exceeded.

There's no 'opt out' for individuals wishing to work longer than an average 48-hour week, but breaks and periods of availability (POA) don't count as working time.

Night work
Night working is limited to 10 hours in any 24-hour period where any work is carried out between the hours of midnight and 4.00 am. The 10-hour limit may be exceeded if this is permitted under a collective or workforce agreement.

Breaks
When driving is being carried out, the break provisions under EU drivers' hours rules (EC/561/2006) take precedence. Drivers aren't permitted to work for more than six consecutive hours without a break. Where working hours total between six and nine hours a day, a break of at least 30 minutes is

required. A further 15-minute break (45 minutes in total) is required if total working time exceeds nine hours. The break periods can be divided, but the duration of each break must be at least 15 minutes.

Rest

The rules on rest periods are the same as the EU (EC/561/2006) or AETR (see the glossary in section 7) drivers' hours rules.

Record-keeping

Records must be kept for two years after the period in question.

Periods of availability

Generally speaking, a period of availability is waiting time, the timing and duration of which is known about in advance by the mobile worker. (For a definition of 'mobile worker', see the glossary in section 7.) This must be known before departure or just before the start of the period in question.

To meet the requirements of a POA, a mobile worker shouldn't be required to remain at their workstation (for example, in the cab), although they may do so if they wish to or need to do so for security or safety reasons. However, they must be available to

- answer calls to start work
- resume driving on request.

Mobile workers don't need to be formally notified about a POA or its duration. It's enough to know about it in advance – for example, if

- someone (who doesn't have to be their employer) has told them
- they've arrived too early for their allocated slot
- they always experience a delay at one of their regular customers.

There are no requirements as to the minimum or maximum length of a POA.

Changes to a POA

If a mobile worker is told in advance that a POA is to be, for example, 60 minutes long, but this is extended to 90 minutes, then only the first 60 minutes qualify as a POA, with the remaining 30 minutes being other work. This only applies if the mobile worker isn't notified in advance of the additional 30 minutes of waiting.

If the mobile worker is told that the POA is to be, for example, 60 minutes long, but they are then told to start work after only 30 minutes, only 30 minutes qualify as a POA, with the other 30 minutes being recorded as either driving or other work.

Examples of a POA

Situations when a period of time could be recorded as a POA (provided the 'known in advance' precondition is met) include

- accompanying a vehicle being transported by boat or train

- waiting at frontiers

- when driving or travelling as part of a team, the time spent sitting next to the driver while the vehicle is in motion (unless the mobile worker is taking a break or performing any other work, such as navigation). This time (or part of it) could also count as a break – but would need to be recorded as such

- waiting for someone to load or unload their vehicle, if they know about the length of the delay at the start of the period because

  - someone has told them

  - they've arrived too early for their slot

  - they always experience a delay at one of their regular customers

- where a mobile worker reports for work but is informed that they aren't required to undertake any duties for a specified period (although they need to remain on site to answer calls and be ready to take up work)

- if the vehicle breaks down and the mobile worker is told how long it will take to be rescued.

Examples of situations where a period of time should **not** be recorded as a POA are

- where a driver is diverted due to a road closure – he or she would still be driving, so the period couldn't be counted as a POA

- delays due to congestion (ie stuck in a traffic jam) – these would not count as a POA because the driver would be stopping and starting the vehicle

- if a mobile worker is monitoring activity by others (for example, at a filling station or unloading the lorry) – this time would count as working time, rather than a POA.

These are examples only. Further information on periods of availability can be obtained by contacting DVSA or by visiting **www.gov.uk**

⊕ Operator licensing and the driver's responsibilities

Goods vehicle operator's licence

In Great Britain, most users of commercial goods vehicles weighing over 3.5 tonnes must have a goods vehicle operator's licence. This applies even if they use a hired vehicle or only use a vehicle for one day.

The licence authorises an operator to use a maximum total number of motor vehicles and trailers from a specific operating centre or centres where the vehicles are normally kept when not in use. You need to

- satisfy the traffic commissioner that your operating centre(s) is/are suitable
- list information about the vehicles that will be kept there
- provide evidence that you're entitled to use the operating centre if you don't own it.

There are three types of operator's licence

- Restricted, which allows an operator to carry his/her own goods in connection with his/her business
- Standard National, which allows an operator to carry his/her own goods and goods for other people for hire or reward in Great Britain
- Standard International, which allows an operator to carry his/her own goods and goods for other people for hire or reward, both in Great Britain and on international journeys.

Each vehicle operating under these licences must display a disc in the windscreen. The discs are colour-coded

- orange for Restricted
- blue for Standard National
- green for Standard International.

Licence applications are made to statutorily independent traffic commissioners, who are appointed by the Secretary of State for Transport. Great Britain is divided into six traffic areas: see section 7 for details of these traffic areas and contact details for the area offices. An operator must hold a licence in each traffic area where it has an operating centre or centres. A free guide for operators, summarising the legislation, is available at **www.gov.uk**

If you wish to appeal against a traffic commissioner's decision or require further details of the appeals procedure, a free booklet can be obtained from

Upper Tribunal Administrative Appeals Chamber
Traffic Commissioner Appeals
7th Floor, Victory House
30–34 Kingsway
London
WC2B 6EX
Tel 020 3077 5860

The booklet is also available from your local traffic area office. Information about traffic commissioner public inquiries is available at
www.gov.uk/being-a-goods-vehicle-operator

Northern Ireland operations

Northern Ireland has a separate system, administered by the Road Transport Licensing Division of the Driver and Vehicle Agency (DVA). It isn't necessary for operators in the province to obtain a short-term 'O' licence before entering Great Britain. Holders of current 'O' licences or Northern Ireland Road Freight Operator Licences are permitted to carry goods in each country. For more information, visit **www.nidirect.gov.uk/information-and-services/motoring**

The driver's responsibility for the receipt, carriage and delivery of goods

The driver is responsible for the contents of their vehicle and needs to ensure that the vehicle is loaded correctly for stability and ease of access. The goods should be delivered to the appropriate persons at the agreed time, but don't allow a deadline to make you exceed the speed limits for the area or conditions. Always allow sufficient time to reach the premises.

The goods should arrive in the condition they were in when collected or loaded onto the vehicle. Don't let lack of attention cause damage to the goods during loading or unloading. The goods should be delivered in accordance with any agreed conditions set for that contract. Operators can limit their liability for lost, delayed or damaged goods by issuing conditions of carriage.

Encouraging customers to check (where possible) and sign for handover of goods will prevent incorrect deliveries. Any required paperwork should be kept to enable work records to be maintained. If a customer isn't around to check and sign for a delivery, the delivery note and goods should be returned to the depot.

It's good practice for a carrier to sign a receipt or consignment note acknowledging acceptance of the goods to be carried. A signed receipt for delivery of the consignment should also be obtained from the consignee. The absence of such documents can complicate matters in the event of any dispute involving incorrect goods or damage in transit.

Know the regulations

In addition to the rules and regulations that apply to drivers' hours, vehicles and loads, you should make sure that you comply with any regulations that affect your

- health
- conduct
- vehicle
- driving
- licence
- safety.

It's essential that you know and keep up to date with the regulations and the latest official advice.

⊙ Driving in Europe

Document requirements

When driving on international journeys in Europe, you must carry your national driving licence, insurance certificate and vehicle registration document. You'll also need to carry your passport with you at all times – many countries require visitors to do so as a valid form of identification. Other documentation may also be required for some countries.

International carriage of goods by road

Any goods being carried for hire or reward on international journeys under the provisions of the Convention on the Contract for the International Carriage of Goods by Road (CMR) **must** be recorded on CMR consignment notes. These consignment notes confirm that carriage is being undertaken in agreement with the CMR Convention. There are four copies:

- red – kept by the consignor (sender)
- blue – for the consignee
- green – travels with the vehicle
- white with black border – retained by the originator.

Usually, the carrier completes the CMR consignment note. However, most of the information relates to the consignor, so it's a good idea for them to complete the documents. When the goods have been delivered, the consignee is asked to sign the consignment note. Under the CMR Convention, the carrier is responsible for any loss or damage to the goods after accepting them and before delivering them.

Where it's necessary to divide a consignment, separate consignment notes can be made for the individual parts of the consignment.

The CMR Convention regulates the responsibilities and potential liabilities of the carrier when engaged in international transport for hire or reward. It applies to every contract for the carriage of goods by road when the place taking over responsibility for the goods and the place designated for delivery, as specified in the contract, are situated in two different countries. One of these countries must be the contracting country, irrespective of the place of residence and the nationality of the parties.

The Convention doesn't apply to

- any carriage performed under the terms of any international postal arrangements
- any funeral consignments
- any furniture removal.

Consignment notes for own-account carriage by road
Own-account operators aren't required to use CMR consignment notes for international journeys. Any journey that can be shown to be on own account, not for hire or reward, need only have a simple consignment note.

Customs procedures and documentation
Since 1993, goods being shipped to EU countries are no longer classified as exports. They're known as despatches, as long as they're of EU origin and in free circulation within the EU. They're classed as having community status, can be transported between EU member states and are no longer subject to customs procedures. These goods require an invoice, a transport document or a completed copy 4 of the single administrative document (SAD).

Exports outside the EU
A declaration of entry must be made to HM Revenue and Customs if exporting to non-EU countries (with certain exceptions).

Illegal immigrants

Legislation requires road hauliers to operate an effective system to protect their vehicles against the carriage of illegal immigrants. Hauliers may be liable for penalties if their vehicles bring illegal immigrants into the UK. Each individual responsible person (for example, the vehicle owner, hirer and driver) can receive a penalty of up to £2000 for each illegal immigrant carried.

An effective system comprises three separate areas: vehicle security, vehicle checking and documentation.

Vehicle security

The vehicle owner should ensure that the outer fabric of the vehicle doesn't permit unauthorised access (for example, through cuts or tears) and that it can be properly secured. They should provide security devices, depending on the type of vehicle.

- Hard-sided vehicles (for example, box trailers) – the rear doors and any external storage compartments should be secured with an integral lock, padlock or seal. All locks and padlocks should be robust and maintained in working order. Seals should be numbered and spares should be provided in case it becomes necessary to resecure the vehicle during its journey.

- Soft-sided vehicles (for example, curtain-sided trailers) – a security (TIR) cord should be provided, in good condition, with a padlock or seal to join the cord after fitting. Any external storage compartments should be treated as above.

TIR procedures

TIR stands for 'Transports Internationaux Routiers', which, when translated, means International Road Transport. It's a transit system allowing goods to travel across one or more international borders with the minimum of customs involvement.

TIR can be used in the EU for movements that

- begin or end in a non-EU country
- are destined for an EU member state via a third country, **or**
- consist of consignments for split delivery to destinations in the EU and in non-EU countries.

You can't use TIR for transit movements that are entirely within the EU.

Seals

One of the most important features of the TIR system is that containers and vehicles must be sealed by customs. The seals will be checked at customs offices en route to make sure that they haven't been broken or tampered with. Before removing the seals, the customs office at the destination will check that the seals applied to the container or vehicle are intact and as described.

If you discover that an official seal has been tampered with or broken, you must notify customs immediately. If the breakage is found on your own premises, you should report the facts to your local control office. If it's found on a vehicle or container in which you're carrying goods under customs control, you should report to customs at your destination as soon as you arrive there. If there's also extensive damage to the vehicle or container and/or the goods, report to your nearest customs office at once.

The customs officer may ask you to explain how any seal breakage and damage occurred. In all cases of unauthorised seal breakage, you must obtain a customs officer's permission before you remove or unload the goods originally secured by that seal.

An unforeseen incident that occurs during a transit operation must be brought to the attention of customs at the first opportunity. Wherever possible, prior authorisation must be obtained from customs if seals have to be broken or the goods need to be transferred from one vehicle to another. An account of the incident must be noted on the transit declaration, then both the goods and the declaration must be presented to the nearest customs authority. When customs are content that the operation may continue, they'll reseal the goods and endorse the declaration accordingly.

Vehicle checking

An effective system must be provided for checking of the vehicle at appropriate times during its journey to the UK. You, as the driver, will normally be responsible for checking the vehicle. You should check the vehicle at the following times:

Final loading

Check the interior of the vehicle when the vehicle is loaded before departure for the UK. This includes checking any external storage compartments if they're fitted. If you're collecting cargo from different places, the check should be made at the final loading point. Immediately after this check, the vehicle (including any external storage compartments) should be secured with appropriate devices.

If you aren't able to carry out this check yourself, you should get confirmation in writing from the person responsible for the final loading that there are no unauthorised persons within the vehicle.

During the journey

You should check that the vehicle's security hasn't been breached after any stops made while travelling to the port of embarkation, particularly if the vehicle has been left unattended. Physically examine security cords, seals and locks for any signs of tampering. The underside of the vehicle should also be checked, as would-be illegal immigrants sometimes hide on vehicle axles or in storage areas beneath vehicles.

Final check

Where the immigration control for traffic travelling to the UK operates in a control zone outside the UK, penalties can be imposed if illegal immigrants are found in vehicles at any time within the control zone. These control zones are currently operating at Calais, Coquelles and Dunkirk. If you're using these routes, a final check must be carried out before entering the control zone.

If you're travelling through other ports, the final check should be made immediately before boarding the ferry to the UK. The final check should include the security cord (if fitted) and any locks or seals. Also check the underside of the vehicle, its roof and wind deflector (if fitted). If you haven't been able to secure the vehicle properly, the final check should include a thorough manual check of the vehicle's interior.

Checks provided by port operators

Make use of vehicle checks provided by port operators. These aren't foolproof, however, and may not always detect the presence of illegal immigrants. You're responsible for carrying out the final vehicle check.

Documentation

The operator should provide you with a document including

- instructions on how to secure the vehicle
- details of when and how to check the vehicle
- advice on what to do if illegal immigrants are suspected of being in the vehicle, or if the vehicle's security is breached or compromised.

This document must be carried with the vehicle, so that it may be produced immediately for immigration officers if requested. It should also include a checklist (see illustration), which acts as a reminder for you to carry out the checks required and enables you to keep a record of the checks you've made. In the event that illegal immigrants are carried, these documents will help to show that a checking system was operated as required under the legislation.

Methods of entry

There are several common ways in which access is gained to vehicles. Some are listed below.

- Unauthorised entry is often gained to soft-sided (including curtain-sided) vehicles because a security cord (properly joined with a seal or padlock) is absent. Entry to hard-sided vehicles may be gained if their doors aren't locked or sealed.
- Security cords can be cut and rejoined. Physically checking the cord by pulling on it will usually bring this to notice.
- Seals and padlocks can be broken and rejoined. This can often be revealed by physically checking the seal or padlock.
- Entry gained by cutting the canvas side or roof of the vehicle can be identified through proper checking (particularly at the final check).
- Some illegal immigrants hide beneath vehicles – for example, on an axle or in panniers. Consequently, checking these areas is vital.

These examples aren't exhaustive. Illegal immigrants will look for any possible means of entering a vehicle, especially if it can be achieved in a few minutes.

REMEMBER, penalties can only be avoided by operating an effective system to protect vehicles and ensure that illegal immigrants aren't carried.

Company name:

Loaded at:

Date:

Vehicle number:

Trailer number:

CHECK / Date	After loading	1st stop	2nd stop	Final CHECK[3]	Extra (Check if time between third-party check + embarkation > 15 min)
Vehicle/trailer inside	Yes / No				
Tilts and roof checked for damage	Yes / No	Yes / No	Yes / No	Yes / No	Yes / No
External compartments checked	Yes / No	Yes / No	Yes / No	Yes / No	Yes / No
Below vehicle checked	Yes / No	Yes / No	Yes / No	Yes / No	Yes / No
TIR cord tight and in place and checked[1]	Yes / No	Yes / No	Yes / No	Yes / No	Yes / No
Seal in place and checked[2]	Yes / No	Yes / No	Yes / No	Yes / No	Yes / No
Padlock in place and checked[2]	Yes / No	Yes / No	Yes / No	Yes / No	Yes / No
Seal/padlock number					
Third-party check e.g. CO2, PMMW				Yes / No	
Cabin check				Yes / No	Yes / No
Time checked					
Driver's signature					

1 The TIR security cord should be checked physically for evidence of tampering, in particular for signs that it has been cut and rejoined.

2 Seals and padlocks should be checked physically to ensure they haven't been cut or broken and repaired. If a padlock is difficult to open or close, this may suggest it has been tampered with.

3 If travelling through Calais, Coquelles or Dunkirk, the final check should be carried out before entering the UK control zone. If using another port, the final check should take place immediately before boarding the ferry.

→ Your health and conduct

Health issues

Many incidents happen as a result of inattention or distraction while driving. Your health can play a big part in this: even apparently simple illnesses can affect your reactions. You should be on your guard against the effects of

- flu symptoms
- hay fever
- a common cold
- tiredness.

Worries, stress or anger can also affect your driving ability. Always make sure that you're calm and fit to drive before you get behind the wheel.

Fatigue

Fatigue can lead to reduced concentration and can also impair your reaction time. To avoid fatigue, it's important to take proper rest before starting duty and to take adequate rest breaks during driving and between duty periods. Always take planned rest breaks and, if necessary, take more rest than is required by law.

The introduction of

- air-suspension driver's seats
- floating cab suspension
- air suspension on vehicles
- quieter, smoother diesel engines
- more widely adopted soundproofing materials

has produced a comfortable 'cocoon' where you'll spend most of your working day. This can easily cause tiredness.

Be on your guard against boredom on comparatively empty roads or motorways, especially at night. Always

- take planned rest breaks
- keep fresh air circulating around the driving area
- avoid allowing the driving area to become too warm
- avoid driving if you aren't 100% fit
- avoid driving after a heavy meal.

If you start to feel tired, stop at the next lay-by or pull off the motorway (or slip road) as soon as it's safe and legal to do so. Walking around in the fresh air can refresh you in the short term, but this is no substitute for adequate rest.

Falling asleep

Much research has been undertaken, on behalf of the Department for Transport, into sleep-related vehicle incidents (SRVIs). This research has shown that about 40% of SRVIs involve commercial vehicles. SRVIs are more likely to result in serious injury than the average road incident, because they often involve running off the road or into the back of another vehicle, and they're made worse by the high speed of impact (because there's no braking beforehand). SRVIs are more evident in male drivers up to 30 years of age, who often deny or ignore that they're suffering from the effects of sleep loss or sleepiness.

Sleepy drivers are normally aware of their sleepiness. However, drivers who are already mildly sleepy, because of previous sleep disturbance or insufficient sleep, are more vulnerable to any additional sleep loss and may not perceive an **increase** in sleepiness. If you begin to feel sleepy, stop in a safe place before you get to the stage of fighting sleep. Sleep can ensue more rapidly than you would imagine.

There's a particular risk when driving between midnight and 6.00 am, because this is when the 'body clock' is in a daily trough. There's another, smaller trough between about 2.00 pm and 4.00 pm.

Effects of shift work

Shift work can affect your rest and sleep cycles. It's tempting to continue as usual when at home – for example, undertaking domestic duties or socialising. However, you need to make sure that you don't do this at the cost of rest/sleep. Be flexible: you may need to change the times/days when jobs are done.

Shifts that mean your routine differs from those of friends and family can leave you feeling isolated. It's important to make the effort not to lose contact with them. Things you can do to help include

- talking to them about shift work
- making them aware of your schedule, so they include you when planning social activities
- where possible, planning mealtimes, weekends and evenings together
- making the most of your free time
- inviting others who work similar shifts to join you in social activities.

Drugs

The problem of drug abuse has now reached the point where well-known multinational companies have introduced random drug testing for their drivers. Those drivers who fail such tests may face instant dismissal.

It's illegal to drive in England and Wales if

- you're unfit to do so because you've taken legal or illegal drugs
- you have more than the specified levels of certain illegal drugs in your blood, even if they haven't affected your driving
- you have more than the specified levels of certain prescription medicines in your blood and you haven't been prescribed them.

You should note that the levels of illegal drugs specified in the legislation are very low, and are only there to allow for cases of accidental exposure. The government has a zero-tolerance approach to people who drive after taking illegal drugs.

Legal drugs include prescription medicines and over-the-counter medicines such as cold or flu remedies. If you're taking these medicines and you aren't sure whether you should drive, talk to your doctor, pharmacist or healthcare professional.

The effects of drugs can last for up to 72 hours. If the police think you might have taken drugs, they can stop you and make you do a 'field impairment assessment'. This is a series of tests; for example, asking you to walk in a straight line. They can also use a roadside drug kit to screen for cannabis and cocaine.

If the police think you're unfit to drive because you've taken drugs, you'll be arrested and you'll have to take a blood or urine test at a police station. If this test shows that you've taken drugs, you could be charged with a crime.

> For more information about the drug-driving laws, visit
>
> **www.gov.uk/drug-driving-law**

Alcohol

It's an offence to drive with

- a breath alcohol level higher than
    - (in England and Wales) 35 microgrammes per 100 millilitres of breath
    - (in Scotland) 22 microgrammes per 100 millilitres of breath
- a blood alcohol level higher than
    - (in England and Wales) 80 milligrammes per 100 millilitres of blood
    - (in Scotland) 50 milligrammes per 100 millilitres of blood.

This means that the limits in Scotland are lower than those in England and Wales.

Be aware that alcohol can remain in the body for around 24–48 hours, so you could fail a breath test the morning after a night of drinking.

If you're convicted of a drink-driving offence while driving an ordinary motor vehicle, a driving ban will result in you losing your HGV entitlement and your livelihood.

> **REMEMBER,** don't drink if you're going to drive.

Smoking in work vehicles

Following the introduction of legislation in 2006 and 2007, you mustn't smoke in vehicles used for work purposes in certain prescribed circumstances. Separate regulations apply to England, Wales and Scotland. Your vehicle must have 'No smoking' signs displayed inside the cab area.

Smoking restrictions also apply to all work premises.

Further information can be found at **www.gov.uk/smoking-at-work-the-law**

Seat belts

Certain exemptions apply to the wearing of seat belts. You don't have to wear one if you have a medical exemption certificate or if you travel less than 50 metres while making deliveries or collections. It's compulsory for drivers and passengers, in vehicles constructed or adapted to carry goods, to wear their seat belts while making deliveries or collections when travelling a distance of more than 50 metres.

You can remove your seat belt while carrying out a manoeuvre that involves reversing, but don't forget to put it back on when you've finished.

If children are travelling as passengers in the vehicle, they must wear a child restraint appropriate to their size. The only exception is for an occasional short journey, when, if a child restraint isn't available, an adult seat belt must be worn.

The number of passengers shouldn't exceed the number of seats fitted with seat belts and child restraints.

> **REMEMBER,** where seat belts are fitted, they must be worn.

Health and safety

It has been estimated that up to a third of all road traffic incidents involve somebody who is at work at the time. This equates to around 12 fatalities and 155 serious injuries in Great Britain every week. Incidents involving goods vehicles account for around 8% of all deaths and injuries caused by road traffic incidents in Great Britain.*

The total value of prevention of British road traffic incidents in 2016 was estimated to be £16 billion.* This includes an estimate of the cost of damage-only incidents but doesn't allow for unreported injury incidents.

Companies can suffer substantial downtime as a result of road traffic incidents, and staff may need time to recover. This leads to more vehicles off the road and lost business. It's the responsibility of all drivers to try to reduce the number of incidents on the road. Road safety is of paramount importance.

Incidents at work

Incidents at work aren't restricted to road traffic incidents. The haulage and distribution industry has a high rate of other types of incident. If road traffic incidents are excluded, studies show that, over a five-year period, 60 employees were killed, 5000 were seriously injured and 23 000 suffered injuries severe enough to keep them off work for three or more days.**

Almost all deaths at work arise from one of the following:

- being struck by a moving vehicle
- falling loads
- falling from a vehicle.

Many major injuries happen during loading and unloading. They're caused by

- slips and trips
- collapsing or overturning vehicles
- being struck by moving or falling objects
- falls from less than two metres
- manual handling.

* Figures taken from 'Reported Road Casualties Great Britain: 2016', produced by DfT and published by National Statistics

** 'Health and Safety in Road Haulage', published by HSE.

Together, manual handling and slips/trips account for two-thirds of other reportable injuries.

Parking a vehicle on soft ground when loading or unloading is particularly dangerous. The ground may shift under the weight of the vehicle, causing the vehicle to become unstable or roll over.

Drivers very often need to work at height on a vehicle, and falling from a vehicle is one of the most common causes of injury. Managers should consider the following points when trying to minimise the risks.

- Reduce the need for people to work at height or provide equipment for safe access, such as scaffolds, handrails, access steps, gantries and platforms.

- Position the load so that the items to be unloaded first are the most accessible. This will reduce the need to climb onto the load.

- Allow enough time to complete loading and unloading. This will reduce the risk of slips, trips and falls, as drivers will be less rushed.

- Provide training in how to avoid slips and trips.

- Make sure incidents and defects with safety equipment are reported and rectified.

- Ensure safe handling of loads at delivery and collection sites by communicating with clients and suppliers before arrival.

- Make sure that appropriate cleaning equipment is provided, as well as waste disposal facilities to keep the area tidy. Diesel spills, oil and grease may be picked up on the soles of footwear and spread to other surfaces, making them slippery. Contaminants need to be removed, so there must be safe access for cleaning and maintenance.

- Consider the effects of weather conditions. Falls may be caused by high winds, rain, snow and ice. These conditions can make surfaces slippery and affect balance.

- Be aware that yards may have potholes and uneven surfaces.

Deliveries and collections

Deliveries and collections can be dangerous activities. Injuries may result from manual handling, being hit by a vehicle or falling. Reasonable steps should be taken to prevent incidents. This involves communication between the supplier, haulage company and the person receiving the load (the 'duty holders').

These parties have a responsibility to inform one another, decide on appropriate safety measures and ensure these measures are put into practice. Such measures may include

- wearing high-visibility clothing
- designating a responsible person who will be in overall charge of the loading and unloading of visiting vehicles
- knowing what to do if a load has shifted
- ensuring the correct methods of loading and unloading, including the correct equipment, are used
- training drivers in general safety, plus what to do if a site doesn't conform to acceptable safety standards. A driver should be able to recognise a dangerous practice and refuse to load or unload
- encouraging drivers to report any incidents and telling them whom to contact
- using platforms with slip-resistant surfaces, handrails and access steps that remain with the vehicle
- using work restraint systems, such as a harness and lanyard, that make it impossible for a worker to get into a dangerous position from which they could fall.

To ensure safety, it's important to observe speed limits imposed by the company when driving on site.

Falls from vehicles

Every year, several hundred people die or are seriously injured falling from vehicles. To minimise the risk of falling from a vehicle, follow this advice.

- When entering the vehicle, always open the door fully, use both grab rails to enter the cab, and make sure all the steps are used.
- When exiting the cab, turn around and use both grab rails, making sure all the steps are used.
- Don't jump from the lorry or load. Use any steps provided, ensuring that they're safe for you to use.
- Always use all equipment provided to avoid work at height. If work at height is unavoidable, then use fall-arrest systems if possible, especially when roping and sheeting.
- Keep the lorry tidy – avoid creating tripping hazards.

- Wear suitable footwear for the job.

- Make sure that steps and work areas are well lit.

- Use edge protection on tail lifts (where it's fitted).

- Don't walk backwards near the rear or side of the vehicle bed.

- Only use equipment such as ropes, straps, curtains, sheets and nets if you're sure it's well maintained.

To help improve the working environment, you should report any

- damaged or broken sheeting devices

- damaged, loose or inadequate steps and handholds

- slippery surfaces; for example, those that are oily or greasy.

Other activities
Many more activities have become the subject of health-and-safety regulations. These include

- limits on the weight of objects that should be lifted manually; for example, packages that are being loaded or unloaded

- provision of protective clothing

  - reflective jackets

  - boots

  - gloves

  - warm clothing

  - hard hats where appropriate to the nature of the work.

Asbestos
During vehicle maintenance, drivers should be aware of the dangers to health from asbestos dust – especially when dealing with components known to contain this material, such as

- brake shoes

- clutch plates

- tank or pipe lagging.

Safe working practice

Extra care must be taken when working

- near or over inspection pits (danger of falling)
- in refrigerated vehicles (which may have wet or slippery floors)
- under hydraulically raised tipper bodies (danger of being crushed – use props)
- near engines emitting exhaust fumes (breathing problems)
- with solvents or degreasing agents (lung and skin problems)
- close to vehicle batteries (risk of burns or explosion)
- at the rear of a vehicle fitted with a tail-lift mechanism (foot injuries)
- in or near paint-spray shops (lung problems from vapour).

Before you open your cab door, check all around and in your mirrors to ensure you don't hit other people, obstructions or vehicles. Always make sure you check that the parking brake is properly applied before either leaving or working near your vehicle. You should also make sure that the engine and ignition system are switched off.

First aid at work

There are regulations governing the provision of adequate first-aid facilities and first aiders on any work premises. The extent of what needs to be provided depends on the number of staff, type of business, risk assessments, etc. Examples of the various risk levels are shown below.

Low-risk areas – shops, offices, libraries.

Medium-risk areas – light engineering and assembly work, food processing, warehousing.

High-risk areas – most construction sites, slaughterhouses, chemical manufacturing, extensive work with dangerous machinery or sharp instruments.

There should be some form of first-aid facilities in every workplace. At the very least, a first-aid kit should be available and all staff should know where it's kept. The minimum first-aid provision on any work site is

- a suitably stocked first-aid box
- an appointed person to take charge of first-aid arrangements and to keep the first-aid box suitably stocked.

The appointed person should be available at all times when people are at work on the site, but they shouldn't attempt to give first aid for which they haven't been trained. Several short courses are available that include details particular to first aid at work, and anyone can take a general first-aid course (see 'First aid' in section 4 for details of some course providers).

Many small injuries occur in the workplace; these are often very minor, and most don't require hospital treatment. However, to avoid the risk of infection, any wound should be cleaned and properly covered at the first opportunity – especially if

- the work area is dirty or dusty
- the work involves
  - using machinery or tools
  - handling of goods (ie manual loading/unloading)
  - working with foodstuffs
  - dealing with livestock
  - using chemicals or other possible contaminants.

If you incur a minor injury such as a cut or graze while on site, or if you're helping someone else who has incurred such an injury, you need to take certain precautions to protect yourself as well as the person you're helping. To minimise the risk of infection, you should

- wash and dry your hands before giving any treatment
- protect yourself by wearing disposable gloves
- carefully and gently clean the cut or graze and surrounding skin to remove any dirt and surface debris
- gently pat the area dry
- cover the area with a sterile dressing.

You shouldn't use adhesive plasters, as these can cause skin irritation.

Record-keeping

The company or site should have an accident book or some other method of logging and recording details of injuries, such as

- the name and job of the injured person
- the date, place and time of the incident

- details of the injury/illness and any treatment given
- what happened to the casualty immediately afterwards (for example, back to work, home, hospital)
- the name and signature of the person dealing with the incident.

You should always make sure that any book or log is completed properly, so that a record exists should complications develop from the injury at a later date. The information recorded can also help to identify accident trends and possible areas for improvement in the control of health-and-safety risks.

Personal protection

Even if the activities involved in collection, transport and delivery of your payload have no requirement for such things as headgear, ear protection or safety glasses, two essential safety items for use at all times are

- a high-visibility jacket or vest to maximise your visibility
- protective footwear to guard feet against drop or crush injuries.

High-visibility clothing

High-visibility clothing is especially important when loading or unloading – there could be other vehicles reversing in the area around you or forklift trucks in operation.

You should also make sure that you're clearly visible during rest stops, vehicle checks or breakdowns. At these times, you may be outside your vehicle, adjacent to moving traffic.

Protective footwear

Footwear is an important consideration in the prevention of incidents at work. Steel toecaps help to protect drivers from falling objects, and slip-resistant shoes help to prevent slips, trips and falls. It's important to clean mud, etc off shoes to stop surfaces becoming slippery in the first place.

Certain types of protective footwear can also guard against things like corrosive substances, oil or heat. It's important to make sure you have the most appropriate footwear for your job.

Personal protective equipment

Your operator should provide you with any personal protective equipment (PPE) that's needed to perform your duties, but it's your responsibility to ensure that you use it properly, for your own safety, even if it's only required occasionally for a specific task. In addition to a high-visibility jacket and protective footwear, important protective items might include

- hard hat or other protective headgear
- heat- or corrosion-resistant gloves
- safety glasses/protective goggles
- face mask/breathing apparatus
- ear protectors/plugs.

For example, wet cement can cause skin irritation and burns, so gloves and overalls with long sleeves and trousers should be worn while loading or unloading it. In the event of contact with the cement, the area of skin should be washed with both warm and cold clear running water.

If you transport animals, you may also have to pass through infection-control areas or decontamination procedures such as foot dips, walk-through disinfectant baths or hosing areas, for which you should have the appropriate waterproof clothing and footwear. Make sure that you carefully follow any instructions or procedures provided by your operator.

Personal safety awareness

Consider your personal safety throughout any journey – especially if the load you're carrying has high commercial value (for example, tobacco or alcohol). There's always the possibility of an attempted theft or hijack. Be aware of what's going on around you, especially if you have a regular delivery route.

During breaks, walkaround checks or when locking/unlocking your vehicle, etc, proceed with caution – watch for anything unusual, such as people who seem to be loitering or taking an interest in your activities. Activating the vehicle alarm could make any potential assailant back off or leave the scene. Follow any instructions given by your operator, stay aware and stay safe.

Defusing an awkward situation

Occasionally, you may experience a situation where another person displays a confrontational attitude – for example, following a road traffic incident.

If a situation does develop, stay in your vehicle if you can, as it gives some physical protection. If you're already out of your vehicle when a situation develops, you can use body language to help calm things down by

- speaking in gentle, mild tones – you'll seem less threatening

- keeping your hands raised and open at midriff level while talking, and not pointing

- not standing too close or making body contact, as this can be misinterpreted.

Don't aggravate any situation by losing your temper or focusing on who was to blame.

Most situations can be defused by following three steps, in the specific order shown below. You need to be

- **calming** – listening and encouraging them to keep talking for as long as they need

- **assuring** – repeating their main points back to them to show understanding

- **controlling** – offering a solution or a way out that's mutually acceptable.

If the situation deteriorates at any time, return to step one. Continue to show your willingness to listen until the other person has calmed sufficiently, then move on through the process gradually until resolution is reached.

➡ Your vehicle

The law

The law relating to vehicles is extensive. Manufacturers, operators and drivers must all obey specific regulations.

The manufacturer is responsible for ensuring that the vehicle is built to comply with the Construction and Use Regulations.

The operator is responsible for making sure that a vehicle

- continues to comply with those regulations
- meets all current requirements and new regulations as they're introduced

- is tested as required
- displays all required markings, discs and certificates
- is in a serviceable condition, including equipment, fixtures and fittings.

In addition, the operator must operate a system of reporting and recording any faults that might affect the roadworthiness of the vehicle. This reporting system should enable drivers of the vehicle to report such defects, both verbally and in writing, and have them rectified before the vehicle is used again. This should include problems associated with the tachograph or speed limiter.

Operators should make drivers aware of their legal responsibilities regarding vehicle condition. It's important for all operators to ensure that company procedures for defect reporting are fully understood by their drivers. The driver shares responsibility for vehicle roadworthiness with the operator. This means that a driver may be liable for prosecution if they're considered partly or wholly responsible for the existence of any defect found. They could also lose their driving licence.

The operator shouldn't cause or permit a vehicle to be operated in any way other than the law allows. It's recommended that written records of faults and corrections to any vehicle should be kept by the operator, as a historical reference, with other documents for that vehicle. Where drivers are expected to make minor repairs themselves (for example, light-bulb replacement), operators should bear in mind that they may need basic training.

Daily walkaround check

A daily walkaround check should always be carried out before you start your journey. As the driver, you're legally responsible for the condition of your vehicle while it's in use on the road. You must

- take all reasonable precautions to ensure that legal requirements are met before driving any vehicle
- check that the vehicle is fully roadworthy and free from significant defects before driving it
- ensure that any equipment, fixtures or fittings required are present and serviceable, including a height-restriction plate in the cab, which should be visible to the driver
- not drive the vehicle if any fault develops that would make it illegal
- ensure that all actions while in charge of the vehicle are lawful.

See this link for a diagram of a walkaround check:
www.gov.uk/guidance/carry-out-daily-heavy-goods-vehicle-hgv-walkaround-checks

The daily walkaround check should include the items in the following list – some of which need to be checked from inside the vehicle. Check

- brakes
- steering
- lights and indicators
- windscreen wipers and washers
- horn
- mirrors
- speedometer
- tachograph
- tyres and wheel-securing nuts/markers
- fuel tanks/caps

- number plates
- reflectors and reflective plates
- bodywork
- exhaust system
- spray-suppression equipment
- any coupling gear
- speed limiter
- correct plating
- current test certificate (if required)
- proper licensing, with the appropriate valid disc(s) displayed
- insurance
- seat belts
- any load being carried.

It's advisable to wear gloves when checking fuel caps, connecting trailer lines, etc, to help eliminate the risk of infections or conditions such as dermatitis or eczema. Your hands will remain clean and you'll preserve a smart appearance for customers, as well as keeping the cab area and controls free of dirt.

When a defect, such as a faulty fog light, is found on a walkaround check, you should make a record of the defect and have it fixed before going onto the public highway. If you discover a serious defect, such as fuel leaking out of a tanker, a supervisor should be informed immediately.

You should look out for anything fitted to the vehicle that isn't required by law but is

- unserviceable
- in a dangerous condition
- not fitted so as to comply with the regulations.

Reporting defects
The results of daily walkaround checks should be recorded. In addition, the driver must monitor the roadworthiness of the vehicle while it's being driven and be alert to any indication that the vehicle is developing a fault (warning lights, exhaust emitting too much smoke, vibrations, etc).

Drivers should report any defects on the vehicle's defect report sheet and make sure that faults are rectified before using the vehicle. Details should include

- the vehicle registration or identification mark
- the date
- details of the defect or symptoms
- the name of the driver/reporter.

The reporting system should include a prioritising procedure, depending on the seriousness of the defect. Where road safety would be compromised, the procedure should enable urgent correction of the defect and allow the vehicle to be taken off the road immediately. Ideally, there should be systems in place to avoid disruption to the business, perhaps by having the facility to hire a similar vehicle at short notice.

It's recommended that any reporting system should incorporate 'nil' reporting, whereby the driver makes out a report sheet confirming that the daily check has been carried out and no defects have been found. Nil reports aren't required under the conditions of operator licensing, but they're a useful means of confirming that daily checks are being made.

Vehicle maintenance records must be kept, covering the previous 15 months. If you're an owner-driver with no-one to whom you can report defects, then you just need to keep defect records yourself for the prescribed 15-month period.

Roadside checks

'Red' (rebated) diesel fuel is restricted to use for authorised purposes only. Any driver whose vehicle is found to be illegally operating on this fuel will face severe penalties for attempting to evade excise duty. Roadside checks are frequently carried out by HM Revenue & Customs officers. Other checks might include the type and legality of any load being carried.

DVSA

DVSA (DVA in Northern Ireland) and the police carry out frequent spot checks of vehicle condition. Where serious defects are found, the vehicle is prohibited from further use until the defects are rectified. Details of the prohibition are notified to the traffic commissioner.

DVA/DVSA officers may be accompanied by staff from other agencies or departments; for example, local-authority environmental health departments check vehicles' exhaust emissions. These staff have the power to prosecute the driver and/or operator if excess emissions are found.

Staff from Trading Standards departments make checks on vehicle weights, and have the power to prohibit a non-compliant vehicle and/or prosecute the driver and/or operator. Department for Work and Pensions staff check for benefit fraud.

Prohibitions

A DVSA examiner can prohibit any goods vehicle that contravenes the Construction and Use Regulations (including overloading) or that's being used in contravention of the drivers' hours and record-keeping regulations.

An examiner issues a prohibition in respect of the vehicle when an offence or defect, relating either to the vehicle or to the driver, is found at an inspection. This inspection could take place either at the roadside or where the vehicle is parked.

Most prohibitions come into force immediately, but some, issued in respect of less serious roadworthiness defects, are delayed so that they come into force up to 10 days from the date of the offence being found. The length of the delay depends on the risk to road safety posed by the defect.

In all cases, the fault or defect must be rectified before the prohibition will be lifted. Therefore, a prohibition issued in respect of a construction-and-use offence (including overloading) will only be lifted following an inspection of the vehicle. In the case of more serious roadworthiness offences, this frequently means a full inspection of the vehicle at a goods vehicle testing station.

Overloaded vehicles must have the excess weight removed, and must then be reweighed and found to be at or below the legal weight limits, before the prohibition will be lifted. Some prohibitions issued in respect of drivers' hours regulations are for a specific period (for example, 24 hours), after which time the driver can continue their journey without having to be released by an examiner.

Impounding

Any laden HGV operating on a public road for the carriage of goods (either for hire or reward or in connection with any trade or business) without an operator's licence can be detained by a DVSA examiner. Goods vehicles used on the road by illegal operators can be impounded and removed to a secure storage facility.

Note: an illegal operator is one who requires an operator's licence but chooses to deliberately and knowingly operate illegally.

Cockpit drill

Make the following checks for the safety of yourself, any passengers and other road users.

Every time you get into your vehicle, check that

- the driving seat and head restraint are correctly adjusted, so that you can sit with the correct posture, reach all controls comfortably and take effective observation
- all interior and exterior mirrors are clean and correctly adjusted
- the lenses and screens of rear-view video equipment are clean and clear
- gauges and warning systems are working correctly (never start a journey with a defective warning device or when a warning light is showing)
- the parking brake is applied
- the gear selector is in neutral (or in 'Park' if driving an automatic vehicle)
- you have sufficient fuel for your journey or until you can next refuel
- your mobile phone is switched off
- the doors are working correctly and are closed before moving off.

Before starting your journey, make sure that you know and understand

- the controls: where they are and how they work
- vehicle size: its width, height and weight
- handling: the vehicle's characteristics
- brakes: whether an anti-lock braking system (ABS) is fitted.

Road-speed limiters

Vehicles that require speed limiters

Goods vehicles requiring speed limiters are those

- with a maximum gross weight of more than 12 tonnes, first used on or after 1 January 1988, which, if a speed limiter were not fitted, would be able to achieve speeds exceeding 56 mph (90 km/h)

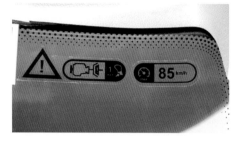

- with a maximum gross weight of more than 7.5 tonnes but not exceeding 12 tonnes, first used on or after 1 August 1992, which, if a speed limiter were not fitted, would be able to achieve speeds exceeding 60 mph (96 km/h)

- with a maximum gross weight of more than 3.5 tonnes but not exceeding 7.5 tonnes, first used on or after 1 January 2005.

If your goods vehicle is fitted with a speed limiter, this will be set at no more than 56 mph (90 km/h).

Exemptions

The requirement for a speed limiter doesn't apply to any vehicle that's

- being taken to a place where a speed limiter is to be installed, calibrated, repaired or replaced

- completing a journey in the course of which the speed limiter has accidentally ceased to function

- used for police, fire or ambulance purposes

- used for naval, military or air-force purposes when used by the Crown or owned by the Ministry of Defence

- being used for no more than six miles on a public road in any calendar week, between land occupied by the vehicle keeper.

The legislation surrounding speed limiters is complex. For more information, contact DVSA.

Speed-limiter technology

There are two main types of speed limiter. One type has a mechanical or electrical actuator, while the other works through the vehicle's engine management system.

Parts

The system consists of

- a road-speed sensor – this may or may not be part of the tachograph system
- an electronic cable
- an electronic control unit (ECU) – this may or may not be part of the vehicle's engine management system
- an actuation device – this may be a pump, relay or valve
- a plate that's fitted to the vehicle to show the set speed.

Connections

Only authorised speed-limiter centres may carry out installation, repairs and calibration. These centres will seal all connections between the speed sensor, ECU and actuation device, to ensure the system is tamper-proof.

Principles of operation

The speed limiter works by receiving a road-speed signal either from the tachograph or from a sensor fitted to another system on the vehicle, such as the ABS. Occasionally, a specific sensor for the speed-limiter system may be fitted. The vast majority of vehicles are fitted with speed limiters that take the road-speed signal from the tachograph.

Irrespective of the type of sensor used, the information is transmitted to the ECU, which in turn controls the equipment used to regulate the power output or revolutions of the vehicle's engine. This is normally achieved by reducing the amount of fuel supplied to the engine.

Maintenance

No day-to-day maintenance is required. However, any failure of the speed limiter must be reported to the operator of the vehicle, who should arrange for it to be repaired at the end of the journey upon which the vehicle is engaged.

Safety of loads on vehicles

The Road Traffic Act 1991 created new offences relating to the state of vehicle loads. All loads carried must be secure whatever the journey, to protect people involved in loading, unloading and driving the vehicle, as well as all other road users and pedestrians. Prosecutions for unsafe loads are brought against drivers and operators in the UK every year. There are stiff penalties, such as disqualification or even, in the most serious circumstances, imprisonment.

All equipment used for securing loads must be inspected regularly for damage or wear. Inspection arrangements must be in accordance with the manufacturer's instructions.

Special attention should be paid to webbing and rope restraints, to ensure there's no visible deterioration (such as fraying) due to constant use. They should also be inspected to ensure they haven't been cut or damaged in any other way; for example, through misuse or by deliberate interference. Detailed information on load types and appropriate restraints can be found in section 2.

Anti-theft measures

Unfortunately, theft of vehicles and trailers is common. You're responsible for your vehicle, so you should make every effort to reduce the risk of it being stolen.

- Don't discuss the details of your load with any unauthorised person.
- Never leave the keys in the cab while it's unattended, even if you're at the rear of the vehicle.
- You can't afford to give a lift to anyone, however plausible their story or however innocent they look.
- Whenever possible, try to avoid using the same route and making the same drops and rest stops.
- Have all major components (plus glass) security etched with the Vehicle Identification Number (VIN).
- Only park in secure, well-lit, reputable overnight lorry parks or designated parking areas if your rest stops can be planned this way. This is especially important if you wish to leave a semi-trailer unattended. Don't park a semi-trailer in a lay-by.

- One simple but effective measure that many drivers adopt at overnight stops is to park with the rear doors of their vehicle or its trailer/container hard up against another vehicle. This works well on most occasions.
- Avoid parking in obviously vulnerable areas if at all possible.
- When leaving your vehicle (for example, for a statutory break), park safely. Try to park your vehicle within sight and check for signs of interference when you return to it.
- Keep your mobile phone with you, if you have one.
- Ensure that all doors are locked and the windows secure if you sleep in the cab overnight.
- Always ask to see the identity card of any officer who might stop you.
- Have an approved alarm system and/or immobiliser fitted to the vehicle by a reputable security specialist.
- Avoid leaving any trailer unattended unless it's on approved secure premises.
- Fit a kingpin or drawbar lock to any trailer that has to be left unattended.

Whenever you return to your vehicle, carry out a further walkaround security check before driving away. Check that your vehicle hasn't been entered, or tampered with in any way, in your absence. Be aware of your own safety at all times. If you witness any suspicious behaviour around your vehicle, it's important that you call the police and inform your employer.

Operators should seek the advice of their local crime-prevention officer, especially if engaged in the transit of high-value merchandise. Fleet operators that regularly carry vulnerable or dangerous loads are encouraged to use roof markings to help police air-support units identify stolen vehicles.

⊕ Your driving

Legal requirements

You must always drive within the law and comply with

- speed limits
- weight limits
- loading/unloading restrictions
- waiting restrictions
- stopping restrictions (clearways)
- lighting regulations
- restrictions of access to
  - pedestrian precincts
  - residential areas
  - traffic-calming zones
  - play streets
- all traffic signs
- road markings
- traffic signals at
  - junctions
  - level crossings
  - fire or ambulance stations
  - lifting or swing bridges
- signals given by authorised persons
  - police officers
  - traffic wardens
  - traffic officers
  - DVSA officers
  - local-authority parking attendants
  - school crossing patrols
  - persons engaged in road repairs

- motorway regulations
- regulations governing specific locations
  - tunnels
  - bridges
  - ferries
- pedestrian crossing rules.

Driving licences

A category C driving licence is a necessity if you wish to earn your living driving HGVs. It's also essential that, when you drive any vehicle other than a goods vehicle, your driving continues to be of the highest standard. If you accumulate penalty points on your car or motorcycle licence, your goods-vehicle licence will be at risk.

Speed limits

Your vehicle may be fitted with a speed limiter, which will generally prevent you from exceeding motorway speed limits. However, it won't stop you exceeding lower speed limits. Observing speed limits is part of your responsibility.

The speed limits that apply to different classes of vehicle on different types of road can be found in The Highway Code. On motorways with more than two lanes, trailers mustn't be towed in the outside lane unless other lanes are closed.

Speeding offences

Police forces and local authorities are now using the most up-to-date technology in an effort to persuade drivers to comply with speed limits.

Fixed cameras that photograph vehicles exceeding the speed limit have been in use for a number of years, but improved detection equipment can now lock on to individual vehicles in busy traffic flows. In addition, new electronic systems display the registration number and speed of any offending vehicle at selected motorway locations, with a view to 'showing up' the driver concerned.

Drivers whose speed is considerably higher than the legal speed limit can expect a fine equivalent to at least 150% of their weekly wages. Remember, though: the aim is to improve driving standards, not to increase prosecutions.

Red-light cameras

Cameras have been installed at many traffic-incident 'black spots' to record drivers who fail to comply with traffic signals. These cameras are also intended to act as a deterrent and to improve safety for road users in general.

Whether it relates to an alleged speeding offence or traffic-signal offence, any photograph produced as evidence will be difficult to dispute if it shows the

- time
- date
- speed
- vehicle registration number
- length of time a red signal had already been showing.

Red Routes

On many roads in London and other large UK towns and cities, yellow lines have been replaced with red lines. A network of priority Red Routes for London was approved by Parliament as a means of addressing traffic congestion and widespread disregard of parking restrictions in the capital. Red Route measures currently apply to 580 kilometres (360 miles) of London's roads.

Yellow-line exemptions don't apply on Red Routes. During the day, loading is only allowed in marked boxes. Overnight and on Sundays, most controls are relaxed to allow unrestricted stopping. However, it's important to check the signs carefully, as the hours of operation for Red Routes vary from area to area.

In London, Red Route controls are enforced by Metropolitan Police traffic police community support officers (PCSOs). There's a fixed fine for illegally stopping on a Red Route, with no discount for early payment.

The police or traffic wardens are able to provide limited dispensations for the rare occasions when loading provisions aren't adequate. These will be available from the local police station.

There are five main types of Red Route marking. The image above shows the layout of the lines on the road. You'll find all the signs more clearly laid out, along with their respective lines, in the DfT publication 'Know Your Traffic Signs'.

Double red lines

Double red lines ban all stopping 24 hours a day, seven days a week. For example, you aren't allowed to stop for

* loading or unloading
* dropping off passengers
* visiting shops.

Single red lines

Single red lines ban all stopping during the daytime; for example, 7.00 am to 7.00 pm, Monday to Saturday. Outside these hours, unrestricted stopping is allowed.

Parking boxes

Parking boxes allow vehicles free short-term parking and can be used for loading.

* **Red boxes** allow parking or loading outside 'rush' hours (for example, between 10.00 am and 4.00 pm), for periods of 20 minutes to one hour.
* **White boxes** allow parking or loading at any time, but a stay may be restricted to 20 minutes or one hour during the day.

At other times, such as between 7.00 pm and 7.00 am, and on Sundays, unrestricted stopping is allowed in either type of parking box.

Loading boxes

Loading boxes mark the areas where only loading is allowed. 'Loading' is defined as when a vehicle stops briefly to load or unload bulky or heavy goods. These goods must be so heavy or bulky that it isn't easy to carry them any distance, and it may involve more than one trip. If that isn't the case, then your vehicle should be parked legally and the goods carried to the premises. Picking up portable items, such as shopping, doesn't constitute loading.

- **Red boxes** allow loading outside 'rush' hours (for example, between 10.00 am and 4.00 pm), for a maximum of 20 minutes.

- **White boxes** allow loading at any time, but a stay is restricted to a maximum of 20 minutes during the day.

At other times, such as between 7.00 pm and 7.00 am, and on Sundays, unrestricted stopping is allowed in either type of loading box.

Clearways

Clearways are found on major roads. There won't be any red lines, but Red Route clearway signs will indicate that stopping isn't allowed at any time.

Further Red Route information can be found in section 4 of this book. You can also visit **tfl.gov.uk/modes/driving/red-routes** or call Transport for London Customer Services on **0343 222 2222**.

Congestion charging

Congestion charging operates in central London to help reduce the volume of traffic and make journey and delivery times more reliable. The congestion charge applies from 7.00 am to 6.30 pm, Monday to Friday, excluding public holidays. Failure to pay the charge will lead to a fine.

Exemptions

Groups that are exempt from the charge include

- disabled people who hold a Blue Badge
- drivers of electrically powered vehicles
- vehicles with nine or more seats
- roadside recovery vehicles
- all two-wheeled vehicles
- London licensed taxis and minicabs.

(Note: for information about these vehicles and minimum emissions standards, see **tfl.gov.uk/modes/driving/ultra-low-emission-zone/motorcycles-mopeds-and-more**)

Residents who live within the congestion-charging zone pay a reduced rate.

Drivers in some categories of exemption need to register with Transport for London (see below for contact details).

Discounts
Businesses and other organisations operating a fleet of 25 or more vehicles are entitled to a discount when they register with a dedicated fleet scheme.

For more information, to register or to make a payment, ring the Congestion Charge line on **0343 222 2222** or visit the website **tfl.gov.uk/modes/driving/congestion-charge**

Congestion charging is gradually being introduced in other UK towns and cities.

Low and Ultra Low Emission Zones
London also has a Low Emission Zone (LEZ) and an Ultra Low Emission Zone (ULEZ). The zones cover most of Greater London and operate for 24 hours a day, all year round. Charging days run from midnight to midnight, so if you entered the zone before midnight and were still driving through it at 1.30 am you'd need to pay the charge for both days. To see if your vehicle is affected, visit **tfl.gov.uk**

Section four
➜ Driver skills

This section covers

- Professional driving
- Driving at night
- Motorway driving
- All-weather driving
- Avoiding and dealing with congestion
- Helping the environment
- Road traffic incidents
- First aid
- Breakdowns

⊙ Professional driving

This section provides specialist advice on good driving practice for drivers of heavy goods vehicles (HGVs). Other useful information can be found in 'The Official DVSA Guide to Driving – the essential skills'. Every professional driver must be familiar with the rules of the road, as published in 'The Official Highway Code'.

The rules for all types of road users have recently been updated in The Highway Code to improve the safety of people walking, cycling and riding horses.

Study the latest edition carefully and make sure you understand your responsibilities towards more vulnerable road users.

Essential skills

A professional driver should develop the skills necessary to make clear, positive decisions about situations encountered on the road. The following are the main skills you'll require.

Control

You must have the physical skills to keep control of your vehicle at all times. You should know how your vehicle and its load will handle in any situation you encounter by understanding its capabilities and limitations.

Awareness

You need to know what's happening around you, so that you're always conscious of any potential hazards. This will give you the time to deal with hazards as they occur.

Planning

Proper planning will enable you to act early when approaching junctions or hazards. This will prevent unnecessary braking and gear-changing, helping you to make progress in traffic. Loaded large vehicles take longer to gain speed than smaller vehicles. Other road users will appreciate your ability to avoid late signalling, constant braking and slow acceleration away from hazards.

Anticipation

By knowing the correct way to deal with situations as they occur, you'll develop anticipation of how to react in those instances. You'll also have a better insight into the way others respond to those same situations.

You should drive skilfully and plan ahead, so that your vehicle is travelling at the appropriate speed and in the correct position for the next manoeuvre you need to make. You should never have to take action hastily. By adopting the correct techniques, you'll create the time and room needed to complete manoeuvres safely.

Other road users

Everyone suffers when collisions happen. But people in charge of vehicles that can cause the greatest harm in a collision bear the greatest responsibility to take care and reduce the danger they pose to others. As a driver of a large vehicle, you will have a responsibility to reduce danger to motorcyclists, cyclists, pedestrians and horse riders.

Remember that other people on the road might make mistakes. You have to accept that other road users are not always aware of the extra room or time you need due to the size of your vehicle.

Young children
Young children are particularly unpredictable and might run out into the road suddenly. If you're passing pedestrians who are walking on the pavement but close to the kerb, you must be aware that the size of your vehicle will cause a draught. This could unsteady a small child or, indeed, an adult. Always check your nearside mirror as you pass pedestrians, particularly if you're pulling up on the left. Take care that your nearside mirror doesn't strike the head of any pedestrian.

Take extra care on congested roads, particularly in shopping areas or when near ice-cream vans or mobile shops.

In school areas, you may see a pole with two flashing amber lights, one above the other. This means that children will be crossing the road to or from school. Slow down and watch out for them. Drive slowly until you're clear of the area.

Older people
Some older pedestrians may have poor eyesight and/or hearing difficulties. This might make them indecisive and they may sometimes become confused. They also might take longer to cross the road. You need to understand this and allow them more time.

Older drivers might be hesitant or become confused at major junctions or gyratory systems. Don't intimidate them by driving too close or revving your engine.

Learner drivers

Learner drivers who aren't used to all driving situations and other types of road user might drive excessively slowly or be hesitant. Be patient and give them room.

Cyclists

You need to allow cyclists as much room as you would a car. They might swerve unexpectedly or be blown off course by a gust of wind. If they're approaching a junction or roundabout, you must be aware that they might turn right from the left-hand lane, crossing the path of other traffic. If you see a cyclist ahead of you glancing to their right, they're probably about to turn right. Allow for this.

The size and shape of your vehicle makes it essential that you're aware of the presence of cyclists **all around** you. Use your nearside mirror as you pass a cyclist to check that you've done so safely. When you're waiting at a junction, be aware that they might move up on either side. If they're positioned in front of your nearside mirror, between the kerb and your front nearside wheel, they'll be difficult to see. You should allow them to move away before you drive off.

Cyclists are much narrower than other vehicles and can be difficult to see, especially when you're emerging from a side road. Look carefully at all times before emerging.

Motorcyclists

Much of what has been said about cyclists also applies to motorcyclists. They're very vulnerable because, like cyclists, they're much smaller than other vehicles and are difficult to see. However, they also travel much faster than cyclists, so situations develop much more quickly.

The main cause of motorcycle collisions is other drivers. Many incidents occur because drivers fail to notice motorcyclists, so look out for them when

- emerging at junctions – a motorcyclist may be travelling on the major road and may be hidden behind other traffic. They can be completely hidden from view in the blind spots caused by your vehicle door pillars, mirrors etc. They may also be hidden by signs, trees or street furniture
- turning into a road on your right – a motorcyclist may be following, overtaking or approaching you. Oncoming motorcyclists can be particularly difficult to see, as they may be hidden behind larger vehicles
- straddling lanes; for example, to turn left or to negotiate a roundabout
- changing lanes or moving out to pass slower-moving or parked vehicles.

Motorcyclists often ride between queues of slower-moving traffic to make progress. This is commonly known as filtering. When you're in heavy, slow-moving traffic, always look for cyclists and motorcyclists before you change direction.

Riders may change direction suddenly to avoid loose, slippery or uneven surfaces. They can also be affected by weather conditions. For example, in windy weather, a motorcyclist may be buffeted and blown off course, especially on exposed stretches of road. Think about how motorcyclists may be affected by the weather conditions and make allowances for them.

If there's a slow-moving motorcyclist ahead of you, be patient and stay behind. They might be changing direction, turning, or unsure of their destination.

Pay special attention to motorcycles and mopeds displaying L plates (or D plates in Wales). The riders of these machines may have very little experience on the road, so they're particularly vulnerable.

Horses and other animals
Horses are easily frightened by

- noise (for example, revving engines or hissing air brakes)
- headlights or flashing lights
- vehicles passing too close to them.

Large vehicles can be particularly intimidating. If you see horse riders ahead, either on the road or on the grass verge, plan your approach carefully. Slow down safely and don't rev your engine. You should allow for the fact that some riders might be learners and may not have full control if the animal is startled. Novice riders may sometimes be on a leading rein and have someone walking with them.

When you pass horses and riders, do so slowly, leave plenty of room and be ready to stop if necessary. Always check your nearside mirror to make sure that you've completed the manoeuvre safely. Don't flash your headlights unnecessarily and remember that the hiss of air from your brakes could cause horses to shy or bolt.

If someone in charge of animals signals you to stop, do so and switch off your engine.

Guide dogs

A guide dog usually has a distinctive 'loop' type of harness. The dog is trained to wait until the road is clear before crossing.

The presence of a guide dog doesn't only indicate a visual impairment. Some people with hearing difficulties may also have a guide dog with a yellow or burgundy jacket. If you see a pedestrian with such a dog, they may not be able to hear your vehicle approaching. When a person is both deaf and blind, they may carry a white stick with a red band and their dog may have a red-and-white checked harness.

Effective observation

Mirrors

When you're learning to drive, get into a routine of checking your mirrors. It's important to know about traffic conditions all around you, not just what's going on ahead. Before you change direction or alter your speed, you should assess how your actions will affect other road users.

Blind spots

Because of your vehicle's size and design, you might not be able to see much by looking around, especially if the vehicle is fitted with a sleeper cab. This makes it all the more important to be constantly aware of vehicles in your blind spot on either the offside or the nearside. Be especially aware if your vehicle is left-hand drive, or if you're driving a right-hand-drive vehicle in countries outside the UK.

A sideways glance is often helpful, especially

- before changing lanes on a motorway or dual carriageway
- where traffic is merging from the right or left
- when approaching the main carriageway from a motorway slip road.

Types of mirror

To help overcome blind spots, many large vehicles are fitted with additional mirrors and, sometimes, cameras.

Class II rear-view mirrors These are the standard external rear-view mirrors.

Class IV wide-angle mirror This gives the driver a wider view to the side of the lorry. These mirrors are made from convex glass and reflect a smaller image, which can make it more difficult to judge the speed and distance of any object.

Class V side close proximity mirror This mirror is mounted above the nearside door and shows the area immediately around the front nearside wheel. It can help you to judge the vehicle's position relative to the kerb when parking, and also helps you to see obstructions or vulnerable road users close to the nearside of the vehicle.

Class II rear-view mirror

Class IV wide-angle mirror

Class V side close proximity mirror

Class VI 'Cyclops' mirror

Class VI 'Cyclops' mirror This mirror shows the area immediately in front of the vehicle. It can reveal pedestrians, cyclists or motorcyclists who would otherwise be outside the driver's field of view, especially

* at pedestrian crossings
* in slow-moving, congested traffic.

If you wish to operate any goods vehicle weighing over 3.5 tonnes in London, the vehicle will have to comply with London's Safer Lorry Scheme. This requires lorries to be fitted with

* Class V and Class VI mirrors, to give the driver a better view of cyclists and pedestrians around their vehicle
* side guards to protect cyclists from being dragged under the vehicle's wheels in the event of a collision.

For more information, visit **tfl.gov.uk**

Some vehicle manufacturers are replacing mirrors with externally mounted cameras. They should be used in such a way that the driver has at least the same level of awareness that they would have had if mirrors were fitted.

Use of mirrors
You should use your mirrors well before you signal your intention or make any manoeuvre, such as

* moving away
* changing direction
* turning left or right
* overtaking
* changing lanes
* slowing or stopping
* speeding up
* opening the cab door.

You should also check the mirrors frequently and use them to assess what road users around you are doing, or might do next.

Your mirrors should be

- clean and free from dust or grime
- properly adjusted to give a clear view behind. This is particularly important when you're transporting an oversized load that projects over the normal width of the vehicle.

You must check frequently down the sides of your vehicle.

Check the offside

- for overtaking traffic – especially cyclists or motorcyclists – coming up behind or already alongside. Do this before signalling
- before changing lanes, overtaking, turning right or moving to the right.

Check the nearside

- before you turn left; look for cyclists or motorcyclists filtering up the nearside of your vehicle
- for traffic on your left when moving in two or more lanes
- before moving back to the left after passing another road user, pedestrian(s) or parked vehicles
- to verify the position of the rear wheels of your vehicle or trailer in relation to the kerb
- before changing lanes and after overtaking, turning left or moving closer to the left when leaving roundabouts.

> **REMEMBER,** just a simple glance isn't enough. You need to check carefully.

Moving away

When moving away, look all around to make sure that it's clear **before** your vehicle starts to move. You must also check your nearside and close proximity mirrors, if fitted. Don't rush these checks; only move away when you're sure that it's safe to do so.

Your driving position

Due to the height of your cab, you may have a better view from your driving position than other road users. You can take advantage of this. For example, when approaching a blind bend, by using your added height to see over hedgerows or other obstructions, you can scan ahead for potential hazards.

Observation at junctions

Your zone of vision is the area you can see as you look forward and to the side from your driving position. As you get closer to a junction, your zone of vision into the other road usually improves. You may need to get very close before you can see enough of the new road to know whether it's safe to proceed.

Sometimes, despite having a higher seating position than most drivers, your view at a junction will be restricted by some form of obstruction. To overcome this, you may

- be able to see approaching traffic reflected in shop windows
- have to ease forward until your zone of vision opens up and you can assess whether it's safe to emerge.

If a vehicle is approaching from the right and apparently indicating to turn into the junction where you're waiting, don't pull out until they've started to turn in, because there may be another reason for their signal.

Some road users are more difficult to see than others. Cyclists and motorcyclists, in particular, may be travelling fast and can easily be hidden from view by other traffic. Look carefully and assess the situation. Don't emerge until you **know** that it's clear.

Pedestrians can act unpredictably at junctions, sometimes stepping or even running out, oblivious to your presence. Use your close proximity mirror to check that no-one is standing immediately in front of your vehicle before you edge forward or emerge. Remember that you should give way to people crossing or waiting to cross at a junction.

Safe distances

Never drive at such a speed that you can't stop safely in the distance you can see to be clear. You need to take account of the effects of

- the weather
- the road surface
- any load.

Keep a safe separation distance between your vehicle and the one in front. In reasonable weather conditions, leave at least a two-second time gap. On wet roads, you'll need to at least double this distance, so allow a four-second time gap.

The two-second rule
You can check the time gap by watching the vehicle in front pass a stationary object, such as a bridge, pole or sign. As the vehicle passes that landmark, start saying to yourself **'Only a fool breaks the two-second rule'**. If you haven't finished saying this sentence by the time you reach the same point, then you're too close.

On some motorways, this rule is drawn to drivers' attention by chevrons painted on the road surface. The instruction 'Keep at least two chevrons from the vehicle ahead' also appears on a sign at these locations.

In congested traffic, moving at slower speeds, it may not be practicable to leave as much space, but you'll still need to leave enough distance to pull up safely.

If you find that a vehicle is driving too close behind you, gradually reduce your speed to increase the gap between your vehicle and the one ahead. You'll then be able to brake more gently if the vehicle ahead slows, and this will reduce the likelihood of the vehicle behind colliding with your rear. If another vehicle pulls into the safe separation gap that you've left, ease off your speed to establish the gap again.

Look well ahead
On a road where the national speed limit applies, or on a motorway, look well ahead for brake lights and hazard warning lights. These could indicate that traffic ahead is slowing down sharply for some reason.

Traffic signals

By planning well ahead, you'll reduce the effort needed to drive a goods vehicle. Anticipating traffic speeds ahead and easing off the accelerator may allow you to keep your vehicle moving. This can reduce the need to brake, to make multiple gear changes, to come to a stop, or to apply the parking brake. By driving like this, you'll be more able to make steady progress and it will keep your fuel costs down.

Approaching traffic lights

Signals on green

Look well ahead and gauge how much traffic is waiting on each side of the junction you're approaching. Ask yourself the following questions.

- How long has the green light been showing?
- If the signals change, can I stop safely?
- If I have to brake hard, will following traffic be able to stop safely?
- Are any vehicles waiting to turn across my path?
- How will the road surface and weather conditions affect my braking distance?

Signals on amber

The amber signal means **stop**. When the lights change to amber, you may only continue if

- you've already crossed the stop line
- you're so close to the stop line that to pull up might be unsafe or cause an incident.

Signals on red

The red traffic signal means that you **MUST** stop. However, you may be able to time your approach so that you're able to keep your vehicle moving as the signal changes to green. This is especially important when driving a laden vehicle uphill. Look well ahead for traffic lights.

Signals not working

If you come to traffic lights that aren't working, or there's a sign to show that they're out of order, treat the junction with great care, because no-one has priority.

> **REMEMBER,** a green light means go if the way is clear. Check that other vehicles using the junction have stopped at their red light. Only drive past a green light if you can clear the junction safely. (!)

Don't

- accelerate to try to get past the signals before they change
- wait until the last moment to brake – harsh braking could result in loss of control.

Harsh accelerating or braking could also cause your load to move.

Signalling

You should

- signal to let other road users know your intentions
- give other road users time to respond safely to your signal.

Road users include

- drivers of oncoming vehicles
- drivers of following vehicles
- motorcyclists
- cyclists
- crossing supervisors
- police directing traffic
- pedestrians
- horse riders
- road repair contractors.

Give signals

- clearly and in good time
- that are shown in The Highway Code.

Your signals should be readily understandable by all other road users. Try not to mislead anyone by giving a signal that could confuse; for example, when intending to pull up just after a junction on the left. (Another road user might misunderstand this signal if it's given too early.) Don't use your headlights as a signal to give or claim priority. This might lead other road users into a hazardous situation.

Any signal that doesn't appear in The Highway Code is unauthorised and could be misinterpreted by another road user.

Using the horn

You'll rarely need to sound the horn. Use it only if you're moving and you need to warn other road users of your presence – for example, at a blind bend or a hump bridge. Sounding the horn doesn't give you priority, nor does it relieve you of the responsibility to drive safely.

Don't use the horn

* when stationary
* between 11.30 pm and 7.00 am in a built-up area, unless there's danger from a moving vehicle
* as a rebuke or simply to attract attention (unless it's to avoid an incident or collision).

Avoid long, aggressive blasts on the horn, which can alarm pedestrians.

REMEMBER, some pedestrians might have hearing problems and so may not hear your warning.

Driving through tunnels

When you approach a tunnel

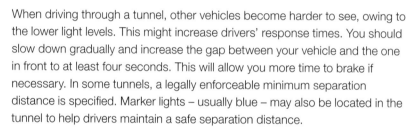

- switch on your dipped headlights

- observe the road signs and signals

- switch on your radio and tune it to the indicated frequency.

Many tunnels have radio transmitters to give drivers information and advance warning of any incident, congestion or roadworks. This information is particularly useful in European tunnels, some of which are many miles long.

If you're wearing sunglasses, take them off before you drive into a tunnel.

When driving through a tunnel, other vehicles become harder to see, owing to the lower light levels. This might increase drivers' response times. You should slow down gradually and increase the gap between your vehicle and the one in front to at least four seconds. This will allow you more time to brake if necessary. In some tunnels, a legally enforceable minimum separation distance is specified. Marker lights – usually blue – may also be located in the tunnel to help drivers maintain a safe separation distance.

If you're carrying dangerous goods, remember that the height of the vehicle and the need to have an escort must be considered when approaching a tunnel.

If the tunnel is congested

- keep your distance, even if you're moving slowly or stationary. If you have to stop, leave at least a 5-metre gap between you and the vehicle in front

- if possible, listen to messages on the radio.

- follow any instructions given by tunnel officials or variable message signs.

If you break down or are involved in a collision in a tunnel

- switch on your hazard warning lights

- switch off the engine

- leave your vehicle

- give first aid to any injured people, if you're able

- call for help from an emergency point.

If your vehicle is on fire and you can drive it out of the tunnel, do so. If not

- pull over to the side and switch off the engine
- leave the vehicle immediately
- **don't** open the engine cover fully. You may be able to direct the nozzle of a fire extinguisher through the small gap available when the release catch on the cover is undone
- should the fire appear to be large, **don't** try to tackle it. Get well clear of the vehicle and leave it to the fire brigade. Don't take any risks.

Emergency diversion routes

Sometimes, it's necessary to close a section of motorway or other main road to traffic. When this happens, a temporary sign may advise drivers to follow a diversion route. This route will bring traffic back onto the same road at some point after the closed section.

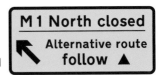

To help drivers navigate the route, black symbols on yellow patches may be permanently displayed on existing direction signs, including motorway signs. The sign alerting drivers to the road closure will identify the symbol they should follow.

A number of different symbols may be used, as in some places more than one diversion route may be in operation. The range of symbols used is shown below.

If you're driving a high-sided or extra-wide vehicle, you may need to check a map, satellite navigation equipment or other route information for details of any low or narrow bridges that may be present on the diversion route. If your vehicle is too large to fit under any bridge, you'll have to find an alternative route.

⊕ Driving at night

Driving an HGV at night, often over long distances, requires additional skills. The problems you need to overcome include

- not being able to see so far ahead
- dazzle, caused by the headlights of oncoming vehicles
- shadows created by patchy street lighting
- poor lighting on other vehicles (for example, pedal cycles)
- tiredness and fatigue, especially between midnight and 6.00 am, when your 'body clock' is in its daily trough.

Incidents have occurred because the driver of a large vehicle was either overcome by tiredness or failed to see an unlit, broken-down vehicle. Long night-time journeys, particularly on motorway routes with little to relieve the monotony, require planning and close attention to proper rest and refreshment stops.

Tiredness

All drivers are vulnerable to tiredness, especially at night. Don't ignore sleepy feelings. Always play it safe: stop for a break before you reach the stage of fighting sleep.

Don't

- drive without taking a proper rest period
- allow the cab to become too warm
- eat a heavy meal just before setting out
- take your eyes off the road to change radio channels or a music track
- use a mobile phone or headphones when driving.

Try to

- keep plenty of cool, fresh air moving through the cab
- walk around in the fresh air during a rest stop.

Remember, if you feel your concentration slipping, pull up at the next safe, convenient place and take a break.

Night vision

A goods vehicle driver's eyesight is tested at a higher standard than the eyesight of car drivers or motorcyclists. An optician can make sure that your night vision meets the required standard. Have your eyesight checked regularly and avoid

- wearing tinted glasses at night
- using tinted windscreen coverings.

Lighting-up time

You should switch on whichever vehicle lights are appropriate for the conditions, regardless of the official lighting-up times. If the weather conditions are poor or it becomes overcast early, switch on your lights. **See and be seen.**

You must also drive at an appropriate speed, so that you can stop in the distance that you can see to be clear. At night, this will usually be the distance illuminated by your headlights or by street lights.

Unlit vehicles

At night, you **MUST NOT** park a large vehicle on a public road or in a lay-by without using parking lights. You can only park without lights in an off-road parking area.

Vehicles under 2500 kg laden weight are permitted to park in 30 mph zones without lights at night time. Look for unlit vehicles when driving in built-up areas, especially when the street lighting is patchy.

Builders' skips on the road are required to be lit and show reflective plates to oncoming traffic. However, both of these measures can be either neglected or subject to vandalism, so be aware that some skips may be unlit.

Adjusting to darkness

When you step out from a brightly lit area into darkness, such as when leaving a motorway service area, your eyes will take a short while to adjust. Use this time to check and clean your vehicle's lights, reflectors, lenses and mirrors.

At dawn

Other drivers may have been driving through the night and may be less alert. Switch on your lights and leave them on until you're satisfied that other road users will see you.

It's harder to judge speed and distance correctly in the half-light at dusk and dawn. The colour of some vehicles also makes them harder to see in these conditions.

Oversized loads at night

Oversized loads are usually parked overnight. However, in certain circumstances the police authority responsible for that particular area may consider that the load would be more safely moved when there's less traffic on the road. Look for any signals given by the escort of such vehicles.

If you have permission to move any load at night, and that load projects beyond the normal size of the vehicle, all additional marker lights and hazard warning lights should be on.

Vehicle lighting

It's essential that all lights are clean and operating correctly. In addition to the driver needing to see ahead properly, it's essential that other road users are able to recognise the size of your vehicle and its direction of travel.

All regulation markers and rear lights must be lit and clear of dirt and obstructions such as ropes, sheets and overhanging projections.

Auxiliary lighting

Goods vehicle drivers must conform to regulations governing the use and fitting of any auxiliary lights, especially with regard to their mounting height.

Any lights showing to the front should be white (or, as allowed on some vehicles, yellow) unless they're side marker lights, which are required by law to be fitted to certain longer vehicles.

If your vehicle is fitted with any additional working lights (for example, to assist with coupling/uncoupling or loading), remember to switch them off when the vehicle is being used on the road.

High-intensity rear fog lights and additional front fog lights should only be used when visibility is less than 100 metres (about 330 feet). They must be switched off when visibility improves.

Amber hazard beacons are sometimes required if the load projects beyond specified limits or if the vehicle is travelling at slower speeds than normal.

Avoid the 'Christmas tree' effect (use of decorative lighting in or on the cab). It can be distracting and confusing to other road users at night. Also, any red light used in the cab mustn't show to the front of the vehicle.

Parked vehicles

Any goods vehicle exceeding 2500 kg laden weight must have its parking lights on when parked on the road, or in a lay-by, at night. Lights aren't required when your vehicle is parked at night in an off-street location, such as a lorry park.

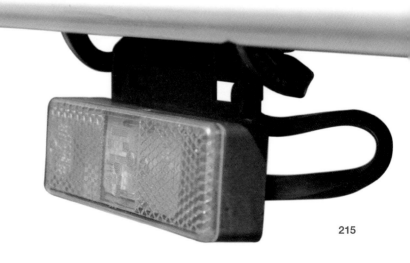

Driving in built-up areas

Always use dipped headlights in built-up areas at night. They help others to see you and assist your own vision if the street lighting varies or is defective.

At night, vulnerable road users, especially those wearing dark clothing, may be difficult to see. Vulnerable road users include

- pedestrians
- runners
- cyclists.

Take extra care when approaching pedestrian crossings. Drive at a speed that will allow you to stop safely if necessary.

Make sure that you obey the speed limits, even if the roads appear to be empty.

Maintenance work

Essential maintenance is often carried out at night. Be on the alert for diversion signs, obstructions and coned-off sections of road when you're driving at night.

In larger cities, street cleaning often takes place at night, so look out for these slow-moving vehicles.

Driving in rural areas

If there's no oncoming traffic, you should use full-beam headlights when driving in rural areas, so that you can see as far ahead as possible. Dip your lights as soon as you see oncoming traffic to avoid dazzling the oncoming driver or rider.

If there's no footpath, look out for pedestrians in the road. The Highway Code advises pedestrians to walk facing oncoming traffic, but not all pedestrians follow this advice. Additionally, The Highway Code advises that large groups of people on organised walks should walk on the left.

Fog at night

It would be unrealistic to suggest that a professional goods vehicle driver shouldn't drive in fog. However, if the fog is so dense that you just can't see safely to drive, you should seriously consider the wisdom of setting out.

If you start your journey when it's foggy and you're delayed, you'll be committing an offence if you exceed your permitted driving hours, because the delay was foreseeable.

Make sure that you know and understand the meaning of the different colours of reflective road studs used on motorways and dual carriageways (see The Highway Code, Rule 132). In thick fog, especially at night, these can help you to keep a safe and correct position.

Overtaking at night

It takes considerable time to complete an overtaking manoeuvre in an HGV, so you must only attempt this when you can see well ahead and are sure that it's safe to do so. This means that, unless you're driving on a motorway or dual carriageway, the opportunities to overtake at night will be limited. Without street lighting, you won't be able to tell whether there's anything ahead (such as bends, junctions or hills) that might prevent you from seeing an oncoming vehicle.

If you do decide to overtake, make sure that you can do so without cutting in on the vehicle being overtaken or causing oncoming vehicles to brake or swerve.

Sometimes, the driver of a vehicle you've just overtaken will flash their headlights. This is an unofficial signal, commonly used to indicate that it's safe for you to move back to the left. However, you should use your own judgement about when it's safe to move back to the left, because the signal may not have been meant for you.

Never close up on the vehicle ahead before attempting to overtake. This will restrict your view of the road ahead.

Headlights and separation distance

Make sure that your lights are on dipped beam when you're following another vehicle. Avoid driving so close to the vehicle ahead that your lights dazzle the driver. You should maintain a separation distance that ensures the beam of your headlights falls short of the vehicle in front.

If a vehicle overtakes you, dip your headlights as soon as it starts to pass you.

➡ Motorway driving

Basic preparation

Motorways are statistically the safest roads in the UK. However, motorway incidents can involve a large number of vehicles and, due to the vehicles' high speed, they can result in more serious injuries and damage than incidents on other roads.

The higher speed and greater volume of traffic on motorways cause situations to change much more rapidly than on other roads. For this reason, you need to

- stay alert
- be fit to drive
- avoid distractions.

Otherwise, you may not be able to respond safely to any sudden change taking place ahead of you.

Fitness to drive

Don't drive if you're

- tired
- unwell
- taking medicine that makes you feel drowsy
- worried or unable to concentrate.

Any of these factors can affect your reactions – especially in the event of an emergency.

Rest periods

You must observe mandatory rest periods in your daily driving schedule. On long journeys, try to plan a break at a motorway service area or refreshment stop. This is especially important at night, when tiredness can easily set in.

It's illegal to stop for a rest on the hard shoulder or slip roads of a motorway. If you start to feel tired, open the windows, turn down the heating and leave the motorway at the next junction. When you reach a service area, have a hot drink, wash your face (to refresh yourself) and walk around in the fresh air, or perhaps take a short nap (15–20 minutes) before driving on.

A substantial meal, accompanied by the warmth of the cab, the constant resonance of the engine and long, uninterrupted stretches of road, especially at night, can make you feel sleepy. These are precisely the conditions you need to avoid.

Regulations

Motorways are subject to specific rules and regulations that must be observed by all goods vehicle drivers. Study the relevant sections of The Highway Code.

You also need to know, understand and obey motorway warning signs and signals.

Vehicle checks

Before driving on the motorway, you should carry out routine checks on your vehicle. These are especially important because of the long distances and prolonged high speeds involved. For more details on vehicle maintenance, see section 2.

Tyres
All the tyres on your vehicle (and any trailer) must be in good condition. Tyres can become very hot during sustained high-speed running, and this can cause faulty tyres to disintegrate. Check for excessive heat when you stop for a break.

Inspect both the inside and outside visible faces of tyres for signs of

- wear
- damage
- bulges
- separation
- exposed cords.

Make sure that your vehicle has wheels of the correct size. Smaller-diameter wheels will turn faster, and this may cause the tyres to overheat on longer journeys. Make sure that all the tyres are suitable for the load being carried, and make a habit of checking the tyre pressures regularly when the tyres are cold.

If a tyre bursts or shreds, you may be able to see this in your mirrors. If you see smoke from the tyres, you should stop as soon as it's safe to do so. If a tyre bursts, hold the steering wheel firmly and allow the vehicle to slow down gradually. On a motorway, try to get to the hard shoulder, but don't turn sharply. Stay aware of any traffic to your left and switch on your hazard warning lights.

Mirrors
Make sure that all mirrors are clean and properly adjusted.

Windscreen
All glass must be

- clean
- clear
- free from defects.

Keep the windscreen-washer reservoir topped up and the jets clear. Make sure that all wiper blades are in good condition.

Laminated windscreens may crack. If you notice a crack or chip during a walkaround check, report it immediately. A small crack can quickly become larger if the screen flexes during a journey, particularly if the road is uneven or potholed.

Spray-suppression equipment
Check all spray-suppression equipment fitted to the vehicle and any trailer. Make sure that it's serviceable before setting out, especially if bad weather is expected.

Instruments
Check all gauges and warning lights, such as those for

- anti-lock brakes (ABS)
- air pressure
- oil pressure
- coolant temperature.

Lights and indicators

To comply with the law, all lights must be in working order, even in daylight. Make sure that headlights and reflectors are clean and there are no blown bulbs. High-intensity rear fog lights and marker lights (if fitted) must be working. Indicator lights must operate properly and flash at the correct speed.

Reversing lights should operate automatically on selection of reverse gear.

Fuel

Make sure that you have enough fuel to complete your journey or the means to refuel at a service area before you run out.

Engine oil

The engine operates at sustained high speeds on a motorway, so you should check the level of engine oil before you set out. If the engine doesn't have enough oil, this can result in costly damage and could cause a breakdown at a dangerous location.

Coolant

Check the level of coolant in the vehicle before you begin your journey, to prevent the engine from overheating.

Joining a motorway

Access points

There are three ways that traffic can join a motorway. All access routes will be clearly signed.

At a roundabout

The entrance to a motorway from a roundabout will be signposted. Motorway direction signs have blue backgrounds and are clearly displayed to prevent non-motorway traffic from accidentally joining the motorway.

Main trunk road becomes a motorway

There will be clear advance direction signs so that prohibited traffic can leave the main route before the motorway regulations apply.

Via a slip road

Slip roads leading directly onto a motorway will be clearly signed to prevent prohibited traffic from joining the motorway.

Effective observation

Before joining the motorway from a slip road, try to assess traffic conditions on the motorway. You may be able to do this as you approach from a distance. Alternatively, if you need to reach the entry point by means of a bridge over the motorway, you can look down and get advance information about the traffic conditions on the motorway. This should help you to plan your approach.

If it's clear, you should build up your speed and merge safely into the left-hand lane of the motorway. It it's busy, plan your approach and try to avoid having to stop at the end of the slip road. If the motorway is extremely busy, you may have no choice but to stop and filter into the traffic. Don't use the size of your vehicle to force your way onto the motorway. Use your mirror and signal as you pull out onto the main carriageway, when it's safe to do so. Watch particularly for motorcyclists: they can be difficult to see because of their narrow profile and they can approach quickly. They may also be hidden behind slower-moving traffic that they're overtaking.

Before you move across to join the motorway, a quick sideways glance may be necessary to check your blind spots and to ensure that you've correctly assessed the speed of any traffic approaching in the left-hand lane. If your vehicle is left-hand drive, be particularly aware of your blind spots and check them carefully.

Don't

* pull out into the path of traffic in the left-hand lane if this will cause it to slow down or swerve
* drive along the hard shoulder before filtering into the left-hand lane.

There are a small number of locations where traffic merges onto the motorway from the right. You should move over to the left as soon as it's safe to do so. At these specific locations, no offence is committed if a goods vehicle initially travels in the right-hand lane, but you should move to the left as soon as you can do so safely.

Approaching access points

After passing a motorway exit, there will often be an entrance or access point for traffic joining the motorway. Look well ahead. If vehicles are joining the motorway

- be prepared to adjust your speed and make room for them to join safely
- move to the next lane, if it's safe to do so, to allow room for the joining traffic.

Lane discipline

Keep to the left-hand lane unless overtaking slower vehicles.

Goods vehicles that are required to be fitted with a speed limiter aren't allowed to enter the right-hand lane of a three-lane or multi-lane motorway unless signs indicate otherwise. Details of which vehicles are required to be fitted with a speed limiter are given in section 3. On two-lane motorways, these vehicles **are** permitted to use the right-hand lane for overtaking.

Take care not to allow your vehicle to wander, however slightly. An HGV already occupies most of the available lane width, and any move away from a mid-lane position may cause an overtaking driver or rider to assume that you're starting to pull out into their path.

Use the Mirrors – Signal – Manoeuvre (MSM)/Position – Speed – Look (PSL) routine well before signalling to move out. Don't start to pull out and then signal.

Sideswiping

'Sideswiping' is a term that describes when a driver makes an unsafe lane change and collides with another road user already in that lane. The increase in the number of left-hand-drive vehicles on UK roads has made sideswiping more common. Despite additional kerbside mirrors, there remains an area where the driver may not be fully aware of the presence of a vehicle or motorcycle. Be extra careful and signal well in advance of your manoeuvre. This allows any unseen vehicles to move into view.

Overtaking

Look well ahead to plan any overtaking manoeuvre. Consider the effect a speed limiter will have on the speed available to you.

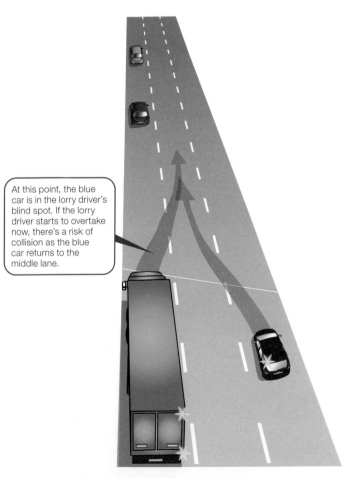

At this point, the blue car is in the lorry driver's blind spot. If the lorry driver starts to overtake now, there's a risk of collision as the blue car returns to the middle lane.

Remember to check the blind spots before changing lanes

On a three-lane or four-lane motorway, make sure that you check for any vehicle in the right-hand lane(s) that might be about to move back to the left. Most of the traffic coming from behind will be travelling at a much higher speed, and motorcyclists may be particularly difficult to see.

When you overtake, pay particular attention to the position of the road user you're overtaking. Check your nearside mirror carefully before pulling back in, to make sure that you've passed safely. Motorcyclists, in particular, are more vulnerable and may be affected by buffeting from your vehicle.

If another large vehicle starts to overtake you but doesn't have sufficient speed to get past, be prepared to reduce your speed so that you don't block the motorway any longer than necessary. Don't flash your headlights at the overtaking vehicle after it's passed – let the driver decide when it's safe to move back in.

Slow vehicles

Observe signs showing a crawler/climber lane for large vehicles. This will suggest a long, gradual climb ahead.

If a slow-moving, oversized load is being escorted, look for any signal the escort might give. They may permit you to move into the right-hand lane to pass the obstruction.

Separation distance

On motorways, you should

- look further ahead than on other roads
- allow a safe separation distance.

In good conditions, you'll need at least a two-second separation gap from the vehicle in front.

In poor conditions, you'll need to allow at least double the stopping distance you would need in good conditions.

In snow or icy conditions, the stopping distance can be **10 times** that needed in good conditions.

Seeing and being seen

Make sure that you start out with a clean windscreen, mirrors and windows. Use the washers, wipers and demisters to keep the screen clear.

In poor conditions, use dipped headlights. High-intensity rear fog lights mustn't be used unless visibility is less than 100 metres (about 330 feet). They should be switched off when visibility improves, unless fog is patchy and danger still exists.

Keep reassessing traffic conditions around you. Watch for brake lights or hazard warning lights that show the traffic ahead is either stationary or slowing down. If you see a stationary queue of traffic ahead, keep well back and briefly flash your hazard warning lights to let traffic behind you know there's a problem.

Motorway signs and signals

Motorway signs are larger than normal road signs. This is so that they can be read from further away, helping you to plan ahead.

Know your intended route. Be ready for the exit that you need to take and prepare for it in good time.

Where there are major roadworks or in an emergency, diversions may be in operation. Drivers will be advised to follow an alternative route, which may be signposted by black symbols on yellow patches. These symbols may be

- square
- diamond-shaped
- circular
- triangular.

Follow the symbol shown on the route signs. See 'Emergency diversion routes', earlier in this chapter, for more images of the symbols used.

Motorway signals

Signals warn of dangers ahead, such as

- incidents
- fog
- icy roads
- delays
- standing traffic.

Flashing amber lights

Look out for flashing amber lights and signs, either on the central reservation or overhead. These warn you of

- lane closures
- roadworks
- other hazards.

They might also show a temporary speed limit. You should

- slow down to the speed limit
- be ready to slow down even further to pass the obstacle or danger
- look out for signs giving further advice
- do not speed up until you see the sign ending the temporary restriction (or there are no more flashing amber lights).

Red flashing lights

Some signs have red flashing lights.

If red lights flash on a signal and a red X is showing, it means the lane is closed. You **MUST** follow the instructions on signs in advance of a closed lane so that you can move safely to an open lane.

You **MUST NOT** drive in a closed lane. A sign will show you when the lane is open again by displaying a speed limit or the word 'END'.

When red flashing light signals and closure of all lanes are shown on a sign, it means the road is closed. You **MUST NOT** go beyond the sign in any lane or use the hard shoulder to avoid the road closure unless directed to do so by a police or traffic officer.

Lane and road closures indicated by red flashing lights are enforced by the police.

Weather conditions

Because of the high speed of traffic on motorways, it's important to take into account the effects that weather may have on driving conditions.

Rain

Visibility can be severely reduced by the spray thrown up by vehicles travelling at speed. You should

- use dipped-beam headlights so that other drivers can see you
- reduce speed when the road surface is wet. You need to be able to stop in the distance that you can see to be clear
- allow a larger separation distance. Leave a four-second gap as a minimum
- check that any spray-suppression equipment fitted to your vehicle is undamaged
- continue to take extra care after it stops raining. The roads may still be slippery even if the sun comes out.

Side winds

Be aware of the effects that strong side winds can have on other road users, especially

- after passing motorway bridges
- when passing motorcyclists
- when passing vehicles towing trailers, such as caravans or horse boxes.

Sometimes, such as on elevated and exposed sections of road, there are side-wind warning signs to alert you to the hazard.

If you're driving a high-sided vehicle such as a

- furniture removal van
- box van carrying comparatively light merchandise
- curtain-sided vehicle

take special notice of warnings on signs or in the media. Avoid known problem areas; for example, viaducts or high suspension bridges.

Motorcyclists are especially vulnerable to side winds on motorways, so give them plenty of room when overtaking them. Check your nearside mirror to observe them as you overtake them and after you complete the manoeuvre.

Ice or frost

In cold weather – especially at night, when temperatures can drop suddenly – be on the alert for any feeling of lightness in the steering. This may suggest frost or ice on the road. Watch for signs of frost along the hard shoulder as well. A warm cab can isolate you from the real conditions outside.

Motorways that appear wet may, in fact, be frozen. Your cab dashboard may have a sensor that warns you of low temperatures.

Allow up to **10 times** the normal distance for braking in icy conditions. Remember, all braking should be carried out gently to reduce the risk of losing control.

Fog

If there's fog on the motorway, you must reduce your speed so that you can stop in the distance that you can see to be clear.

You should

- slow down
- use dipped headlights
- use high-intensity rear fog lights if visibility is less than 100 metres (about 330 feet)
- keep a safe distance from the vehicle in front.

Don't

- speed up as soon as the fog starts to thin. Fog is often patchy and you could run into dense fog again within a short distance
- closely follow the rear lights of the vehicle in front.

Fog affects your judgement of speed and distance. You may be travelling faster than you realise. In fog, multiple collisions on motorways are often caused by drivers who

- travel too fast
- drive too close
- assume there's no stationary traffic ahead
- ignore signals.

If you see fog warning signs but visibility is good, there may be foggy conditions ahead. Be prepared and reduce your speed in good time.

REMEMBER, motorcyclists can be much more difficult to see in fog.

When driving in fog, obey any signals that tell you to leave the motorway. Look for incidents ahead and for emergency vehicles coming up behind you (possibly on the hard shoulder). Police cars may be parked on the hard shoulder with their lights flashing. This might mean that traffic has stopped on the carriageway ahead.

Breakdowns on the motorway

If your vehicle develops a problem, leave the motorway at the next exit or pull into a service area. If you can't do this, pull onto the hard shoulder (or into an emergency area) and stop as far to the left as possible.

If you stop on the hard shoulder, switch on your hazard warning lights. If it's dark, make sure that the vehicle lights are on, unless there's an electrical problem.

You should leave your vehicle through the left-hand door. Do not put out a warning triangle or try to repair your vehicle, even if the repairs are minor. Get behind a safety barrier where there is one; they provide extra protection.

Calling for help

Use the emergency telephone to get help and advice.

If you haven't managed to stop near an emergency phone, look for a telephone symbol and arrow on marker posts 100 metres (328 feet) apart along the edge of the road. The arrow directs you to the nearest phone on your side of the carriageway.

Take care while getting to and from an emergency phone. Stay behind the safety barrier where there is one.

Face the traffic when you use the phone so that you'll be aware of anything coming towards you.

Mobile phones

If you're unable to use an emergency telephone, use a mobile phone if you have one. You should call National Highways on **0300 123 5000**. Before you call, make sure that you can provide precise details of your location. Identify your location from the marker posts on the hard shoulder before you phone.

Waiting for help

Keep well away from your vehicle and moving traffic while you're waiting. If there's a safety barrier, stay behind it.

On a motorway with no hard shoulder

If there is no hard shoulder, or if it's being used as an extra lane, then you should pull into an emergency area. Emergency areas are marked by blue signs with an orange SOS telephone symbol and they may have orange surfacing.

Switch on your hazard lights and leave your vehicle through the left-hand door. Get behind the safety barrier and use the emergency telephone to call for help.

If you cannot get out of your vehicle and get to a safe place, or if you've stopped in a live traffic lane

- stay in your vehicle with your seatbelts and hazard lights on
- call 999 immediately.

Falling loads

If anything falls from either your vehicle or another vehicle that would be a hazard to traffic

- stop on the hard shoulder or in an emergency area
- call 999
- do not attempt to recover the fallen items yourself
- do not stand on the carriageway to warn oncoming traffic.

Rejoining the motorway

To rejoin the carriageway after a breakdown from

- a **hard shoulder**, build up speed, indicate and watch for a safe gap in the traffic. Be aware that vehicles, obstructions or debris may be present on the hard shoulder
- an **emergency area**, you MUST use the emergency telephone provided and follow the operator's advice for exiting the emergency area. A lane may need to be closed so that you can rejoin the carriageway safely.

For more information about safer driving on motorways, visit

nationalhighways.co.uk/road-safety/breakdowns

Leaving the motorway

There will be a series of signs as you approach each exit.

At one mile, you'll see

- the junction number
- the road number
- the one-mile indicator.

Half a mile from the exit, you'll see signs for

- the main town or city served by the exit
- the junction number
- the road number
- the half-mile indicator.

Finally, 300 yards (270 metres) before the exit, there will be countdown markers every 100 yards.

A lorry travelling at 56 mph (90 km/h) has just over 60 seconds from the one-mile sign to the exit. Even at a speed of 50 mph (80 km/h), there's still only 72 seconds from the one-mile sign to the exit.

Plan well in advance, in order to be in the left-hand lane in good time. Large vehicles in the left-hand lane may prevent a driver in the second lane from seeing the one-mile sign, leaving very little time to move to the left safely.

Don't start to overtake unless you're confident you can complete the manoeuvre safely, before you reach the exit. If traffic is queuing, watch out for motorcyclists filtering between other vehicles or coming up on your nearside.

Don't

- steer sharply to join the slip road suddenly or at the last moment
- drive over the white chevrons that divide the slip road from the main carriageway.

Occasionally, there are several exits close together, or a service area close to an exit. Look well ahead and plan your exit in good time. Watch out for mistakes by other drivers – especially those who leave it too late to exit safely.

Queuing traffic

At some locations, traffic can be held up on the slip road. Look well ahead and be prepared for this. **Don't queue on the hard shoulder.**

Illuminated signs have been introduced at a number of locations to give advance warning of traffic queuing on the slip road or in the left-hand lane. Watch out for indicators and hazard warning lights when traffic is held up ahead.

Use the MSM/PSL routine in good time and move to the second lane if you aren't leaving the motorway by that exit.

End of the motorway

There are 'End of motorway regulations' signs

- at the end of slip roads
- where the road changes and is no longer subject to motorway regulations.

These signs remind you that different rules apply to the road that you're joining. Watch out for other signs advising you of

- speed limits
- dual carriageways
- two-way traffic
- clearways
- motorway link roads
- part-time traffic signals.

Reduce speed

After driving on the motorway for some time, it's easy to become accustomed to the speed. When you first leave the motorway, 40 mph can seem more like 20 mph.

You should

- be aware of how your judgement of speed can be affected
- check the speedometer to see the real speed.

Start reducing speed when you're clear of the main carriageway. Motorway slip or link roads often have sharp curves that need to be taken at lower speeds.

Be prepared for the change in traffic at the end of the motorway. Look well ahead for traffic queuing at a roundabout or traffic signals. Remember, as soon as you leave the motorway, you could find more vulnerable road users, such as

- pedestrians
- cyclists
- motorcyclists
- horses and riders.

Contraflows and roadworks

Where essential roadworks are being carried out, streams of traffic travelling in opposite directions may have to share one carriageway. These are known as contraflow systems. The object is to allow traffic to continue moving while repairs or resurfacing take place on the other carriageway or lanes.

Red-and-white marker posts are used to separate opposing streams of traffic. The normal white reflective studs marking lanes are replaced by temporary yellow-and-green fluorescent studs.

Signs
Take notice of advance warning signs, gantry signs or flashing signals (often starting five miles before the roadworks). Get into the correct lane in good time. Don't leave it until the last moment, as this can greatly increase the chance of a mistake and an incident. Obey warning signs indicating lanes that mustn't be used by HGVs (this applies to vehicles over 7.5 tonnes maximum authorised mass (MAM)).

Drivers of goods vehicles carrying oversized loads **MUST** comply with the advance warning notices. These will tell you either to leave the motorway or to stop and telephone the police, then wait for an escort through the roadworks.

Travelling through roadworks

A 50 mph (80 km/h) mandatory speed limit is usually imposed on the stretch of motorway affected. When you reduce your speed to travel through roadworks, it may seem as if you're travelling more slowly than you really are. It's important to observe the speed limit and not just slow down to the speed that feels safe to you.

When you're approaching or driving through roadworks or contraflow systems, you should

- look well ahead to avoid the need to brake sharply
- keep a safe distance from the vehicle in front; you'll need time to brake if that vehicle stops suddenly
- look out for road workers on the site and those who are placing or removing signs
- obey any signs directing you to stay in your lane
- avoid sudden steering movements
- be aware that lanes may be narrower than normal. You must take care not to let your vehicle 'wander' out of your lane.

If all drivers observe the speed limit when travelling through these areas, it helps to keep traffic moving, rather than 'bunching up'. This is good for journey times, as well as for the environment.

Exiting roadworks

Stay within the speed limit even when you're leaving the coned area. There may be road workers' vehicles leaving the roadworks at this point. Don't speed up until you're clear of the roadworks and you pass a sign indicating that the temporary speed limit has ended.

Road traffic incidents

Serious incidents can occur when vehicles cross into the path of the other traffic stream in a contraflow system. You must

- keep your speed down
- keep your distance
- stay alert.

Breakdowns

If your vehicle breaks down in roadworks, remain with the vehicle. These sections of motorway are usually under closed-circuit television (CCTV) monitoring. A recovery vehicle, which is provided free of charge where there are roadworks, will be with you as soon as possible.

Be on the lookout for broken-down vehicles causing an obstruction ahead.

⊕ All-weather driving

Goods need to be delivered 24 hours a day, all year round. With that in mind, you should employ safe driving techniques to ensure that you, your vehicle and the goods in your care always arrive at their destination safely and with the minimum of delay. You'll need all your skills to achieve this during periods of bad weather.

It's important that you take notice of warnings of severe weather, such as

- snow or blizzards
- floods
- fog
- high winds.

If a goods vehicle becomes stranded, it may well block the road and prevent essential rescue and medical services from getting through. In the case of fog, other vehicles could collide with the stranded vehicle.

Don't venture out in severe weather conditions without being properly prepared.

Your vehicle

Your vehicle must be in a roadworthy condition at all times. This means carrying out regular safety checks and following recommended maintenance schedules. For more details on vehicle maintenance, see section 2.

Tyres

Check the tread depth and pattern. Goods vehicle tyres must have a tread depth of at least 1 mm across three-quarters of the breadth of the tyre and in a continuous band around the entire circumference.

Examine tyres for cuts, damage and signs of cord visible at the side walls. Also check between double wheels for any debris that may have become trapped. If double-wheel tyres are touching or rubbing, this may indicate either under-inflation of the tyres or overloading of your vehicle.

Brakes

It's essential that the brakes operate correctly at all times. If you detect any faults, you should stop in a safe place and only continue your journey when the fault has been repaired.

Oil and fuel

Use the correct grades of fuel and oil for any extreme weather conditions.

Prolonged hot weather will place additional demands on the engine's lubricating oil and more frequent oil changes may be necessary. In excessively dusty conditions, such as those that can be encountered on off-road sites, you should strictly follow the schedules for oil-, fuel- and air-filter changes. In extremes of cold, it may be necessary to use diesel fuel with additional anti-waxing additives to prevent the fuel lines from freezing up.

Before making a journey in very cold weather, you should make sure that you have sufficient fuel in case of delays. It's a good idea to make an extra check of the fuel tank and mountings to be sure that their condition is good and the fuel lines aren't damaged or frozen.

Icy weather

Most diesel engines have pre-heaters. These help the engine to start when it's cold, by heating glow plugs in the cylinders. Wait until the indicator light on the dashboard goes out before you operate the starter.

Make sure that the whole of the windscreen is clear before attempting to move off in frosty conditions. You may be able to avoid having to use a scraper or canned de-icer if you

- park under cover overnight
- use the cab night heater.

If you're driving at night, be alert for any drop in temperature that could cause untreated roads to become icy. If the steering feels light, you're probably driving on a frozen road surface, so ease your speed as soon as it's safe to do so. All braking must be gentle and carried out over much longer distances, especially when driving articulated vehicles or those with a trailer.

You'll have to allow more time for your journey, because overall speeds will need to be lower. Stopping distances will also be much longer, so you should allow **10 times** the normal separation distance from any vehicle ahead.

Allow for the fact that other road users might get into difficulties. Remember that motorcyclists and cyclists are especially vulnerable on slippery roads.

Avoid any sudden

- braking
- steering
- acceleration.

Heavy rain

Replace worn windscreen wipers if they aren't clearing the windscreen properly – you'll need to be able to see clearly ahead. Make sure that the windscreen is demisted and that the washer reservoirs are filled with suitable screenwash fluid, especially in winter weather conditions.

Allow at least twice the separation distance you would allow in dry conditions. If you have to brake, do it while the vehicle is stable and preferably travelling in a straight line. Avoid sudden or harsh braking.

When driving through deep water, drive slowly in a low gear with high engine speed to prevent water from entering the engine through the exhaust system.

Your tyres may lose grip because of the build-up of a layer of water between the road surface and the tyres. (This is known as aquaplaning.) If your steering suddenly feels light, ease your foot off the accelerator and slow down gently without braking. When the tyres regain their grip, the steering should feel normal again.

Other vehicles could be temporarily blinded by spray from your vehicle, so take care when you need to change lanes. When overtaking cyclists in heavy rain, make sure that spray from your vehicle doesn't affect their control. Leave plenty of room when passing them and check your left-hand mirror to see whether they're still in control.

Obey advisory speed-limit signs on motorways. Other road users will have more difficulty seeing when there's heavy rain and spray. All spray-suppression equipment on your vehicle should be secure and in good condition.

Construction sites

Take care when driving on off-road gradients, or when getting down from the cab. If your vehicle is fitted with a switch that locks the differential mechanism on the drive axle (the 'diff-lock'), engage it. This will ensure that the power is transmitted to all driven wheels and will assist traction. Remember to disengage the diff-lock as soon as you return to normal road surfaces again. Neglecting to do so can

- seriously affect handling and stability
- cause severe and expensive damage to the differential and axle
- cause excessive tyre wear.

It's an offence to deposit mud on the road to the extent that it could endanger other road users. You may need to hose down the wheels and undergear of your vehicle before leaving a site. You should also check between double wheels for any large stones or building bricks wedged between the tyres. Such objects can fly out at speed, with serious consequences for following traffic.

Snow

Heavy falling snow can severely reduce visibility. Use dipped headlights and reduce your speed. Keep your windscreen, headlights and indicators clear of snow. If snow builds up on the front of your lights, it will reduce their effectiveness.

Allow a much longer stopping and separation distance – up to **10 times** the distance you would allow on dry roads.

Road markings and traffic signs can become obscured by snow. Take extra care at junctions.

Deep snow can lead to the closure of high-level roads. Don't attempt to use such roads if

- broadcasts tell goods vehicle drivers to avoid those routes

- warning signs indicate that the road is closed to goods vehicles or other traffic

- severe weather conditions are forecast.

Some rural roads in exposed places have marker poles at the side of the road. These mark the edge of the road, which would otherwise be hidden by the snow.

During prolonged periods of snow, fitting snow chains to the driven wheels often proves to be of value. Remember, a stranded goods vehicle could

- prevent snow ploughs from clearing the route
- delay emergency vehicles
- block the road for other road users.

Ploughs and vehicles spreading salt or other de-icers

Keep well back from gritter vehicles spreading salt or other de-icers. If they're on the road, bad weather could be on the way. If you overtake, you may find yourself running into deep snow or skidding on an untreated section of road that would have been cleared or treated had you followed on behind them.

Deep snow

If your vehicle becomes stuck in deep snow, engage the diff-lock (if one is fitted) to try to regain some traction. Switch it off as soon as the vehicle is moving and before attempting a turn.

Another technique for freeing a vehicle stuck in the snow is to use the highest gear you can as you try to move off. Then try alternating between reverse and the forward gear, rocking the vehicle until forward motion is possible. Avoid continuous revving in a low gear. This will only result in the drive wheels spinning and possibly creating an even deeper rut.

It's often helpful to keep a couple of strong sacks in the cab to put under the drive wheels if the vehicle becomes stuck. A shovel may be helpful if the journey is likely to involve crossing areas where snow is known to be a hazard during the winter.

When operating independent retarders, care must be taken while descending snow-covered gradients. The retarders could cause the rear wheels to lock. Some retarders are managed by the ABS to help avoid this problem.

Fog

Don't drive in dense fog if you can postpone your journey, and avoid driving at night if there's fog. Don't start a journey that might need to be abandoned because it becomes too dangerous to proceed any further.

Finding a safe place to park an HGV off the road in dense fog can be very difficult. You mustn't leave a goods vehicle on public roads where it would be a danger to other road users.

Lights

Use dipped headlights in any reduced visibility. You need to see and be seen.

If high-intensity rear fog lights and front fog lights are fitted, you can use them when visibility is less than 100 metres (330 feet). Switch off front and rear fog lights when visibility improves, but beware of patchy fog.

Keep all lenses and reflectors clean. You may need to check them more often in poor weather conditions. Make sure that all lights are working correctly.

> **REMEMBER,** don't use high-intensity rear fog lights unless visibility is less than 100 metres (330 feet).

When travelling in fog, don't

- drive too close to the centre of the road
- confuse centre lines and lane markings
- drive without using headlights
- speed up because the fog appears to thin out – it could be patchy and you could run into it again

- use full-beam headlights when following another vehicle – your lights may dazzle the driver and make it difficult for them to see.

Follow this advice:

- Slow down. Keep checking the speedometer to see your true speed. Fog can make it difficult to judge speed and distance.
- Keep a safe separation distance from any vehicle ahead, in case it stops suddenly. A large vehicle travelling ahead of you may temporarily displace some of the fog, making the conditions seem clearer than they really are.
- Don't speed up if a vehicle appears to be close behind.
- Only overtake if you can be sure the road ahead is clear.

When driving an HGV, your high seating position may enable you to see over low-lying fog. Don't speed up in case there are smaller vehicles, cyclists or motorcyclists in front that may be hidden from view.

Reflective road studs and markings
Reflective road studs may be provided to help drivers in poor visibility. The colours used for these studs are

- **red** on the left-hand edge of the road
- **white** to indicate lane markings or the middle of the road
- **green** at slip roads and lay-bys
- **amber** to mark the central reservation on a dual carriageway or motorway
- **fluorescent yellow/green** to indicate temporary lane layouts; for example, at roadworks where a contraflow system is in place.

On rural roads, there are black-and-white marker posts, with red reflectors on the left-hand side of the road and white reflectors on the right-hand side of the road. These mark the edge of the road and are especially useful at night or at other times when visibility is reduced.

Rumble devices

The continuous white line between the left-hand lane and the hard shoulder of a motorway, and on the left-hand edge of some trunk roads, incorporates a rumble strip. This produces an audible sound and a vibration designed to warn drivers when their vehicle runs onto the line and is at risk of leaving the road.

Raised strips can also be found across the road on the approach to some hazards, such as a bend or junction. They provide an intermittent audible and vibratory warning to the driver, encouraging them to slow down.

High winds

In severe weather conditions, you should plan your journey well in advance (24 hours ahead, if possible). Listen to the radio for relevant local reports or check the weather forecast, especially if you're the driver of

- a high-sided vehicle; for example, a removal van or a long-wheelbase box van
- a vehicle with a curtain-sided body or trailer
- a vehicle transporting a load with large, flat surfaces that are susceptible to wind pressures (such as a portable building)
- a vehicle towing a box trailer
- an unladen van of any description.

Take notice if your route includes any locations that are frequently subject to high winds, such as

- high-level bridges or roads
- exposed viaducts
- exposed stretches of dual carriageway or motorway.

Watch out for warning signs indicating high winds. In these conditions, beware of fallen trees or damaged branches that could fall on your vehicle.

Take notice of advance warnings and always remember that

- the route may be closed to certain HGVs
- there may be additional delays due to lane closures. This is done on some high-level routes to create empty 'buffer' lanes, which provide a safety margin for vehicles in case they're blown off course and into the next lane
- you may need to use an alternative route
- if you ignore the warnings, your vehicle and its load could be affected by the winds. It could be blown off course, into another vehicle, off the road or even blown over. This would place you and other road users in danger.

Bear in mind that ferry sailings are likely to be affected by gale-force winds, resulting in delays or cancellations.

Other road users

In windy conditions, other road users are likely to be affected when

- overtaking your vehicle
- you overtake them.

The road users who are most affected include cyclists, motorcyclists and drivers of double-deck buses, horse boxes, high-sided lorries, and vehicles towing caravans or trailers. Motorcyclists and cyclists are particularly vulnerable to the effects of wind pressure produced by a passing vehicle. Check your nearside mirror(s) as you overtake to make sure they still have control of their vehicle. In addition, look out for vehicles or motorcyclists being blown off course and into your lane.

Although cars are relatively stable in high winds, buffeting can still affect them to some extent.

Don't ignore warnings of severe winds. If your vehicle is blown over, you could delay the emergency services from reaching an even more serious incident.

⊙ Avoiding and dealing with congestion

The increase in the number of vehicles on the roads has caused a level of congestion that can lead to frustration and longer journey times. This affects higher-speed roads and motorways as well as urban areas. However, there's an opportunity for all drivers to alleviate the problem to some extent by changing their driving habits.

Journey planning

Time of day

If possible, try to plan journeys to avoid the busiest times of day. Much congestion is generated by work/school-related travel, causing delays in the early morning, late afternoon and early evening. If you don't have to travel at these times, try to avoid doing so. This will both ease the congestion for traffic governed by work/school schedules and allow you a more pleasant journey, with less likelihood of delays.

Route planning

Make sure that you know where you're going by planning your route beforehand. If possible, include alternatives in your plan, in case you find your original route is blocked. This is especially important if the route is unknown to you. You could

- use a map – you may need to use maps of different scales, depending on how far and where you're travelling
- refer to a satellite navigation system (but don't rely on it exclusively)
- consult a motoring organisation or use one of the route planners available on the internet

A satellite navigation system will identify your route for you

- print out or write down the route, using both place names and road numbers to avoid problems if a particular place isn't adequately signed.

Be aware of the size of your vehicle in relation to the width of certain access points or narrow town roads – it can be very difficult or even impossible to manoeuvre a large vehicle if, for example, a one-way street or sharp turn is found to be too narrow, or where weight or height restrictions apply.

Where permitted, satellite navigation systems are a useful tool. They encourage efficiency, thereby improving fuel consumption and reducing emissions. However, you should never rely on them exclusively. Most are designed only for cars and smaller vehicles, and these systems won't filter out routes with features such as narrow lanes, weight restrictions or low bridges – all of which physically restrict or prohibit the passage of larger vehicles. Only systems that are specifically designed for use in HGVs, coaches and mobile homes will have the facility to identify and filter out roads that would be difficult, unsafe or impossible for such vehicles to use.

Even those systems that are designed for large vehicles may not have been updated with the latest information at any given time. Road situations can change very quickly, so it's possible that there will be delays or diversions that a satellite navigation system can't detect. It's best to identify narrow roads, height restrictions, tight turnings or overhanging buildings for yourself by manually planning your route before starting your journey.

Remember that any in-vehicle navigation system can reduce your concentration on the road and your level of control of the vehicle. It's advisable to restrict any visual or manual interaction with the system to an absolute minimum (see Rule 150 in The Highway Code). In the interests of safety, you should find a safe and legal place to stop before programming the system.

Your vehicle radio may pick up local warnings of any emergencies, delays or diversions on your route. This extra information will help you to make any necessary adjustments to your route plan.

Your journey

Leave plenty of time, especially if you're connecting with other forms of transport. Concern about reaching your destination in time can lead to frustration and an increased tendency to take risks. Delivery schedules need to allow for some delays, so the driver isn't forced to take unnecessary risks to stay on time.

Carry your map or directions with you, so you can check positions or identify alternative routes if you're delayed or diverted, but **don't** attempt to look at a map or read directions while you're driving.

Mobile phones

A mobile phone can be useful in case of delays or breakdowns. However, remember that it's illegal to use a hand-held mobile phone while you're driving. This includes while you're waiting in a queue of traffic.

Find a safe place to stop before making a call. If you're driving on a motorway, you must leave the motorway before using a hand-held phone.

Hazard perception

Looking well ahead to see what other road users in front of you are doing will enable you to plan your driving. If you see any changes that could cause you to slow down or alter course, ease off the accelerator and slow down gradually, rather than leaving it late and having to brake harshly. Slow down early – the traffic situation ahead will often have cleared by the time you get there.

Constant speed

When you can see well ahead and the road conditions are good, you should try to drive at a constant speed. This is the time to use cruise control if it's fitted to your vehicle.

Whether or not you have cruise control, choose a speed that's within the speed limit and one that you and your vehicle can handle safely. Make sure that you also keep a safe distance from the vehicle in front. Remember to increase the gap on wet or icy roads. In foggy conditions, you'll have to slow down so you can stop in the distance you can see to be clear.

At busy times, some stretches of motorway have variable speed limits shown on gantries above the lanes. These maximum speed limits are shown in red circles and are mandatory for traffic using the lanes to which they apply. They're in place to make traffic move at a constant speed, as this has been shown to reduce bunching and, over a longer distance, reduce congestion. Your overall journey time normally improves by keeping to the constant speed even if, at times, it may appear that you could have travelled faster for short periods.

Lane discipline

You should drive in the left-hand lane of a dual carriageway or motorway if the road ahead is clear.

If you're overtaking a number of slower-moving vehicles on a three-lane motorway, it may be safer to remain in the centre lane until you complete the manoeuvre, rather than continually changing lanes. Return to the left-hand lane once you've overtaken all the vehicles or if you're delaying traffic behind you. Don't stay in the middle lane when you've finished overtaking.

Try to avoid overtaking another large vehicle where the difference in speed between the two vehicles is slight, because it causes a slow overtake. It can take several minutes for you to complete the manoeuvre, during which time you're delaying faster vehicles and potentially causing frustration, which can lead to a dangerous situation. A long, slow overtake will not improve your journey time by much, but it will use more fuel than if you'd remained behind the slightly slower vehicle.

You mustn't normally drive on the hard shoulder. However, at roadworks and certain places where signs direct, the hard shoulder may become the left-hand lane.

Using sign information

Look well ahead for signals or signs, especially on a motorway. Signals situated on the central reservation apply to all lanes.

On very busy stretches of road, there may be overhead gantries with messages about congestion ahead and a separate signal for each lane. The messages may also give an alternative route, which you should use if at all possible.

If you aren't sure whether to use the alternative route (for example, you're unsure whether you can reach your destination if you use the route suggested), take the next exit, pull over at the first available safe place (a lay-by or service area) and look at a map. You can always rejoin the motorway if you feel that's the best course of action once you've had time to consider the options.

Remember, on a motorway, once you've passed an exit and encounter congestion, there may not be another opportunity to leave and you could be stuck in slow-moving or stationary traffic for some time.

If you need to change lanes to leave the motorway, do so in good time. At some junctions, a lane may lead directly off the motorway. Only get in that lane if you wish to go in the direction indicated on the overhead signs.

Traffic control on motorways

On some sections of motorway, technology is in place to reduce congestion and improve journey times. This varies the speed limit as the volume of traffic increases. Drivers may also be allowed to use the hard shoulder as an extra lane during busy periods.

Controlling traffic on the motorway

Motorways that have 3 or more lanes can have variable speed limits shown on overhead signs. These speed limits are shown inside a red circle and are legally enforceable.

On some motorways, the hard shoulder is permanently used as an extra lane. Emergency areas with emergency telephones are provided at least every 2500 metres, in case of an emergency or breakdown, and drivers receive regular information updates via overhead signs. These signs display information on the current mandatory  variable speed limit, as well as indicating whether lanes are closed.

On some sections of motorway, the hard shoulder is used to provide extra capacity during busy periods. The hard shoulder is marked with a solid white line and drivers are only allowed to use it as a running lane when the overhead signs say that it's available. If the sign above the hard shoulder displays a red X or is blank, you must only enter the hard shoulder in an emergency, or when told to do so by the police, traffic officers or an emergency sign.

Driving on a smart motorway

Overhead signs display speed limits to manage traffic and give information about incidents or driving conditions. They also tell you which lanes are available for you to use. Obey the signs; they're there to keep the traffic moving.

- Red crosses show when lanes, including the hard shoulder, shouldn't be used. If you see a red X above a lane, don't drive in that lane.

- If a speed limit is displayed directly above the hard shoulder, you can drive on it. If you see a red X or no speed limit displayed above the hard shoulder, you should only use it in an emergency or breakdown.

Traffic officers

Working in partnership with the police, traffic officers are extra eyes and ears on motorways and some 'A' class roads in England and Wales. They're a highly trained and highly visible service, patrolling the motorway to help keep traffic moving and make your journey as safe and reliable as possible.

Traffic officers wear a full uniform, including a high-visibility orange-and-yellow jacket, and they drive a high-visibility vehicle with yellow-and-black chequered markings. Every traffic officer will have a unique identification number and photographic identity card. They normally patrol in pairs.

The vehicles contain a variety of equipment for use on the motorway, including temporary road signs, lights, cones, debris removal tools and a first-aid kit.

Role of a traffic officer

Traffic officers

- help motorists to arrange a recovery when their vehicle has broken down
- offer safety advice to motorists
- clear debris from the carriageway
- undertake patrols in clearly identifiable vehicles
- support the police and emergency services during incidents
- provide mobile/temporary road closures
- manage diversion routes following a road traffic incident.

If you have an emergency or break down on the motorway, the best action to take is to use an emergency roadside telephone. These telephones are answered by control-centre operators, who are able to monitor any stranded motorists on CCTV screens and despatch the nearest available traffic-officer patrol to assist.

Powers of traffic officers

Unlike the police, traffic officers don't have any enforcement powers. However, they're able to stop and direct anyone travelling on the motorway.

It's an offence not to comply with the directions given by a traffic officer. For more information, see The Highway Code, Rules 107 and 108.

Urban congestion

Congestion in urban areas leads to

* longer journey times
* frustration
* pollution from standing and slow-moving traffic.

Red Routes

Red Routes keep traffic moving and so reduce the pollution that comes from stationary queuing vehicles. Stopping and parking on a Red Route is allowed only within marked boxes and at certain times. There's a fixed penalty for an offence and illegally parked vehicles may be towed away.

There are five main types of Red Route marking.

Double red lines Stopping isn't allowed at any time, for any reason. Double red lines are normally placed at road junctions or where parking or loading would be dangerous or cause serious congestion.

Single red lines Parking, loading or picking up/ setting down passengers isn't allowed during the day (generally 7.00 am to 7.00 pm). Stopping is allowed outside these hours and on Sundays.

Red boxes Parking or loading is allowed at off-peak times during the day (normally 10.00 am to 4.00 pm). Some boxes allow loading and some allow parking; the rules are clearly shown on a sign beside the box.

White boxes Parking or loading may be allowed at any time; the restrictions are clearly shown on the sign beside the box.

Red Route clearway There are no road markings, but clearway signs indicate that stopping isn't allowed at any time, apart from in marked lay-bys.

For more details about Red Routes, see 'Your driving', in section 3.

⊕ Helping the environment

Reducing your fuel consumption

If you follow the principles of fuel-efficient driving set out in the following pages, you'll become a more environmentally friendly driver. Your journeys will be more comfortable and you could considerably reduce both your fuel bills and those emissions that cause damage to the atmosphere. As a professional driver, you'll set an example to other road users in helping to keep the environment 'green'.

It's vital that operators monitor and manage the fuel used by their vehicles. A fuel management programme can help to reduce fuel consumption across the fleet, and use of safe and fuel-efficient driving techniques will contribute to the cost savings.

For example, reducing fuel consumption by 1000 litres per year will

- save 2.6 tonnes of carbon-dioxide emissions per year
- save £1000 per year for the operator (assuming a price of £1.00 per litre, excluding VAT).

Driving in a more fuel-efficient way is better for the environment and can improve the image of both the company and the transport industry as a whole by showing that they're making an effort to reduce their carbon footprint.

Becoming a fuel-efficient driver

Fuel-efficient driving is a recognised and proven style of driving that contributes to road safety while reducing fuel consumption and emissions.

One of the main ways to improve road safety is to plan ahead, so that you're prepared in advance for potential hazards. By improving your hazard perception and planning skills, you can make maximum use of your vehicle's momentum and engine braking. Doing this saves fuel and so helps to reduce damage to the environment.

For example, keeping your vehicle moving at a walking pace, instead of repeatedly stopping and moving off again, will use less fuel. Similarly, descending a hill without using the accelerator uses little or no fuel, as the engine management system will regulate the supply of fuel to the engine.

Although it's beneficial to save fuel, you mustn't compromise either your safety or the safety of other road users when attempting to do so. Road safety is always the most important consideration. At all times you should be prepared to adapt to changing conditions, and it may be that you'll have to sacrifice fuel saving for safety.

Hazard awareness and planning

You should scan all around as you drive. Check the far distance, middle distance and foreground. Also check behind and to the sides of your vehicle through frequent use of all of your mirrors. Your high seating position allows you to see well ahead, giving you the opportunity to see hazards early and act in good time.

Early recognition of potential hazards is important, but you also need to act correctly on what you've seen. You must be able to

* anticipate problems
* take appropriate action in good time, to ensure that you're travelling at the correct speed when you reach the hazard.

By doing this, you'll avoid late braking and harsh acceleration, both of which lead to higher fuel consumption. Harsh braking is also a major cause of 'bunching', so avoiding this will help traffic to flow more smoothly.

Whenever you drop down a gear, fuel consumption increases. Forward planning helps to eliminate excessive gear changes; for example, when approaching junctions or roundabouts. Remember that it isn't always necessary to use every gear. Reducing the number of gear changes (for example, by using 'block' gear changing) not only improves fuel consumption but also saves time and physical energy, which in turn can mean less fatigue for the driver.

Keep a safe distance from the vehicle in front, as this will help you to plan your driving. Try to leave sufficient room, so you don't have to brake immediately or harshly when traffic in front of you slows down. Simply taking your foot off the accelerator will slow your vehicle, and fuel consumption will be reduced. However, you may sometimes wish to use your brakes to activate your brake lights, so that vehicles behind will know that you're slowing down.

If you have to make a prolonged stop, say for more than two minutes at a level crossing or roadworks, you may consider it best to stop the engine while you wait.

Route planning

Plan your route to give you the easiest way to access your destination, avoiding known hold-ups and roadworks.

- Refer to a satellite navigation system but don't rely on it exclusively, as it may have out-of-date or incomplete information at any given time, even if the system you're using is specifically designed for large vehicles.
- Always know where you're going – you'll use lots of fuel by getting lost.

Make sure you avoid any narrow roads, areas where it may be difficult to manoeuvre a large vehicle, and areas with weight, width or height restrictions.

Driving away

Avoid overrevving your engine when you start your vehicle, and try to pull away smoothly.

Choosing your speed

Always keep within the speed limit. Exceeding the speed limit by only a few miles per hour will mean that you use more fuel. More importantly, you'll be breaking the law and you'll increase the risk of serious injury if you're involved in a collision.

The accelerator

Try to use the accelerator smoothly and progressively. When appropriate, take your foot off the pedal and allow the momentum of the vehicle to carry you forward. Taking your foot off the accelerator when going downhill can save a considerable amount of fuel without any loss of vehicle control.

Rather than use your brakes for a long period (which brings the risk of brake fade), you should control downhill speed through the use of lower gears and, if fitted, any endurance braking system (commonly known as a 'retarder').

Whenever possible, accelerate smoothly and avoid heavy braking, as this leads to higher fuel consumption and more pollution. Driving smoothly can reduce fuel consumption by about 15%, as well as reducing wear and tear on your vehicle.

Selecting gears

As noted earlier, it isn't always necessary to change up or down through each gear; it's possible to miss out intermediate gears ('block' gear changing). This helps to reduce the amount of time you spend accelerating, and, as this is when fuel consumption is at its highest, it can save fuel.

Accelerate smoothly to an appropriate speed and, as soon as conditions allow, use the highest gear possible without making the engine struggle. Modern vehicles are designed to deliver power even when engine revs are quite low. You'll find that this allows you to make use of the higher gears at low speeds.

Large vehicles are increasingly being fitted with automatic or semi-automatic transmission. These systems can sense the load, speed or gradient and select the best gear for the conditions and for fuel economy.

Braking

Smooth and progressive braking is an integral part of fuel-efficient driving. It will save fuel and reduce wear on the brake linings and tyres. It also minimises the road speed lost when braking, so less fuel is required to resume your travelling speed.

Using a retarder can contribute to fuel efficiency as well as increasing the life of the brake linings. Both bring significant cost savings for operators.

Engine braking

The resistance to movement applied by the engine when your foot is fully off the accelerator is known as engine braking. Engine braking uses little or no fuel, so take advantage of it wherever possible. On long downhill gradients, using lower gears instead of extended use of the brakes can help to avoid brake fade.

Cruise control

Cruise control keeps the vehicle moving at a constant speed. It works by delivering the appropriate amount of fuel for any given situation. This not only improves fuel economy but also reduces mechanical wear and maintenance costs. If it's fitted, it should be used whenever safe and appropriate.

Use of cruise control, effective route planning and keeping the rev counter in the green band will all help to minimise the amount of fuel used.

Remember, cruise control mustn't be used as a substitute for concentration; you must exercise proper control of your vehicle at all times. It isn't advisable to use cruise control in stop/go traffic or in hilly terrain. In these conditions, it may not help fuel economy and it could also be dangerous.

Minimising drag

Aerodynamic styling – for example, a curved trailer roof, side skirts or wind deflectors – helps to minimise wind resistance or 'drag'. Drag can increase fuel consumption by more than 15%, so a correctly adjusted air deflector will save fuel. Roof spoilers should be adjusted to guide airflow over the highest point at the front of the trailer or load. As a guide, for every 10 cm of trailer front exposed to airflow, fuel consumption will increase by 0.1 miles per gallon.

Retrofitted parts can assist vehicle stability in windy conditions and also help to prevent the build-up of road film and dirt.

REMEMBER, if a vehicle has aerodynamic styling, then adding further exterior lights will affect the airflow over the vehicle.

The height and positioning of a load can also influence fuel consumption. Minimising the load height reduces wind resistance, especially when using a flat-bodied vehicle. The position of the load should be calculated to reduce drag while also avoiding any overloading of the axles (see 'Loads and load restraint', in section 2).

Fuel consumption

Check your vehicle's fuel consumption regularly. To make sure that you're getting the most from your vehicle, simply record the amount of fuel you put in, against the number of miles travelled. This will help you check whether you're using fuel efficiently. Keeping the engine revs in the green band will maximise fuel economy.

If you haven't changed your driving style, or the conditions in which you're driving, an increase in average fuel consumption can mean that the vehicle needs servicing or that a fault (such as low tyre pressure) may be developing. A fuel-efficient driver is constantly aware of how much fuel their vehicle uses. If your vehicle has a fuel-consumption display on the instrument panel, use it to monitor the fuel used during your journey. Alternatively, you can simply divide the number of miles travelled by the number of gallons of fuel used.

Overfull fuel tanks can cause fuel to leak through the breather vent. Fuel expands when it heats up, so, if the tank is filled to the brim, leaks can happen when the fuel expands. This can waste fuel and make the road surface dangerous for other road users. Always leave a little room for expansion when you fill your tank.

If your vehicle has a lifting axle, it's possible to save fuel by running with the axle raised. However, when doing this, you must make sure that the weight limits on the remaining axles aren't exceeded. See section 2 for more information about axle loads and weight limits.

Temperature control

Use air conditioning only when you really need it; running it continuously can increase fuel consumption by about 15%.

The alternative to air conditioning may be to open your windows, but this will increase drag – and consequently fuel consumption – when you're driving.

In cold weather, fuel-efficient ways of avoiding ice on the windows include

- pre-setting the night heater to warm up the cab
- parking the vehicle under cover at the end of a shift.

Select for economy and low emissions

There are advantages and disadvantages to all types of fuel. However, most HGVs are now powered by diesel. These engines are very fuel-efficient and produce less carbon dioxide (a global warming gas) than petrol engines. They also emit less carbon monoxide and hydrocarbons than  petrol engines, but they produce more emissions of nitrogen oxides (NOx) and particulates, which are bad for local air quality. Fitting a particulate trap to a vehicle can help to reduce harmful emissions by filtering hydrocarbons, carbon monoxide and particulate matter.

Newer vehicles have to meet strict standards aimed at reducing these emissions, and all diesel vehicles can now use ultra-low-sulphur diesel to reduce pollution.

Some manufacturers reduce emissions of nitrogen oxides by pumping a mixture of urea and water into the exhaust. This is sold as AdBlue and it converts nitrogen oxides to nitrogen gas and water. If your vehicle has an AdBlue tank, make sure you keep it topped up.

Low and Ultra Low Emission Zones

In some areas, you may have to pay a congestion charge to use congested road space.

In London, you may also have to pay the Ultra Low Emission Zone (ULEZ) and/or Low Emission Zone (LEZ) charges. These zones are specified areas of Greater/central London within which diesel-engined vehicles are required to meet specific emissions standards. If a vehicle doesn't meet these standards, a daily charge must be paid in order to drive within the zone.

Find out more about congestion and emission zone charging in London using the Transport for London (TfL) website.

tfl.gov.uk/modes/driving/congestion-charge
tfl.gov.uk/modes/driving/low-emission-zone
tfl.gov.uk/modes/driving/ultra-low-emission-zone

Keep your vehicle well maintained

Follow these suggestions to keep your vehicle well maintained and reduce its impact on the environment.

- Make sure that the engine is maintained correctly. Badly maintained engines use more fuel and emit more exhaust fumes. MOT tests include a strict exhaust emission test to ensure that vehicles run efficiently and don't cause excessive air pollution.

- Have your vehicle serviced as recommended by the manufacturer. The cost of a service may well be less than the cost of running a badly maintained vehicle. For example, even slight brake drag can increase fuel consumption.

- If you do your own maintenance, make sure that you send waste oil, old batteries and used tyres to a garage or local-authority site for recycling or safe disposal. Don't pour waste oil down a drain; it's illegal, harmful to the environment and could lead to prosecution.

- Tears to curtain sides will increase wind resistance and so increase fuel consumption. Make sure they're repaired as soon as possible.

- Use good-quality engine oil. If you use synthetic engine oil, rather than the cheaper mineral oil, you can save fuel.

- Make sure your tyres are properly inflated. Incorrect tyre pressure results in shorter tyre life and may create a danger, as it can affect stability and braking performance. In addition, under-inflated tyres can increase fuel consumption.

- When filling your fuel tank, leave room for expansion. As previously stated, fuel expands when it becomes hot, and, if you fill the tank to the brim, its only method of escape is via the breather vent.

- If at any time you notice that your fuel filler cap is missing, you **MUST** get it replaced before continuing.

Here's a checklist of signs that a commercial vehicle may need workshop attention to stop it wasting fuel. Make this list a part of your regular vehicle examination. Check for

- any fuel or oil leaks, including missing or broken fuel caps
- missing seals in the fuel-tank cap or signs of fuel spills around the filler neck
- low tyre pressure
- tyre wear suggesting faulty steering or incorrect axle alignment

- missing tyre valve caps (dirt in the valves can cause them to leak)
- traces of black smoke in exhaust fumes
- tears in the body curtains, or any body damage
- missing or damaged air-management equipment
- excessive engine-oil consumption (no leaks) suggestive of internal wear.

Your maintenance team will also monitor records showing rapid wear of clutch or brake friction material.

Extra tips on fuel economy

Improving fuel economy

E very time you move off, do so smoothly – avoid harsh acceleration.

C hange down to the appropriate gear, but wait for your speed to decrease.

O n acceleration, try to skip gears where you can.

N ever leave it to chance – maintain your vehicle in good condition.

O bserve and keep within the rev counter green zone.

M inimise brake use – plan ahead and keep monitoring road conditions.

Y our speed should remain constant when possible.

⊕ Road traffic incidents

You can reduce the risk of being involved in a road traffic incident by

- concentrating at all times
- anticipating how situations might develop
- staying aware of what's happening on the road, both around your vehicle and as far ahead as you can see.

It's important to recognise the effects your vehicle can have on more vulnerable road users, such as cyclists, pedestrians and motorcyclists. When travelling at speed, an HGV creates areas of low air pressure along its sides. Higher-pressure air then rushes to backfill this space, creating a suction effect. Cyclists, and pedestrians near the edge of the kerb, are especially vulnerable to the changing air pressure drawing them towards the vehicle – and, in some cases, under its wheels. You should anticipate, at all times, the actions of other road users around you.

You should

- be fit to drive
- concentrate
- stay alert
- observe the changes in traffic conditions
- plan well ahead
- drive at a safe speed, appropriate to the road and traffic conditions
- keep your vehicle roadworthy
- make sure that any load is securely stowed
- avoid the need to rush.

> **REMEMBER,** if your vehicle is involved in a road traffic incident, you MUST stop. It's an offence not to do so.

If you have an incident

If you're involved in an incident, you MUST give your details to anyone who has reasonable grounds for requiring them. These details should include

- your name and address
- the name and address of the vehicle's owner
- the registration number of the vehicle you're driving.

You should obtain the same details from anyone else involved. Also, try to obtain the names and addresses of anyone who **saw** the incident.

You should make a note of

- the time and date of the incident
- the location of the incident (including street names)
- vehicle registration numbers
- weather conditions

- lighting (if applicable)
- any road signs or road markings
- road conditions
- damage to vehicles or property
- traffic lights (colour at the time)
- any indicator signals or audible warning given
- any statements made by the other party or parties
- any skid marks, debris, etc.

Give your details to any other road user involved in the incident

You **MUST** report the incident to the police as soon as possible, and in any case within 24 hours (immediately in Northern Ireland), if

- anyone is injured
- damage is caused to another vehicle or property and the owner isn't present or can't be found
- the incident involves any of the animals specified in law.

If you can't produce your driving licence and insurance documents at the time of the incident, the police may require you to produce them within seven days, at a police station of your choice. If you're on a journey that takes you out of the country and you can't produce the documents within the seven days specified, the police may allow you to do so as soon as is reasonably possible.

Company documentation

If you're involved in an incident or near-miss while at work, a superior must be informed as soon as possible, because it's their legal duty to report it. It's a good idea, therefore, to familiarise yourself with your operator's particular reporting requirements, to make sure that you collect all the necessary details at the time of the incident. Your operator may have a procedure for completing incident reports and there may already be some forms in your vehicle.

Many operators have standardised the procedure for reporting incidents. Drivers carry a 'bump card', which they use to record details at the scene, and the information is then transferred to an official form held at base. Drivers are often supplied with incident packs, which include a bump card, a disposable camera, a guide to reporting incidents, a pen and a torch. Some operators have set up call centres, so that drivers can immediately call in if they're involved in an incident.

You should record the details listed above. Also include

- the purpose of the journey
- the starting time
- a sketch or photograph of the scene
- your account of what happened
- details of any injuries sustained.

In most cases, a senior manager will interview the driver about what happened.

The driver may be found at fault if they

- were driving too fast for the conditions
- failed to anticipate possible difficulties and danger
- failed to give proper signals of their intentions
- failed to comply with The Highway Code.

Reaction in the event of aggression

Be aware that others involved in an incident may initially behave in an agitated or aggressive manner. This is often a symptom of shock, so try to be as reasonable and softly spoken as possible when asking for personal details or insurance information. The fact that you appear calm and in control may be all that's needed to defuse the situation.

Helping at the scene of an incident

If you're the first, or among the first, to arrive at the scene of an incident, your actions could be crucial. Find a safe place to stop, so you don't endanger yourself, any passengers or other road users.

It's essential to

- warn other traffic approaching the scene, by means of hazard warning lights, beacons, cones, advance warning triangles, etc
- reduce the risk of fire by making sure that all naked lights are extinguished and vehicle engines are turned off
- **make sure that someone phones 999**, giving details of any injury or danger to other road users

- protect injured people from any further danger; for example, from traffic or hazardous materials. If they aren't at risk of any further danger, don't move them. If you need to move a casualty to a place of safety, do so carefully – incorrect handling could cause more injury or even prove fatal

- move any apparently uninjured people away from the vehicle(s) to a place of safety

- give first aid if anyone is unconscious. For advice on first aid, see the next subsection

- check for the effects of shock. A person may appear to have no injuries but may be suffering from shock

- keep casualties warm but don't give them anything to drink

- give the **facts** (not assumptions) to the ambulance crew when they arrive.

Don't remove a motorcyclist's helmet unless it's essential to do so; for example, if they aren't breathing normally.

Incidents on the motorway

Traffic travels at higher speeds on motorways and there's increased danger of a collision becoming a serious incident, so it's essential to inform the motorway police and emergency services of any collision as quickly as possible.

You should

- use the nearest emergency telephone – it's free and the operator can quickly inform the emergency services of your exact location. Don't cross the carriageway to get to an emergency telephone. If you use a mobile phone, first make sure that you've identified your location

- try to warn traffic behind if possible, without placing yourself in danger

- move any uninjured people to a place of safety, well away from the main carriageway

- be on the alert for emergency vehicles approaching the incident along the hard shoulder.

Emergency vehicles

Emergency vehicles may approach at any time while you're on the road. You should look and listen for flashing blue, red or green lights, headlights or sirens being used by ambulances, fire engines, police or other emergency vehicles.

When one of these vehicles approaches, don't panic; consider the route it's taking and take appropriate action to let it pass. If necessary, pull to the side of the road and stop. Be aware of other road users and make sure that you don't endanger them in any way.

If you see or hear emergency vehicles in the distance, be aware that there may be an incident ahead and other emergency vehicles may be approaching.

In addition to the usual emergency vehicles you would expect to see using blue flashing lights (fire service, police, ambulance), there are others that aren't so common. These include bomb-disposal and blood-transfusion vehicles. A green flashing light is used by a doctor making an urgent journey.

Dangerous goods

If a road traffic incident involves a vehicle displaying either a hazard information plate or a plain orange rectangle

- give the emergency services as much information as possible about the labels and any other markings

- contact the emergency telephone number shown on the plate of a vehicle involved in any spillage (if a number is given)

- don't use a mobile phone close to a vehicle carrying flammable loads, and keep well away from such a vehicle unless you have to approach in order to save a life

- beware of any dangerous liquids, dusts or vapours, no matter how small the concentration may appear to be. A fine spray of corrosive fluid leaking from a pinhole puncture in a tank vessel can cause serious injuries.

Examples of various hazard labels are shown in section 7.

Fire

Fire can start in a number of places on a goods vehicle; for example

- near the engine
- within the load
- from a fault in the transmission
- from overheating tyres
- from a leak in the fuel system
- due to a fault in the electrical circuits.

It's vital that any fire is tackled without delay. A vehicle and its load can be destroyed by fire within a very short period of time.

If fire is suspected or discovered, it's essential to

- stop as quickly and safely as possible
- get all individuals out of the vehicle, if it's safe to do so
- either dial 999 or get someone else to do it immediately.

Carrying a suitable fire extinguisher in your vehicle may help you to put out a small fire. If you suspect a fire in the engine compartment, take the actions shown in the previous three bullet points. In addition

- don't try to access the engine compartment. This could allow more air to reach the fire and make it worse. You may be able to direct the nozzle of a fire extinguisher through any small gap
- if the fire appears to be large, don't try to tackle it. Get well clear of the vehicle and leave it to the fire brigade
- don't take any risks.

Drivers of vehicles carrying dangerous goods must be trained in how to deal with a fire. Specialist fire-fighting equipment must also be available on the vehicle.

You should

- keep all members of the public and other traffic well away from the incident
- isolate the vehicle to reduce danger to the surrounding area
- make sure that someone contacts, without delay, the emergency telephone number given on either the hazard warning plate or the load documents
- warn approaching traffic.

REMEMBER, stay calm and react promptly.

Fire extinguishers

You should be able to recognise the various types of fire extinguisher and know which fires they're intended to tackle. For example, it's dangerous to tackle a fuel fire with a water fire extinguisher. Attempting to do so may only spread the fire further.

Most extinguishers are designed to smother the source of the fire through the action of either an inert gas or a dry powder. If at all possible

- disconnect electrical leads
- cut off the fuel supply.

Visit this website to find out more about the different types of fire extinguisher and when they should be used.

extinguisheradvice.org.uk/types-of-fire-extinguisher.php

⊕ First aid

Regulations require many HGVs transporting chemicals or other potentially dangerous cargo to carry first-aid equipment. Even if you don't have to carry a kit by law, it's sensible for every goods vehicle driver to have a first-aid kit available.

Consider taking a first-aid training course. One day it could save a life.

Courses are available from

- St John Ambulance
- St Andrew's First Aid
- British Red Cross Society.

First aid on the road

The following information was compiled with the assistance of St John Ambulance, the British Heart Foundation and the British Red Cross. It's intended as a general guide for those without first-aid training but shouldn't be considered a substitute for proper training. Any

first aid given at the scene of an incident should be looked on only as a temporary measure until the emergency services arrive.

1. Deal with danger

Further collisions and fire are the main dangers following a crash. Approach any vehicle involved with care, watching out for spilt oil or broken glass. Switch off all engines and, if possible, warn other traffic. If you have a vehicle, switch on your hazard warning lights. Stop anyone from smoking, and put on the gloves from your first-aid kit if you have one.

2. Get help

If you can do so safely, try to get the assistance of bystanders. Ask someone to call the appropriate emergency services on 999 or 112 as soon as possible. The operator will need to know the exact location of the incident (including the direction of traffic, eg northbound) and the number of vehicles involved. Try to give information about the condition of any casualties; for example, if anyone is having difficulty breathing, is bleeding heavily, is trapped in a vehicle or doesn't respond when spoken to.

3. Help those involved

Don't move casualties from their vehicles unless there's the threat of further danger.

Don't remove a motorcyclist's helmet unless it's essential.

Try to keep casualties warm, dry and as comfortable as you can. Avoid moving a casualty unnecessarily, as this could make their injuries worse.

Give reassurance confidently and try not to leave a casualty alone or let them wander into the path of other traffic.

Don't give a casualty anything to eat or drink.

4. Provide emergency care

If you need to provide emergency care, follow the DR ABC code.		
Danger		Check that it's safe to approach.
Response		Try to get a response by gently shaking the casualty's shoulders and asking loudly 'Are you all right?' If they respond, check for injuries.
Airway		If there's no response, open the casualty's airway by placing your fingers under their chin and lifting it forward.

If you need to provide emergency care, follow the DR ABC code.

Breathing		Check that the casualty is breathing normally. Look for chest movements, look and listen for breathing, and feel for breath on your cheek.
		If there are no signs of breathing, start CPR. Interlock your fingers, place them in the centre of the casualty's chest and press down hard and fast – around 5–6 centimetres and about twice a second. You may only need one hand for a child and shouldn't press down as far. For infants, use two fingers in the middle of the chest and press down about a third of the chest depth. Don't stop until the casualty starts breathing again or a medical professional takes over.
Circulation		If the casualty is responsive and breathing, check for signs of bleeding. Protect yourself from exposure to blood and check for anything that may be in the wound, such as glass. Don't remove anything that's stuck in the wound. Taking care not to press on the object, build up padding on either side of the object. If nothing is embedded, apply firm pressure over the wound to stem the flow of blood. As soon as practical, fasten a pad to the wound with a bandage or length of cloth. Use the cleanest material available.

Unconscious and breathing

Don't move a casualty unless there's further danger. Moving a casualty unnecessarily could worsen any injury they may have sustained. If breathing stops, treat as recommended under 'DR ABC'.

Don't attempt to remove a motorcyclist's helmet unless it's essential; for example, if the casualty isn't breathing normally. Otherwise, serious injury could result.

If an adult or child is unconscious and breathing, but otherwise uninjured, place them on their side in the recovery position (shown here).

- Start with the casualty on their back and sit or crouch to one side of them.

- Place the arm nearest you straight out, at a right angle to their body.

- Roll them onto their side towards you.

- Turn the casualty's other arm palm upwards, and place this hand between the ground and the casualty's cheek.

- With your other hand, grasp the casualty's top leg just above the knee and pull it up at a right angle, keeping the foot on the ground. This will prevent them from rolling over any further.

- Make sure that the casualty's airway remains open and that you monitor their condition until a medical professional takes over.

Dealing with shock

The effects of shock may not be immediately obvious. Warning signs to look for include

- paleness of the face (pallor)
- cold, clammy skin
- fast, shallow breathing
- fast, weak pulse
- yawning or sighing
- confusion
- loss of consciousness (in extreme cases).

Prompt treatment can help to deal with shock.

- Don't give the person anything to eat or drink. Their condition may be severe enough to require surgery, in which case it's better if the stomach is empty.
- Lay them down, with their head low and legs raised and supported, to increase the flow of blood to their head.
- Call 999 or 112 for medical help. Say that you think the person is in shock, and explain what you think caused it (such as bleeding or a heart attack).
- Loosen any tight clothing around the person's neck, chest and waist to make sure it doesn't constrict their blood flow.
- Fear and pain can make shock worse, by increasing the body's demand for oxygen, so, while you wait for help to arrive, it's important to keep the person comfortable, warm and calm. Do this by covering them with a coat or blanket and comforting and reassuring them.
- Keep checking their breathing, pulse and level of response.
- If they lose consciousness at any point, open their airway, check their breathing, and prepare to treat someone who has become unconscious.
- If someone is hysterical, talk firmly and quietly to them.

Burns

Put out any flames, taking care for your own safety. Cool the burn for at least 20 minutes with plenty of clean, cool water. Cover the burn with cling film if available. Don't try to remove anything that's sticking to the burn.

Electric shock

Some accidents involve a vehicle hitting overhead cables or electrical supplies to traffic bollards, traffic lights or street lights. In such cases, make a quick check that it's safe before trying to get someone out of a vehicle.

Don't touch any person who's obviously in contact with live electricity, unless you can use a non-conducting item, such as a piece of dry wood, plastic or something similar – nothing wet should be used. Use this to push away any electrical equipment or loose cables if you can and separate any contact the casualty has with the electricity supply. You mustn't try to give first aid until contact has been broken.

A person can also be electrocuted simply by being too close to a high-voltage overhead cable. Contact the provider (a number may be shown on a nearby pole), then follow their advice.

⊕ Breakdowns

What to do in the event of a breakdown

If your vehicle breaks down, try to move it as far over to the left as possible. If you can get it off the main carriageway without causing danger or inconvenience to other road users, especially pedestrians, do so. Don't park on the pavement – the weight of a goods vehicle can damage paving stones and underground services.

If you have a warning triangle, and you're on a single carriageway road, place it at least 45 metres (147 feet) behind the vehicle. Some form of warning is vital if an electrical problem has stopped the rear lights from working. However, **don't** attempt to place a warning triangle or any other warning device on a motorway, dual carriageway, hard shoulder or slip road.

Don't attempt to work on the offside of the vehicle unless you're protected by a recovery vehicle with flashing hazard warning lights. Even then, take great care on roads carrying fast-moving traffic. Injuries and fatalities have occurred at the scenes of initially simple breakdowns.

If your vehicle is causing an obstruction and possible danger to other road users, inform the police as soon as possible. This is particularly important if the vehicle is carrying dangerous goods or other hazardous materials.

If you suspect that your vehicle has a mechanical problem, don't be tempted to continue your journey. Small defects could become dangerous if they aren't given attention. You could create a more serious situation if your vehicle eventually breaks down in a busy location.

Breakdown insurance

It's wise to take out insurance with a reputable breakdown association. Without the benefit of membership, the cost of towing or repairing an HGV could be substantial.

For safety reasons, vehicles that break down on the motorway are required to be removed as quickly as possible.

Tyre failure

Many goods vehicle breakdowns involve tyre failure. Not only is this dangerous in itself, causing loss of control, but the resulting debris also presents a hazard to other road users.

Front tyre blow-outs

Sudden deflation of the front tyre on a goods vehicle can result in the loss of steering control. You should

- keep firm hold of the steering wheel
- always be aware of anything on your nearside
- signal to move to the left
- try to steer a steady course to the left-hand side of the road (or the hard shoulder on a motorway)
- reduce speed gradually, avoiding any harsh braking
- try to bring the vehicle to rest under control and as far to the left as possible
- use a warning triangle, if you have one (unless you're on a motorway or dual carriageway). Place it at least 45 metres (147 feet) behind the vehicle and switch on the vehicle's hazard warning lights.

Rear tyre blow-outs

If a rear tyre on either the vehicle or a trailer deflates, the effects may not be quite so severe. On a large vehicle, it may not be immediately obvious to you, especially if you have a multi-axle trailer. Use your mirrors to check your trailer frequently during a journey.

Section five

⊙ Preparing for your driving tests

This section covers

- The theory test
- The practical driving tests
- Preparing for your tests
- Booking your part 3a and 3b tests
- The national standard for driving lorries

⊕ The theory test

Before you take your heavy goods vehicle (HGV) practical driving tests, you'll have to pass the theory test. This test is specifically for drivers of large vehicles (it's separate from the theory test for car drivers) and it has two parts: a multiple-choice part with 100 questions and a hazard-perception part with 19 interactive clips.

Examples of the topics included in the multiple-choice part of the theory test are

- height, weight, width and length restrictions, and the actions you need to take
- rules on drivers' hours and rest periods
- braking systems and speed limiters
- the way that the size and shape of your vehicle restrict your view

- sharing the road safely with other types of road user
- recognising any faults on your vehicle
- loading a vehicle safely and securely
- the effect of wind on your vehicle and on other road users around you
- how to deal with other weather conditions, such as rain, ice or fog
- the documents you need, and the legal requirements you must meet, as the driver of an HGV
- reducing your vehicle's impact on the environment
- what to do if you're involved in, or arrive at, an incident
- the meaning of traffic signs and road markings.

To prepare for the multiple-choice part of the theory test, the Driver and Vehicle Standards Agency (DVSA) recommends that you study 'The Official DVSA Theory Test for Drivers of Large Vehicles' (available as a book and eBook, and online at **safedrivingforlife.info**). This contains hundreds of practice questions, as well as essential background information on all the key topics.

DVSA also produces 'The Official DVSA Guide to Hazard Perception', an online product that will help you to practise the hazard-perception part of the test.

Both publications can be purchased online at **safedrivingforlife.info/shop** or by calling **0333 200 2401**.

Once you've passed both parts of your theory test, you can book your practical tests.

Your theory test pass certificate will have a life of 2 years from the date that you passed the first part of the theory test. This means that you have to take and pass the practical tests within this 2-year period. If you do not, you'll have to take and pass the theory test again before you can book your practical tests. If you want to drive professionally, you'll also need to pass the Driver CPC case study test (part 2).

⊕ The practical driving tests

In November 2021, the original Driver CPC part 3 (driving ability) test was split into 2 parts. There are now 2 separate tests

- Driver CPC part 3a – the off-road exercises test
- Driver CPC part 3b – the on-road driving test.

You must pass both tests to drive a heavy goods vehicle, even if you do not intend to drive professionally.

You can choose to take the off-road exercises test (part 3a) with an approved private test provider or with DVSA.

You'll need to book and take the on-road driving test (part 3b) with DVSA.

You must pass the part 3a test before taking the part 3b test.

You should aim for a professional standard when you take your off-road exercises (part 3a) and on-road driving (part 3b) tests. You'll pass if your examiner sees that you can

- drive safely to a high standard
- show expert handling of the controls
- carry out the set exercises accurately and under control
- demonstrate through your driving that you have a thorough knowledge of The Highway Code and vehicle safety.

⊙ Preparing for your tests

Driver training for large vehicles is usually intensive, so it may be necessary for either you or your trainer to book your practical tests before you've reached the standard required to pass. Your instructor may offer you a mock test to give you an understanding of how the tests will be conducted. It may also help you to identify any weaknesses. If you need to work on any problem areas, work with your instructor to overcome them.

Having a test date to aim for can be a good incentive, but driver's skills and understanding develop at differing rates. It's possible that you may need more time and training than you'd planned. If your instructor does not feel that you have competent, safe control of the vehicle by the time of your test, accept that judgement and change your test appointment. Do not leave it too late though, as a late change or cancellation may result in you losing your fee for the driving test.

How will I know that I'm ready?

You're ready for your practical tests when you can drive

- consistently well
- with confidence
- in complete control
- without help or guidance from your instructor.

You'll pass if your examiner sees that you can

- drive safely to a high standard
- show expert handling of the controls
- carry out the set exercises accurately and under control
- demonstrate through your driving that you have a thorough knowledge of The Highway Code and vehicle safety.

Most people fail when they haven't had enough instruction or practice. Make sure that all aspects of the national standard for driving lorries are covered during your training. Advice on choosing an instructor can be found in section 1.

The Highway Code

You must know and understand The Highway Code thoroughly and put it into practice both during the tests and throughout your driving career. Study the latest edition carefully. Questions on The Highway Code form part of the theory test for drivers of large vehicles.

'The Official Highway Code' is available as a book, an eBook and online at **www.gov.uk**. Other useful training materials include 'Know Your Traffic Signs' (book and eBook) and 'The Official DVSA Theory Test for Drivers of Large Vehicles' (book, eBook and online).

It's important that you understand and follow the content of The Highway Code, not just so you know what's required of you as a driver, but also so you know what other types of road user may do, or be required to do, in various circumstances.

⊛ Booking your part 3a and 3b tests

Driver CPC part 3a: off-road exercises test

You must have passed the Driver Certificate of Professional Competence (CPC) part 1 theory test before you can book the Driver CPC part 3a test.

You can book your test with either an approved private test provider or with DVSA. Visit **www.gov.uk** to find a list of approved test providers near you. You can book directly with them. If there are no test providers near you, you can book a test with DVSA instead.

Trainer booking

If you're learning to drive with a training organisation, they'll normally book your test for you. This enables them to arrange courses that include a test appointment.

> **REMEMBER,** If the organisation that runs your training is also your test provider, your assessor must not have been involved in your training.

Special circumstances

When you book your test, you should say if

- your movement is restricted in any way
- you have any disability that might affect your driving.

Your assessor may talk to you about your disability and any adaptations that have been fitted to your vehicle.

Driver CPC part 3b: on-road driving test

You can book your part 3b test online at **www.gov.uk** or by telephone on **0300 200 1122**.

You must pass the part 3a (off-road exercises) test before you can take the part 3b test.

Trainer booking

If you're learning to drive with a training organisation, they'll normally book your test for you. This enables them to arrange courses that include a test appointment.

Special circumstances

When you book your test, you should tell DVSA if

- your movement is restricted in any way
- you have any disability that might affect your driving.

Your examiner may talk to you about your disability and any adaptations that have been fitted to your vehicle.

⊕ The national standard for driving lorries

Based on extensive research and consultation, the driving and riding standards set out everything a 'good' driver or rider needs to know and understand.

The standards form the basis of the tests – both theory and practical – for every category of vehicle. They're also the foundation for all the official learning materials that DVSA publishes for drivers and riders – at all stages of their driving or riding career.

There are various national driving and riding standards, starting with the base standards for driving a car (category B) or riding a motorcycle (category A). They then become more specialised. All of the standards can be found in full at **www.gov.uk**

The national standard for driving lorries is what you'll be most interested in as you prepare for your test. This standard describes the skills, knowledge and understanding that you need to be a safe and responsible driver of a category C vehicle: a lorry.

The standard assumes that, if you want to qualify as a lorry driver, you already hold a current full category B driving licence. It also assumes that you've demonstrated competence against the national standard for driving cars and light vans.

You'll need to show that you've kept up and continued to improve your driving competence since you passed your car test, and that you're ready to move on to a more specialised category of vehicle.

The national standard for driving lorries is split into five 'roles'. Each role covers a different aspect of driving a goods vehicle.

The roles are

Role 1	Prepare vehicle and its occupants for a journey
Role 2	Guide and control the vehicle
Role 3	Use the road in accordance with The Highway Code
Role 4	Drive safely and responsibly in the traffic system
Role 5	Review and adjust driving behaviour over lifetime

Each of the five roles is then broken down into units, which cover specific areas within each role.

The units are further broken down into elements, which cover

- what you must be able to do
- what you must know and understand.

The following tables set out

- the five roles
- their units
- the elements within each unit, and **an example** in that element of
  - what you'll need to be able to do
  - what you'll need to know and understand.

The **full descriptions** of what you'll need to be able to do, know and understand within each element can be found at **www.gov.uk**

Role 1	Prepare vehicle and its occupants for a journey
Unit 1.1	Prepare occupants of vehicle for a journey
	Element 1.1.1 Make sure you're fit to drive

For example

You must be able to assess whether your ability to drive safely and legally is affected, or likely to be affected, by the use of

- over-the-counter medicines
- prescription medicines
- illegal or controlled substances
- alcohol.

You must know and understand how illegal or controlled substances or alcohol impair your ability to drive safely, and

- that, regardless of any legal limits, the desirable level of alcohol to have in your system is zero
- how the strength of alcohol varies in different types of drink
- what a 'unit' of alcohol is equivalent to in different types of drink
- how the body metabolises drugs and alcohol, and the rate at which they're removed from your system
- that any alcohol may make you more likely to fall asleep even if the levels in your blood are below the legal limit.

Role 1	Prepare vehicle and its occupants for a journey

Element 1.1.2 Control the risks associated with carrying passengers, loads and animals

For example

You must be able to make sure that your vehicle is suitable for the load that's being carried and that

- its maximum authorised mass (MAM) isn't exceeded
- maximum permitted gross axle weights aren't exceeded at any time
- there are sufficient load anchoring points
- you have sufficient load securing devices, such as strapping, chains, wedges, chocks or sheeting
- load securing devices are free from defects and, where applicable, can be adjusted fully
- the headboard is strong enough to resist penetration when carrying loads such as poles or girders.

You must know and understand what to consider when loading the vehicle, the best way to secure different loads, and

- what the vehicle's payload is, or how to calculate it based on its MAM and its tare weight
- how to find your vehicle's maximum permitted gross axle weights
- that a vehicle which has compliant maximum permitted gross axle weights at the start of the journey may become illegal as consignments are offloaded
- the devices that may be used to secure a load and how to use them
- which hooks are suitable to be used as load anchorage points and where to find this information
- how to use straps, chains, wedges and chocks to make sure the load cannot move
- that the higher a vehicle's centre of gravity, the less stable the vehicle and its load will be.

Role 1	Prepare vehicle and its occupants for a journey
Unit 1.2	**Make sure the vehicle is roadworthy**
	Element 1.2.1 Make routine checks of vehicle roadworthiness For example **You must be able to** check there's no damage that would • affect your ability to drive the vehicle safely • make the vehicle illegal • have an adverse effect on its environmental impact. **You must know and understand** any rules that apply to the fitting and use of ancillary equipment and how to make sure it can be used safely and with the minimum of distraction.
	Element 1.2.2 Check the vehicle is fit for the journey For example **You must be able to** categorise and report any vehicle defects and know what action to take; for example • remove vehicle from service (safety-critical defects) • report defect and continue in service (non-safety-critical defects). **You must know and understand** the operation of low-fuel, mpg or range indicators and how much fuel is left in the tank when low-fuel indicators operate.
	Element 1.2.3 Make sure vehicle documentation meets legal requirements For example **You must be able to**, where your journey will take you into an area where different rules apply, make sure that you follow those rules. **You must know and understand** that learner drivers, holding a provisional licence, must be supervised by somebody who • is at least 21 years old, and • has held a licence to drive the category of vehicle for at least three years.

Role 1	Prepare vehicle and its occupants for a journey
Unit 1.3	Plan a journey

Element 1.3.1 Plan a journey

For example

You must be able to plan a suitable route, taking into account

- road conditions
- weather conditions
- traffic
- driving experience
- the vehicle you're using.

You must know and understand how congestion charges, and road and bridge tolls, may affect your choice of route.

Role 2	Guide and control the vehicle
Unit 2.1	Start, move off, stop and leave the vehicle safely and responsibly

Element 2.1.1 Start the vehicle

For example

You must be able to carry out pre-start checks on

- doors
- parking brake
- seat
- steering
- seat belt
- mirrors.

You must know and understand that different models of vehicle may have different starting mechanisms, types of instrumentation and other aids, and that it's vital to use the vehicle handbook to find out how they work.

Element 2.1.2 Move off safely and smoothly

For example

You must be able to move off at an angle from behind a parked vehicle or obstruction, safely and smoothly, keeping control of the vehicle at all times.

You must know and understand the importance of applying the footbrake before selecting 'Drive' on an automatic vehicle.

Role 2	Guide and control the vehicle
	Element 2.1.3 Decelerate and bring the vehicle to a stop safely
	For example
	You must be able to use the vehicle's endurance braking system (retarder) when needed.
	You must know and understand the principles of the various endurance braking systems (retarders) that may be fitted to large vehicles; for example
	• electric
	• engine-driven
	• exhaust brakes.
	Element 2.1.4 Park the vehicle safely and responsibly
	For example
	You must be able to apply the relevant Transports Internationaux Routiers (TIR) procedures when travelling internationally, and make sure that
	• TIR cords are fitted securely
	• you know the points in your journey at which you need to check the cords
	• you have the required paperwork available throughout your journey.
	You must know and understand the rules in The Highway Code that apply when leaving your vehicle on different roads and in different lighting and weather conditions.
	Element 2.1.5 Couple and uncouple a trailer and vehicle safely
	For example
	You must be able to make sure that the trailer's brakes are applied prior to coupling and uncoupling.
	You must know and understand why it's important to stow the air lines and electrical connections safely.

Role 2	Guide and control the vehicle
Unit 2.2	Drive the vehicle safely and responsibly

	Element 2.2.1 Monitor and respond to information from instruments, driving aids and the environment
	For example
	You must be able to make effective use of mirrors and other aids to vision to identify and monitor other road users and hazards.
	You must know and understand that you must always act on the basis of what's in front of you, and not just rely on the information provided by satellite navigation systems or other aids.
	Element 2.2.2 Control the acceleration of the vehicle effectively
	For example
	You must be able to drive smoothly and in a controlled and progressive way to avoid destabilising any load.
	You must know and understand whether the vehicle you're driving is fitted with a speed-limiting device and, if so, the effect that this will have on the control of the vehicle.
	Element 2.2.3 Use gears correctly
	For example
	You must be able to select the appropriate gear for the road speed of the vehicle, given the road and traffic conditions.
	You must know and understand the effect that unsuitable gear selection can have on
	• the performance of the vehicle • the driver's ability to drive safely and responsibly • the environment.
	Element 2.2.4 Steer the vehicle safely
	For example
	You must be able to steer the vehicle safely and responsibly in all road and traffic conditions, paying attention to any weight, height, width, length and ground-clearance restrictions.
	You must know and understand where to find the dimensions of the vehicle; for example, MAM or height.

Role 2	Guide and control the vehicle
	Element 2.2.5 Manoeuvre the vehicle
	For example
	You must be able to make sure that if audible reversing warning systems are fitted, they're used only when it's legal to do so.
	You must know and understand that different vehicles will react differently in a possible skid situation, depending on their configuration (such as front-wheel or rear-wheel drive) and on the technologies fitted (such as ABS or ESP).
Unit 2.3	**Drive the vehicle while towing a trailer**
	Element 2.3.1 Drive the vehicle while towing a trailer
	For example
	You must be able to make sure you have the correct licence to drive the intended combination of vehicle and trailer.
	You must know and understand the effect that towing a trailer may have on braking, the concept of brake fade and what to do when descending gradients to make sure you keep in control.

Role 3	Use the road in accordance with The Highway Code
Unit 3.1	**Negotiate the road correctly**
	Element 3.1.1 Maintain a suitable position on the road
	For example
	You must be able to take into account the effect of the road camber on the position of the vehicle, particularly with regard to street furniture and other potential impact sources.
	You must know and understand that on roads with a severe camber, the top of a large vehicle can lean up to 250 mm (around 10 inches).
	Element 3.1.2 Negotiate bends
	For example
	You must be able to select a safe position and speed to enter a bend.
	You must know and understand the importance of coordinating the use of gears, accelerator, brakes and steering to negotiate a bend safely and responsibly.

Role 3	Use the road in accordance with The Highway Code
	Element 3.1.3 Negotiate all types of junctions, including roundabouts, and all types of crossings For example **You must be able to** actively scan for more vulnerable road users at junctions, roundabouts and crossings – for example, cyclists and motorcyclists. **You must know and understand** the rules that apply to • merging into a stream of traffic • crossing the path of an approaching stream of traffic • all types of pedestrian crossing • train and tram crossings.
	Element 3.1.4 Drive on motorways and dual carriageways For example **You must be able to** allow for other road users joining or leaving the motorway or dual carriageway. **You must know and understand** that you mustn't cross the central reservation, or drive against the traffic flow on a motorway or dual carriageway, unless directed to do so by an authorised person or traffic signs.
Unit 3.2	**Comply with signals, signs and road markings**
	Element 3.2.1 Comply with signals, signs and road markings For example **You must be able to** respond correctly to signals given by authorised persons. **You must know and understand** the meaning of, and how to respond to • mandatory traffic signs • warning signs • road markings.

Role 4	Drive safely and responsibly in the traffic system
Unit 4.1	**Interact correctly with other road users**
	Element 4.1.1 Communicate intentions to other road users For example **You must be able to** use horn and lights to communicate with other road users where necessary. **You must know and understand** why you should make sure signals are given in good time and cancelled as soon as possible.
	Element 4.1.2 Cooperate with other road users **You must be able to** manage the risk that other road users may not give you enough space to manoeuvre. **You must know and understand** the importance of predicting the likely actions of other road users, with particular reference to vulnerable road users such as cyclists, motorcyclists, children and the elderly.
Unit 4.2	**Minimise risk when driving**
	Element 4.2.1 Identify and respond to hazards For example **You must be able to** judge the significance of possible hazards and prioritise your responses. **You must know and understand** which kinds of hazard to particularly look for in different environments, such as tractors on rural roads, deer on forest roads or flooding in heavy rain.
	Element 4.2.2 Drive defensively For example **You must be able to** assess your own driving behaviour and identify areas needing work. **You must know and understand** that the stopping distance for larger vehicles is often farther than that for cars and therefore a larger separation distance is required to keep a safe driving space.
	Element 4.2.3 Follow the principles of ecologically responsible (fuel-efficient) driving For example **You must be able to** drive in the highest responsive gear to keep full control and avoid labouring the engine. **You must know and understand** how effective scanning and planning can help you to use smooth acceleration or deceleration to keep momentum.

Unit 4.3	Manage incidents effectively
	Element 4.3.1 Take suitable action if your vehicle breaks down For example **You must be able to** make sure passengers, animals and loads are managed safely. **You must know and understand** the benefits of wearing protective clothing, such as a high-visibility jacket or protective footwear, and your organisation's instructions on this.
	Element 4.3.2 Take suitable action when involved in, or witness to, a collision For example **You must be able to** give clear and accurate information to emergency services. **You must know and understand** the law that applies to • stopping • providing your details • giving statements • producing documents.

Role 5	Review and adjust driving behaviour over lifetime
Unit 5.1	**Learn from experience**
	Element 5.1.1 Learn from experience For example **You must be able to** demonstrate that you've continued to develop and update your driving skills since you took your driving test. **You must know and understand** the advantages of having regular driver development sessions with a competent instructor to keep up to date and remove bad habits.
Unit 5.2	**Keep up to date with changes**
	Element 5.2.1 Keep up to date with changes For example **You must be able to** keep up to date with changes to vehicle technology, especially if you change the vehicle you're using. **You must know and understand** where to find information about changes to vehicle technologies; for example, manufacturers' websites and trade magazines and websites.

Section six
➡ The HGV driving tests

This section covers

- Driver CPC part 3a: off-road exercises test
- The reversing exercise
- Uncoupling and recoupling
- Your test result
- Driver CPC part 3b: on-road driving test
- Safety check questions
- The braking exercise
- The vehicle controls
- Moving off
- Using the mirrors
- Giving signals
- Traffic signs and signals
- Awareness and anticipation
- Making progress and controlling your speed
- Separation distance
- Positioning and lane discipline
- Junctions
- Roundabouts
- Overtaking
- Meeting and passing other vehicles
- Crossing the path of other vehicles
- Pedestrian crossings
- Selecting a safe place to stop
- Your test result

⊙ Driver CPC part 3a: off-road exercises test

Your test vehicle

To avoid wasting your own time and the assessor's, make sure that your test vehicle is in roadworthy condition and meets the minimum test vehicle requirements for the category. See **www.gov.uk** for the rules that apply to the licence category of vehicle you want to bring to your test.

The vehicle you bring must be in the driving licence category that you want to get a licence for. For example, if you want to get a licence for an articulated lorry (category CE), you must use an articulated lorry for the test.

Make sure that the vehicle you intend to drive during the test

* is roadworthy
* is covered by insurance for its present use and for you to drive
* meets the minimum test vehicle requirements for the category in which you want to obtain a full licence
* has ordinary L plates visible to the front and rear (or D plates if you wish when driving in Wales).

Test vehicles in all categories must be fitted with an anti-lock braking system (ABS) and a tachograph. You should also check the vehicle's

* brake lights
* headlights and rear lights
* direction indicators
* lenses and reflectors
* mirrors
* brakes
* tyres
* exhaust system (for excessive noise)
* windscreen, wipers and washers.

Make sure that the cab is clean and free from any loose equipment.

> **REMEMBER,** Your test will be cancelled and you will not get your money back if you do not bring the right documents or if your vehicle does not meet the rules.

What to expect on the day

Arrive in good time for your test, otherwise it may not go ahead and you'll lose your fee. The test will last for up to 30 minutes.

When you arrive for your test, your assessor will ask to see your driving licence, your theory test pass certificate and, if appropriate, your photographic identification (your passport).

They will also ask you to confirm which email address you would like your driving test report sent to.

You'll be asked to sign a declaration that

- your vehicle is insured
- you meet the residency requirement
- your health hasn't changed in a way that might affect your driving since your last licence application.

Your test will not go ahead if you are unable to meet these requirements.

When all the paperwork has been completed, you'll be asked to lead the way to your vehicle.

Your assessor will ask you to complete 2 exercises

- an 'S' shaped reverse into a bay
- showing the uncoupling and recoupling procedure if you're taking a test with a trailer.

Before you start the engine

You should check that

- all doors are properly closed
- your seat is properly adjusted and comfortable, so that you can reach all the controls easily

- you have good all-round vision
- your driving mirrors are properly adjusted
- your seat belt, if fitted, is fastened, correctly adjusted and comfortable
- the parking brake is on
- the gear lever is in neutral.

This is a routine you should have developed while you were learning. Once you've started the engine, if your vehicle is fitted with air brakes, wait until the gauges show the correct pressure or until any device (a buzzer or a flashing light) has stopped operating.

⊙ The reversing exercise

What to expect
....

The reversing exercise tests your ability to reverse your vehicle and trailer in a restricted space. You must be able to do this

- under control and in reasonable time
- with good observation
- with reasonable accuracy.

Your assessor will show you a diagram of the manoeuvring area and explain what's required. You'll need to

- start with the front of the vehicle at a fixed point (in line with cones A and A1)
- reverse inside a clearly defined boundary (marked by yellow lines)
- pass cone B on the offside of your vehicle.

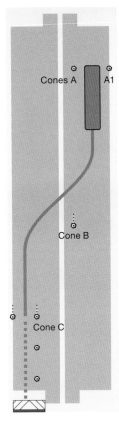

Cones A   A1

Cone B

Cone C

The manoeuvring area

A to A1: one-and-a-half times the width of the vehicle.

A to B: twice the length of the vehicle.

The width of the bay will be one-and-a-half times the width of the vehicle.

Bay cones C: for all vehicles 12 metres or more in overall length, set at 12 metres. For vehicles less than 12 metres long, set to the actual vehicle length.

The stopping area will have both a solid yellow line and a yellow-and-black hatched section, and a barrier will be situated at the end of the reversing bay. The yellow-and-black stopping area will be 75 cm deep.

You should reverse your vehicle into the bay and stop with the extreme rear of your vehicle within the 75 cm-deep yellow-and-black stopping area, in a position to load or unload safely at the simulated loading platform. You may touch the barrier gently.

Technique

You should

- approach the starting point slowly
- drive in a straight line as you approach cones A and A1
- stop before the marker cones A and A1
- reverse under complete control, using effective all-round observation

- show accurate judgement of the size of your vehicle and trailer
- drive with careful coordination of the clutch, accelerator and footbrake until the exercise is completed
- stop with the rear of your vehicle and trailer inside the yellow-and-black area.

Tips

When you're in the bay, you may leave the cab once to check where the back of the vehicle is in relation to the barrier. Make sure the vehicle is safe before leaving the cab.

If you need to take a forward shunt to complete the manoeuvre, take as much room as you need but don't drive beyond a position level with cones A and A1 or cross any boundary lines.

⊕ Uncoupling and recoupling

You should know and be able to demonstrate how to uncouple and recouple your vehicle and trailer safely.

What to expect

Your assessor will ask you to uncouple and recouple your vehicle and trailer on safe, level ground.

You'll be asked to

- demonstrate the uncoupling of your vehicle and trailer
- pull forward and reverse the vehicle alongside the trailer

- realign the vehicle with the trailer before recoupling the trailer
- recouple the vehicle and trailer.

Your assessor will expect you to make sure that the

- coupling is secure
- lights and indicators are working
- trailer brake is released.

Technique

You should be able to uncouple and recouple your vehicle and trailer

- safely
- confidently and in good time
- showing concern for your own and others' health and safety.

Uncoupling

When uncoupling, you should

- make sure that the brakes are applied on both the vehicle and trailer
- lower the landing gear and stow the handle away safely
- turn off any taps fitted to the air lines (sometimes referred to as 'suzies')

- disconnect the air lines and stow them away safely
- disconnect the electrical line and stow it away safely
- remove any dog clip securing the kingpin release handle
- release the fifth-wheel coupling locking bar, if fitted
- drive the tractor unit away slowly, checking the trailer either directly or in the mirrors.

If you're driving a drawbar outfit, you might have to support the trailer drawbar before you pull away. The 'suzies' on a drawbar trailer remain with the trailer and should be left in a safe position; for example, laid over the drawbar.

For drivers of articulated vehicles with close-coupled trailers, the uncoupling sequence is as follows

- make sure that the brakes are applied on both the tractor unit and the trailer
- lower the landing gear and stow the handle away safely
- disconnect the dog clip (if fitted) and release the fifth-wheel coupling
- drive the tractor unit far enough forward so that you can stand on the catwalk
- apply the tractor-unit parking brake
- turn off any taps fitted to the air lines
- disconnect the air lines and electrical connections, and stow them away safely
- drive the tractor unit away slowly, checking the trailer either directly or in the mirrors.

Recoupling

When recoupling, treat the trailer as you would a new trailer that you haven't seen before. You should

- make sure that the trailer brake is applied
- check that the height of the trailer is correct, so that it will receive the tractor unit safely
- reverse slowly up to the trailer until you hear the kingpin mechanism lock into place
- select a low gear and try to move forward in order to check that the locking mechanism is engaged. Do this twice to make sure it's secure

- make sure that the vehicle parking brake is applied

- carry out a visual inspection to check that the fifth-wheel jaws have correctly engaged, that the release handle is in the locked position, and that the kingpin is located correctly in the jaws

- connect any dog clip to secure the kingpin release handle. If the dog clip doesn't fully engage, pull the release handle to disengage the jaws, slowly move the tractor unit away from the trailer, then repeat the fifth-wheel coupling procedure

- connect the air and electrical lines. Turn on the taps, if fitted

- raise the landing gear and stow the handle away safely

- release the trailer parking brake

- check that air is building up in the storage tanks

- check the trailer lights and indicators.

For drivers of articulated vehicles with close-coupled trailers, the recoupling sequence is as follows

- make sure that the trailer brake is applied

- reverse slowly up to the trailer, stop just short of it and apply the tractor-unit parking brake

- check that the height of the trailer is correct, so that it will receive the tractor unit safely

- reverse far enough under the trailer so that you can stand on the catwalk

- apply the tractor-unit parking brake

- connect the air and electrical lines. Turn on the taps, if fitted

- reverse under the trailer and connect the fifth wheel

- select a low gear and try to move forward in order to check that the locking mechanism is engaged. Do this twice to make sure it's secure

- apply the tractor-unit parking brake

- carry out a visual inspection to check that the fifth-wheel jaws have correctly engaged, that the release handle is in the locked position, and that the kingpin is located correctly in the jaws

- connect any dog clip to secure the kingpin release handle

- raise the landing gear and stow the handle away safely
- release the trailer parking brake
- check that air is building up in the storage tanks
- check all the lights and indicators.

Tips

Stopping your vehicle's engine at the correct time during the exercise isn't only safer, but also saves fuel and reduces air and noise pollution.

⊙ Your test result

If you pass the test, you'll get a test certificate. Keep the certificate safe; you'll need to take it to your Driver CPC part 3b (on-road driving) test.

You need to pass the Driver CPC part 3b test within 6 months of getting your certificate. If you do not, you'll need to pass part 3a again.

If you do not pass the part 3a test, you can book another test straight away, but you must leave at least 24 hours before you take the test again.

If you lose your test certificate

If you took your test through an approved test provider, ask them for a replacement. They can charge you up to £15.

If you took your test with DVSA, email the DVSA vocational test team at **module3a@dvsa.gov.uk** to get a replacement.

You'll need a debit or credit card to pay the £15 fee.

Include the following in your email:

- your full name
- your driving licence number
- the date you passed the test
- a telephone number so DVSA can contact you to take your payment.

⊕ Driver CPC part 3b: on-road driving test

This test includes vehicle safety questions and one hour of practical road driving.

How is my driving assessed?

Your examiner will assess any errors you make. These errors will be assessed and recorded depending on their degree of seriousness and marked on the driving test report. You'll fail your test if you commit a serious or dangerous fault. You'll also fail if you accumulate too many driving faults.

Driving fault Less serious but has been assessed as such because of circumstances at that particular time.

Serious fault Recorded when a potentially dangerous incident has happened, or a habitual driving fault indicates a serious weakness in a candidate's driving.

Dangerous fault Recorded when a fault is assessed as having caused actual danger during the test.

At the end of the test, you'll be offered some general guidance to explain your driving test report. Your instructor can be present during this debrief even if they have not accompanied you on your driving test.

Does the standard of the test vary?
No. All examiners are trained to carry out the test to the same standard, regardless of which test centre they work at. You should receive the same results from different examiners or different HGV driving test centres. Test routes are as consistent as possible and include a wide range of typical road and traffic conditions.

Are examiners supervised?

Yes, they're closely supervised. A senior officer may sit in on your test if there are 2 or more passenger seats in your vehicle. Do not worry about this. The supervising officer will not be examining you, but will be checking that the examiner is carrying out the test properly. Just carry on as if they were not there.

Can anyone accompany me on the test?

Due to the shortage of seats in a lorry, this isn't always possible. If there are three or more seats in the cab of your vehicle, and provided a DVSA supervisor isn't observing, your instructor may sit in on your test but can't take any part in it.

What if I need a translator?

All Great Britain driving test candidates must take their test in either English or Welsh. Candidates taking their test in Northern Ireland may bring a translator/interpreter with them on their test. See **nidirect.gov.uk**

How should I drive during the test?

Your examiner will want you to drive safely to a high standard throughout your test. If you make a mistake, try not to let it worry you. It might be a trivial mistake and may not affect the results of the test.

If at any time you're unable to hear or understand the instructions given, ask for them to be repeated. The examiner will not mind. They will try to put you at ease.

What will the test include?

The test will last around one hour. At the test centre, you'll need to satisfy the examiner that you're capable of preparing to drive safely by carrying out simple safety checks on the vehicle you're using on the test.

When you're driving on the road, the test route will cover a variety of road and traffic conditions. The examiner will see how you:

- use the vehicle controls
- move away at an angle, uphill and downhill
- do a controlled stop
- use the mirrors
- give appropriate signals
- show awareness and anticipation of other road users' intentions

- manage your progress and control your vehicle speed
- deal with hazards
- select a safe place to stop.

There will also be 10 minutes of independent driving, designed to test your ability to drive safely while making independent decisions.

On the day of your test

Arrive in good time for your test, otherwise it may not go ahead and you'll lose your fee. The test will last about an hour, so make sure that you will not exceed the number of hours you're allowed to drive by law, and that you have sufficient fuel.

When you meet the examiner you'll be asked to sign a declaration that the vehicle you're using for the test is insured for that purpose and that you meet the residency requirements.

Documents

Make sure that you have these documents and that they're in date

- driving licence
- your theory test pass certificate (unless you're upgrading your licence to tow heavier trailers)
- your part 3a pass certificate.

You must also bring one of the following

- a Great Britain photocard driving licence
- a Northern Ireland photocard driving licence and paper counterpart
- an EU photocard driving licence (and paper counterpart, if you have one)

REMEMBER, If you do not bring these documents with you on the day, you will not be able to take your test and you'll lose your fee.

If you do not have a photocard driving licence, bring your paper licence and a valid passport.

Your test vehicle

Make sure that your test vehicle is in roadworthy condition and meets the minimum test vehicle requirements for the category. See **www.gov.uk** for the rules that apply to the licence category of vehicle you want to bring to your test.

The vehicle you bring must be in the same driving licence category as you used for your part 3a test. For example, if you passed the part 3a test in an articulated lorry (category CE), you must use an articulated lorry for the part 3b test.

Before you start the engine

Before you start your engine, you must always be sure that

- all doors are properly closed
- your seat is properly adjusted and comfortable, so that you can reach all the controls easily
- you have good all-round vision
- your driving mirrors are properly adjusted
- your seat belt, if fitted, is fastened, correctly adjusted and comfortable
- the parking brake is on
- the gear lever is in neutral.

It's best to develop good habits and to practise this routine while you're learning.

After you start the engine

Do not attempt to drive a vehicle fitted with air brakes until the gauges show the correct pressure or when any warning device (a buzzer sounding or a light flashing) is operating.

⊙ Safety check questions

What to expect

The examiner will ask you to carry out safety checks on your vehicle before you start driving.

The questions your examiner could ask include the following:

- Tell me how you would check the condition of the body is safe on this vehicle.

- Show me how you would replace the tachograph disc on this vehicle.

- Tell me how you would operate the loading mechanism on this vehicle.

- Show me how you would check that the wheel nuts are secure on this vehicle.

- Tell me how you would check the condition of the windscreen wipers on this vehicle.

- Show me how you would check that all doors, including cargo doors, are secure.

- Tell me how you would check the condition of the reflectors on this vehicle.

- Show me how you would check the condition of the mudguards on this vehicle.

- Tell me how you would check the condition of the suspension on this vehicle.

- Show me what instrument checks you would make before and after starting the engine on this vehicle.

- Tell me the main safety factors involved in loading this vehicle.

- Show me how you would check for air leaks on this vehicle.
- Show me how you would clean the windscreen using the windscreen washer and wipers.
- Show me how you would set the windscreen demister to clear the windows effectively.
- Show me how you would switch on the rear fog light(s) and explain when you would use it/them.
- Show me how you switch your headlight from dipped to main beam.
- Show me how you would check that the brake lights are working on this vehicle. (I can assist you; if you need to switch the ignition on, please don't start the engine.)

A full list of safety check questions for each licence category, and the correct answers, is published at **www.gov.uk**, under 'Guidance for driving examiners carrying out driving tests (DT1)'.

Tips

Information to help you answer these questions can be found in this book, but you should also be familiar with the vehicle you're using for your test and be able to explain or carry out safety checks on that vehicle.

⊙ The braking exercise

There isn't any emergency-stop exercise in the test, but there **is** a braking exercise.

What to expect

Your examiner will be with you in the vehicle for this exercise. You'll be told in good time when the exercise will start.

You'll be asked to pull up just before you get to a parked vehicle or an object on the kerb, such as a post, street light or tree. You'll need to bring the vehicle to a stop safely, smoothly and under full control, with consideration for other road users.

Technique

You should

- check your mirrors
- signal if necessary
- brake smoothly
- press the clutch in before you stop
- stop accurately, in a straight line and reasonably close to the kerb.

Tips

Use your nearside mirrors, including the Class V close proximity mirror, to help you position reasonably close to the kerb, but don't focus on the mirror so much that you miss any hazard developing around the vehicle.

⊙ The vehicle controls

Being able to control the vehicle confidently and competently is an essential part of driving safely. With practice, you should be able to use all the controls smoothly and easily, so that the vehicle is always completely under your control.

What to expect

Your examiner will watch you carefully to see how you use the

- accelerator
- clutch

- gears
- footbrake
- parking brake
- retarder
- steering
- other controls.

You should understand the functions of these controls and be able to use them

- smoothly
- correctly
- safely
- competently.

Technique

Accelerator

The accelerator controls the mixture of fuel and air that's supplied to the engine. The more you press the accelerator, the more fuel goes to the engine and the more power is generated. Use the accelerator smoothly; harsh or uncontrolled use wastes fuel and increases the amount of harmful emissions the engine produces. It also causes excessive engine noise, which could alarm or distract other road users.

Clutch

The clutch is the connection between the engine and the gearbox, on vehicles fitted with manual transmission. It's a connection over which the driver has control, but using it well requires practice.

You should

- balance the accelerator and clutch to pull away smoothly
- when stopping the vehicle, press the clutch in just before you come to a halt
- avoid jerky and uncontrolled use of the clutch when moving off or changing gear.

If your vehicle has automatic transmission, make sure that your foot is on the footbrake before you select any gear while stationary. This prevents the possibility of uncontrolled movement as the gear engages.

Gears

Increasingly, HGVs are fitted with automatic or semi-automatic transmission. These systems can sense the load, speed or gradient and select the correct gear for the conditions. The driver may only have to ease the pressure on the accelerator, or press the clutch pedal, to allow the system to engage the gear required.

You need to understand the system fitted to your vehicle and be able to use it competently. You should

- move off in the most suitable gear
- change gear in good time
- show an understanding of the type of gearbox you have by using it as appropriate to the road and traffic conditions
- plan well ahead before starting to climb or descend a long hill
- keep your eyes on the road ahead while you change gear
- return your hand to the steering wheel as soon as you've changed gear.

If your vehicle

- has manual transmission, you should avoid coasting with the clutch pedal pressed in or the gear lever in neutral. This is dangerous if you're driving a vehicle with air brakes, because the engine will be idling and the engine-driven compressor won't be able to replace the air being used by the brakes
- loses or gains too much speed before you change gear, you may have difficulty selecting a suitable gear and keeping control of the vehicle.

The gearbox may have one or more crawler gear positions. Using the highest gear possible, matched to the speed of your vehicle and road/traffic conditions, aids fuel economy. If you're driving a vehicle with a range-changer gearbox (see section 2), you should make sure that you've selected the correct range before changing gear.

Footbrake

Most large vehicles are equipped with air-brake systems. These are sensitive, and light pressure on the pedal can provide great braking force at the wheels. This means that good control is needed to avoid harsh braking and inaccurate stopping.

Plan ahead while driving, be aware of the risk of brake fade, and use engine braking when it's safe to do so. Always be aware of the traffic situation behind you and how it may be affected by your actions.

You should brake

- in good time
- smoothly
- progressively.

Parking brake

You should know how and when to apply the parking brake effectively. Some modern vehicles will apply the parking brake when the vehicle is brought to a stop by the footbrake. Be familiar with the system fitted to your vehicle.

You should

- wait until the vehicle has stopped before operating the parking brake
- make sure the parking brake is fully released before moving off
- use the parking brake to prevent the vehicle from rolling back.

Retarder

If your vehicle has a retarder/endurance braking system fitted, use it, where appropriate, to control the speed of your vehicle.

Steering

Most modern vehicles are fitted with power-assisted steering. Power assistance relieves the driver of steering effort, especially at low speeds.

You should

- place your hands on the steering wheel in a position that's comfortable and which gives you full control
- keep your movements steady and smooth
- steer accurately.

If you turn too early at a junction, you risk cutting the corner. This could cause the rear wheels to cut across the path of traffic waiting to emerge when you're turning right, or strike the kerb when you're turning left. If you turn too late, you could put other road users at risk by swinging wide at left turns or overshooting right turns.

Don't attempt to turn the steering wheel while the vehicle is stationary (known as dry steering), because this will cause wear to the steering mechanism and the tyres.

Other controls

There are many controls and switches on your vehicle that have a bearing on road safety. These include

- indicators
- lights
- windscreen wipers
- demisters.

You should know the meaning of all gauges and switches on the instrument panel, such as

- air-pressure gauges
- speedometer
- warning lights and buzzers
- on-board computer displays

- anti-lock braking system (ABS) failure warnings
- bulb failure warnings
- gear-selection indicators.

You should also be able to carry out routine checks on equipment such as

- steering
- brakes
- tyres
- seat belts
- lights
- reflectors
- horn
- rear-view mirrors
- speedometer
- exhaust system
- direction indicators
- windscreen, wipers and washers
- wheel nuts.

Tips

Practise. Make sure that you're familiar with the vehicle you use for your test: you should know where all the controls are without fumbling or searching for them. Having confidence with the controls will allow you to focus your attention on, and cope safely with, the road and traffic situations you meet.

You're responsible for the vehicle you're driving, so you need to be able to check that everything is working properly. Any fault that affects the safety of the vehicle needs to be identified, reported and fixed before you continue your journey – even if it's your driving test.

⊙ Moving off

Being able to move off safely and under control is a skill that all drivers need to master. Large vehicles are generally slow to get moving and have blind areas where vulnerable road users, such as pedestrians or cyclists, can be hidden from view. It's the driver's responsibility to make sure that it's safe to move off, to signal appropriately and to control their vehicle during this manoeuvre.

What to expect

Your examiner will want to see you demonstrate your ability to move off

- on the level
- uphill
- downhill
- at an angle, from a position reasonably close behind a stationary vehicle.

As you move off, your examiner will watch your

- use of all the mirrors
- use of signals
- awareness of other road users
- judgement
- use of the controls.

To test your ability to move off at an angle, you'll be asked to pull up on the left just before you reach a stationary vehicle. You'll then be asked to move away and your examiner will assess the exercise. Sometimes, moving off at an angle will occur naturally during the test. If this happens, you may not be asked to do it again.

You'll also be asked to pull up on uphill and downhill gradients (where possible), so that your examiner can assess how you take account of the gradient while moving away safely. If moving off on a gradient occurs naturally during the test, you may not be asked to do it again.

Technique

When moving away, you need to balance the clutch and accelerator. How much you need to rev the engine will depend on the weight of your vehicle and the circumstances; for example, if you're moving off uphill. However, remember that harsh use of the accelerator wastes fuel.

You should

- use your mirrors
- check the blind spots in front of and around your vehicle
- give a signal, if required
- select an appropriate gear
- use sufficient acceleration, depending on the gradient, without stalling or overrevving the engine
- balance the clutch and release the parking brake without the vehicle rolling away
- move off smoothly
- change to a higher gear as soon as it's safe to do so.

You should be aware of

- other vehicles
- cyclists and motorcyclists
- pedestrians outside the range of your mirrors.

When moving off on a gradient, you should be especially aware of the following points.

On an uphill gradient

- make sure the vehicle doesn't roll backwards
- take account of the vehicle's weight, which will make it slower to accelerate.

On a downhill gradient

- engage the correct gear for the gradient
- hold the vehicle on the footbrake after releasing the parking brake
- when it's safe to move away, coordinate the controls to move off smoothly
- don't allow the vehicle to roll forward until it's safe to move away.

When moving out from behind a parked vehicle, you should

- be especially aware of oncoming traffic
- give a signal, if it's necessary
- steer well clear of the parked vehicle
- check your mirrors, especially the nearside mirror, to confirm that you're clear of the parked vehicle before returning to the left.

Tips

Before moving off, you may have to wait for a gap in passing traffic. Remember that you need to be aware of what's happening on the nearside and in front of your vehicle too. When a safe gap occurs in the traffic, you need to be sure that there's no danger on your nearside or immediately in front of you that would prevent you from moving away safely.

⊙ Using the mirrors

You must always use your mirrors effectively before any manoeuvre and to keep up to date with what's happening behind you.

What to expect

There isn't a special exercise for this aspect of driving. Your examiner will watch you use your mirrors as you drive. You should use them before

- moving off
- signalling
- changing direction
- turning left or right
- overtaking or changing lanes
- increasing speed
- slowing down or stopping
- opening your cab door.

Technique

You should

- check your mirrors before you signal
- signal before you act
- act sensibly on what you see in the mirrors.

Check your offside mirrors for traffic coming up behind and also before

- moving off
- signalling
- changing lanes
- turning or moving to the right
- overtaking.

Check your nearside mirror before turning or steering to the left. At junctions, you need to look for street furniture and pedestrians, cyclists or motorcyclists who may be at risk if the rear of your vehicle cuts in as you turn.

You should also check your nearside mirrors when you pass

- parked vehicles
- cyclists
- other vulnerable road users
- vehicles you've just overtaken
- pedestrians near the kerb.

Use your Class V close proximity mirror and your Class VI front mirror effectively and appropriately. (See section 4 for more information about Class V and Class VI mirrors.)

You need to be aware of the position of your vehicle and the effect it has on other road users.

Tips

Be aware that the mirrors won't show everything: there are some blind areas that they don't cover. Know where these blind areas are and how to deal with them.

⊕ Giving signals

You should only give signals that are in The Highway Code.

What to expect

There isn't a special exercise for this aspect of driving. Your examiner will watch you carefully to see how you give signals as you drive.

Correct signals should help other road users to

- understand what you intend to do next
- take appropriate action.

Technique

You must give clear signals in good time, so that other road users know what you're about to do. This is particularly important with large vehicles, because other road users may not understand the position you need to take

- before turning left
- before turning right
- at roundabouts
- in order to move off at an angle.

You should give signals

- clearly
- at the appropriate time
- with your indicators
- using an official arm signal, if necessary.

Always check that you've cancelled an indicator as soon as it's safe to do so.

Tips

If another road user gives a signal that isn't from The Highway Code, check carefully that

- you understand what they mean
- it's safe for you to take any action that you decide is appropriate.

⊙ Traffic signs and signals

You should have a thorough knowledge of traffic signs, signals and road markings. You should be able to

- recognise them in good time
- take appropriate action.

What to expect

At the start of the drive, your examiner will ask you to follow the road ahead, unless traffic signs indicate otherwise or you're asked to turn. From this point, your examiner will expect you to understand and act correctly on all road signs or signals that you encounter.

Technique

Traffic lights and signals

You should

- comply with traffic lights and signals
- approach at a speed that allows you to stop, if necessary, under full control
- only move forward at a green traffic light if it's clear for you to do so and you won't block the junction.

Authorised persons

You must comply with the signals given by

- police officers
- traffic wardens
- school crossing patrols
- traffic officers
- an authorised person controlling the traffic; for example, at road repairs
- Driver and Vehicle Standards Agency (DVSA) officers.

Other road users

You should look out for signals given by other road users and

- react safely
- take appropriate action
- anticipate their action
- use your brakes and/or give arm signals, if necessary, to warn any traffic following your vehicle.

Tips

You need to be aware that, due to the size of your vehicle, road users behind you may not be able to see signals given by a vehicle ahead of you; for example, if the vehicle is stopping or turning. Therefore, special care should be taken if you need to alter your speed or course because a vehicle ahead of you carries out such a manoeuvre.

⊙ Awareness and anticipation

You should show awareness of, and consideration for, all other road users, while also anticipating possible danger.

What to expect

Your examiner will want to see that you plan ahead while you're driving. As well as reducing risk, this can save fuel, since stopping and moving off again in first gear uses more fuel than if you continue without having to come to a complete stop. For example, you should look well ahead to assess the traffic situation as you approach a roundabout. You may be able to avoid stopping unnecessarily if you can adjust your speed and fit in safely with the flow of traffic.

Technique

You must be aware of other road users at all times. You should plan ahead and show sound judgement, courtesy and consideration. This will allow you to

- predict how their actions will affect you
- take action in good time.

Pedestrians

Look out for pedestrians at all times but especially in shopping areas, where there might be a number of people waiting to cross the road – often at junctions.

You should

- give way to pedestrians when turning from one road into another
- take particular care with very young, disabled and older people. They may not have seen you and might not be able to react quickly to danger.

Cyclists

Take special care

- when crossing bus or cycle lanes
- with cyclists passing on your left
- with child cyclists
- when there are gusty wind conditions.

Moped riders and motorcyclists

Look out for moped riders and motorcyclists moving up alongside your vehicle, especially on the nearside, in slow-moving traffic. They can be difficult to see. Be especially aware when you're waiting to turn or move out from a junction.

Think once
Think twice
Think bike.

Horse riders and animals

The size and noise of your vehicle can easily unsettle a horse. You should

- give riders as much room as is safe
- slow down even if the horse and rider are on the grass verge, rather than on the road
- avoid revving the engine or releasing the air brakes
- look out for young riders who are learning and who might not be able to control their horses (they may be on a leading rein, with someone walking beside them)
- react in good time to anyone who's herding animals
- look out for warning signs; for example, those warning of cattle.

Tips

You need to be aware of how your vehicle may affect other road users. For example, the turbulence a large vehicle creates can buffet pedestrians, frighten animals and destabilise cyclists and motorcyclists. Show courtesy and consideration towards these road users by slowing down and giving them room when you drive past.

⊕ Making progress and controlling your speed

You'll be expected to drive as an experienced driver. Your examiner will watch your driving and expect you to make good progress while also controlling your speed.

What to expect

There isn't a special exercise for this aspect of driving. Your examiner will be looking for a high standard of driving from an experienced driver. You'll need to display safe, confident, positive driving techniques without

- being unduly cautious
- holding up following traffic unnecessarily
- breaking the speed limit that applies to your vehicle.

Technique

You should make good progress along the road, taking into consideration

- the type of road
- the volume of traffic
- the weather conditions and the state of the road surface
- the braking characteristics of your vehicle
- any speed limits that apply to your vehicle
- any hazards associated with the time of day (schools, etc).

You need to

- make reasonable progress where conditions allow
- keep up with the traffic flow when it's safe to do so
- allow for the mistakes of others
- make positive, safe decisions

- take care in your use of speed
- slow down in good time as you approach bends, junctions or other hazards.

Tips

Your test vehicle will be laden and you'll need to be aware of how this will affect it; for example, if it takes more time to pick up speed, you'll need to factor this in when deciding whether it's safe to emerge from a junction or move off on a gradient.

Make sure you leave an appropriate separation distance between your vehicle and the traffic ahead, and be sure that you can stop safely in the distance that you can see to be clear.

⊙ Separation distance

When following another vehicle, you should always leave enough room so that you can stop safely if you have to. How much room you leave will depend on the weather and road conditions. It takes longer to stop on roads that are slippery or have a loose surface than on those with a good, dry surface.

What to expect

There isn't a special exercise for this aspect of driving. Your examiner will watch you as you drive and take account of how you

- maintain a safe separation distance
- anticipate and react to changing road and traffic conditions
- control the vehicle.

Technique

You should always drive so that you can stop safely in the distance you can see to be clear. In good weather conditions, the distance between your vehicle and the one you're following should be at least a two-second time gap (see section 4 for more about the two-second rule). In bad conditions, leave at least double that distance, or a four-second time gap. In heavy, slow-moving traffic, it may not be practical to leave as much space.

You should

- judge a safe separation distance from the traffic in front
- avoid the need to brake sharply if the vehicle in front slows down or stops
- take extra care when your view ahead is limited by large vehicles.

Look for and respond to

- brake lights ahead
- other vehicles' direction indicators
- vehicles ahead braking suddenly.

Tips

If a driver is following you too closely, there's a risk they'll run into the back of your vehicle if you have to stop quickly. To reduce this risk, you should slow down and increase your separation distance. This will give you more room to spread out your braking and gives the driver behind more time to stop safely.

⊕ Positioning and lane discipline

You should normally keep well to the left, without driving too close to the kerb, and position your vehicle correctly for the direction you intend to take. Obey all lane markings – especially road markings for HGVs approaching arches or narrow bridges with restricted headroom.

What to expect

There isn't a special exercise for this aspect of driving. Your examiner will watch carefully to see that you

* normally keep to the left
* keep clear of parked vehicles
* avoid weaving in and out between parked vehicles
* select the correct lane in good time.

Technique

You should plan ahead and choose the correct lane in good time. Obey road markings such as left- or right-turn arrows at junctions and when approaching roundabouts. Position your vehicle sensibly if there aren't any road markings. Follow the rules for driving in one-way streets and avoid driving in bus lanes during their hours of operation.

When driving in lanes, check your mirrors carefully before entering or changing lanes. Position centrally in your lane and don't

* hinder other road users by being badly positioned
* straddle lanes or lane markings
* cut across the path of traffic in another lane at roundabouts.

Tips

Due to the length of your vehicle, there may be occasions when you have to straddle lanes to avoid mounting the kerb or colliding with lampposts, traffic signs, etc. Be aware that other road users might not understand your actions, so signal in good time.

⊕ Junctions

The size of your vehicle means that it's essential to make the correct decisions at junctions. Look well ahead and assess the situation as you approach.

What to expect

There isn't a special exercise for this aspect of driving. Your examiner will watch carefully to see that you check and can judge when it's safe to emerge.

Despite your high seating position, the pillar between your windscreen and side window creates a blind area that could obscure road users such as motorcyclists, cyclists and pedestrians. Parked vehicles or other traffic may also obscure some road users. Don't take any chances; wait until you can see that it's clear before you move away.

If you don't know, don't go.

Technique

You should

- use your mirrors and signal in good time when you approach a junction or roundabout
- assess the situation correctly, so that you can position your vehicle to negotiate the junction safely
- take as much room as you need as you approach a junction if you're driving a long rigid vehicle or a vehicle and trailer combination
- be aware of any lane markings and the fact that your vehicle may have to occupy part of the lane alongside
- get into position as early as is practicable in one-way streets
- make sure that you take effective observation before emerging from any junction.

Take account of the size of your vehicle when turning left or right; position it so that you can

- see into the road
- turn without the rear/trailer wheels mounting the kerb
- turn without any part of the vehicle colliding with bollards or guard rails.

If you're crossing a dual carriageway or turning right onto one, don't move forward unless you can clear the central reservation safely. If your vehicle is too long for the gap, wait until the road is clear on both sides and there's a safe opportunity to go.

Tips

- Watch for motorcyclists coming up from behind as you approach a junction.
- Use your mirrors to check the rear wheels of your vehicle or trailer as you turn into or out of a junction.
- Assess the speed of oncoming traffic correctly before crossing or entering roads with fast-moving traffic.
- Allow for the fact that you'll need more time to build up speed on the new road.

⊙ Roundabouts

Roundabouts vary in size and complexity, but the object of them all is to allow traffic to flow wherever possible. Some roundabouts are so complex or busy that traffic lights are in operation to control the traffic, either permanently or just at peak times, when the traffic becomes very heavy.

At the vast majority of roundabouts, vehicles are required to give way to traffic approaching from the right. However, there are some locations where a 'Give way' sign and markings apply to traffic that's already on the roundabout. You must be aware of these differences and respond appropriately.

What to expect

There isn't a special exercise for this aspect of driving. Your examiner will check that you plan your approach well in advance. Make sure that you get into the correct lane as you approach, bearing in mind that you may have to straddle the lanes. You should know the exit you wish to take and choose the most appropriate route into and through the roundabout, taking into consideration the size of your vehicle.

Technique

You should adjust the speed of your vehicle in good time. Check your speed and select the correct gear to negotiate the roundabout as you approach it. Get into the most appropriate lane (you may have to straddle the lanes). You should

- check your mirrors as part of your forward planning
- look for traffic signs as you approach
- know which exit you intend to take
- count the number of exits before yours
- either follow the lane markings (as far as is possible) or select the lane that's most suitable for the size of your vehicle
- signal your intentions in good time
- avoid driving too close to the right-hand kerb. If you're driving a long or articulated vehicle, you may have to steer to the left to avoid the kerb as you turn.

Turning left

You should

- check your mirrors – nearside and offside
- give a left-turn signal in good time as you approach the roundabout
- approach in the left-hand lane. If you're driving a long vehicle, you might need to take up some of the lane on your right
- adopt a path that ensures that the rear/trailer wheels don't mount the kerb
- give way to traffic approaching from the right
- use the nearside mirrors to make sure that no cyclists or motorcyclists are trapped on the nearside of your vehicle
- continue to signal throughout the turn
- keep checking your mirrors as you turn
- look well ahead for traffic islands or bollards in the centre of your exit road. These could restrict the width available to you.

Going ahead

You should

- approach in the left-hand lane unless it's blocked or clearly marked for left turn only
- check your mirrors
- don't give a signal on approach (other than brake lights, if you need to reduce your speed)
- try to stay in the same lane (this will depend on the size of your vehicle; if you have to straddle the lanes, do so in good time)
- give way to traffic from the right, if necessary
- keep checking your mirrors – both nearside and offside
- indicate left as you pass the exit just before the one that you intend to take
- look well ahead for traffic islands or bollards in the centre of your exit road
- make sure that the rear/trailer wheels don't mount the kerb as you leave the roundabout.

Turning right or full circle

You should

- signal right in good time, before moving over to the right as you approach the roundabout. Watch for any vehicles, especially motorcycles, coming up on the offside of your vehicle
- if you're driving a long or wide vehicle and there's a choice of two lanes for turning right, take up the most appropriate position. This may mean that you have to straddle the lanes. If only one lane is marked for right turns, you might have to occupy part of the lane on your left, not only on approach but also through the roundabout
- keep checking your mirrors as you circle the roundabout
- signal left as you pass the exit before the one you want and move over to the left
- look for any traffic attempting to pass on the nearside of your vehicle.

Mini-roundabouts

You might have restricted room at a mini-roundabout, so check your mirrors constantly. You should

- give way to traffic from the right

- be aware that the rear of a long vehicle can easily clip a car waiting to enter a mini-roundabout
- be aware that it's unlikely that large vehicles will be able to turn at a mini-roundabout without driving over the marked centre area
- position your vehicle correctly as you approach the mini-roundabout, so that you don't mount any kerb
- understand that other road users might not be aware of how much room you need to complete a turn.

Avoid giving signals that might confuse. Because of the limited space and the comparatively short time it takes to negotiate a mini-roundabout, it's important to give only signals that will help other road users.

If you have to drive over a raised mini-roundabout, do so slowly and carefully, so as not to damage your vehicle or its load.

Double mini-roundabouts

Double mini-roundabouts require even more care and planning, since traffic will often back up from one to the other at busy times. Make sure that there's room for you to move forward and that, by doing so, your vehicle won't block the whole system.

Multiple roundabouts

Plan your approach early. You should

- be vigilant in your use of mirrors

- make sure that your eventual exit is clear, so that you don't block the roundabout

- give clear signals

- look out for road users carrying out U-turns.

Complex roundabout systems, incorporating a mini-roundabout at each exit, have been designed in a number of locations. The main thing to remember at such places is that traffic will be travelling in all directions. You must give way to traffic from the right.

Road surfaces

A great deal of braking and accelerating takes place at the entrances to roundabouts. This often makes the road surface slippery, especially when it's wet.

You should

- brake in good time

- make sure that other road users don't have to brake suddenly or swerve when you enter the roundabout.

Cyclists and horse riders

Cyclists and horse riders might take the left-hand lane on approach to a roundabout even when they intend to turn right. Be aware of this and give them plenty of room.

Tips

- Although drivers are advised not to carry out U-turns at mini-roundabouts, be alert for any oncoming traffic doing so.

- At any roundabout, cancel your signal as soon as you've completed the manoeuvre.

- Before you enter a roundabout, watch the vehicle in front of you in case it stops unexpectedly. The driver might be inexperienced or unsure of their route. Don't drive into it while you're looking to the right – this is a common cause of collisions.

⊕ Overtaking

Only overtake where you can do so safely, legally and without causing other road users to slow down or alter course. Be aware of motorcyclists who may be coming up behind you. They're more difficult to see and may be obscured by other vehicles.

What to expect

There isn't a special exercise for this aspect of driving. Your examiner will watch to see that you're able to assess all the factors that will determine whether you can or can't overtake safely, such as

- how far ahead you can see the road is clear
- the capability of your vehicle with the load you're carrying
- the speed of the vehicle ahead
- whether it's legal to overtake on this stretch of road
- whether traffic behind is about to overtake your vehicle.

Technique

Before overtaking, you should look well ahead for any hazards, such as

- oncoming traffic
- bends
- junctions
- road and traffic conditions
- any gradient
- any hazards pointed out by road markings or traffic signs.

You should

- use your mirrors
- give a signal if necessary
- choose a safe opportunity to overtake
- accurately judge the speed of the vehicle that you intend to overtake and the space you need to get past safely
- avoid the need to cut in on the vehicle that you've just overtaken.

Tips

If your vehicle is fully laden, it will be slower to accelerate than when it's empty. Bear this in mind before committing to overtake another vehicle.

⊙ Meeting and passing other vehicles

You should be able to meet and deal with oncoming traffic safely and confidently

- on narrow roads
- where there are obstructions, such as parked cars
- where you have to move into the path of oncoming traffic.

What to expect

There isn't a special exercise for this aspect of driving. Your examiner will watch you and take account of your

- use of your mirrors
- reactions to road and traffic conditions
- handling of the controls.

Technique

Show good judgement when meeting other traffic. Check your mirrors and be decisive when stopping to give way and when moving off. If you have to stop, stop in a position that allows you to move out smoothly when the way is clear. Allow adequate clearance when passing stationary vehicles and slow right down if you have to pass close to them.

You should look out for

- vehicle doors opening
- pedestrians, especially children, crossing from between parked vehicles
- bus stops, where people may be obscured by the bus before they step into the road
- vehicles pulling out without warning.

Tips

Be aware that the wind created by your vehicle may have an effect on vulnerable road users.

⊕ Crossing the path of other vehicles

You should be able to cross the path of oncoming traffic safely and with confidence. For example, you'll need to do this when you turn right at a road junction or enter premises on the right-hand side of the road.

What to expect

There isn't a special exercise for this aspect of driving. Your examiner will watch you and take account of

- your use of mirrors and signals
- where you position your vehicle
- your judgement of oncoming traffic
- your steering control.

You should make safe and confident decisions about when to turn across the path of vehicles approaching from the opposite direction and be confident that your vehicle won't endanger any road user waiting to emerge from the right.

Technique

Use your mirrors and signal, if necessary, before you position your vehicle. You should take account of

- the width of the road
- the size of your vehicle
- any road markings.

You should

- assess the speed and distance of any approaching traffic accurately
- wait if necessary
- make sure that the road or entrance is clear and safe to enter
- show courtesy and consideration to other road users, especially pedestrians.

Tips

Check your offside mirrors before you turn. Motorcyclists or cyclists may not understand what you're doing and may try to overtake as you turn.

⊕ Pedestrian crossings

You should recognise the different types of pedestrian crossing, show courtesy and consideration towards pedestrians, and stop safely when necessary.

What to expect

There isn't a special exercise for this aspect of the test. Your examiner will watch you carefully to see that you

- recognise the pedestrian crossing in good time
- check your mirrors before you take any action
- stop when necessary.

Technique

Controlled crossings
These crossings may be controlled by traffic lights at junctions or by

- police officers
- traffic wardens
- school crossing patrols.

Slow down in good time and stop if you're asked to do so.

Zebra crossings
These crossings are recognised by

- black-and-white stripes across the road
- flashing amber beacons on both sides of the road
- tactile paving on both sides of the crossing
- white zigzag road markings on both sides of the crossing.

Sometimes, they also have a central island.

You should

- slow down and stop if there's anyone on the crossing

- slow down and be prepared to stop if there's anyone waiting to cross
- treat each side as a separate crossing if there's a central island.

Parallel crossings

At some zebra crossings, there is an additional lane for cyclists. This allows cyclists and pedestrians to be kept separate while they're crossing. Drivers should give way to cyclists on the crossing in the same way they do for pedestrians at a zebra crossing.

Pelican crossings

These crossings have traffic signals that are activated by pedestrians pressing a button on the panel at either side of the crossing. There's a flashing amber phase that allows pedestrians who are already on the crossing to finish crossing safely.

There are also white zigzag lines on each side of the crossing and a stop line at the crossing.

You **MUST**

- stop if the lights are red or steady amber
- give way to any pedestrians crossing if the amber light is flashing
- approach all crossings at a controlled speed
- stop safely when necessary
- only move off when it's safe to do so
- be especially alert
  - near schools
  - at shopping areas
  - when turning at junctions.

Puffin crossings

This type of crossing has been installed at selected sites. It has infra-red sensors, which detect any pedestrians on the crossing and hold the lights on red until they've reached the other side. As a result, no flashing amber phase is necessary. The lights operate in the normal traffic-light sequence.

Toucan crossings

This type of crossing is usually found where there are large numbers of cyclists. It allows cyclists to share the crossing with pedestrians without having to dismount. A green cycle light is shown in addition to the pedestrian light when it's safe to cross.

Equestrian crossings

These are especially for horse riders and have higher controls, a fence along the kerb and a wider crossing area. Be especially aware of the danger that excess or sudden vehicle noise, air-brake release or flashing lights could cause.

Tips

Plan ahead. If you see pedestrians at or near a crossing ahead, check your mirrors and slow down in good time. If you control your speed well, the crossing may be clear by the time you reach it and you may not have to come to a complete stop; this can save fuel.

⊕ Selecting a safe place to stop

You should normally stop reasonably close to the kerb. You must be able to select a safe place, where you won't

- cause an obstruction
- create a hazard
- be illegally parked.

What to expect

On several occasions during the test, your examiner will ask you to pull up at a convenient place on the left. When choosing somewhere to stop, you must comply with

- 'no waiting' signs or markings
- 'no parking' signs or markings
- other 'no stopping' restrictions.

Technique

When selecting a safe place to stop

- identify it in good time
- make proper use of your mirrors
- give a signal if it's necessary
- only stop where you're allowed to do so
- don't cause an obstruction
- recognise, in good time, road markings or signs indicating any restriction
- pull up close to, and parallel with, the kerb
- apply the parking brake while the vehicle is stationary.

Tips

Use all your nearside mirrors, including your Class V close proximity mirror, to help you judge how close you are to the kerb.

⊕ Your test result

If you pass

Well done. You've demonstrated that you can drive a laden goods vehicle to the high standard required to obtain a vocational licence.

Your examiner will ask you for your provisional licence, so that an upgraded licence can automatically be sent to you through the post. Once the details have been taken from your licence, it will be destroyed and you'll be given a pass certificate as proof of success until you receive your new licence. You'll receive a copy of your driving test report by email.

If you don't want to surrender your licence, you don't have to, and there will be certain circumstances in which this isn't possible; for example, if you have

- a foreign licence (EU or Northern Ireland)
- changed your name
- a Driver Certificate of Professional Competence (Driver CPC) test in the next few weeks.

In these cases, you'll have to send your provisional licence, your pass certificate and the appropriate fee to the Driver and Vehicle Licensing Agency (DVLA), or the Driver and Vehicle Agency (DVA) in Northern Ireland, and they'll send you your full licence. You must do this within two years or you'll have to take your test again.

Your examiner will also offer you a brief explanation of any driving faults marked. This is to help you overcome any weaknesses in your driving as you gain experience.

Driver CPC

In addition to a full driving licence, you must obtain your Driver CPC before you can drive professionally. See section 1 for more information.

If you don't pass

Your driving hasn't reached the high standard required to obtain the vocational licence. You've made mistakes that caused – or could have caused – danger on the road.

Your examiner will explain why you failed.

You will receive a copy of your driving test report by email. This will show all the faults marked during the test.

You should study the driving test report carefully and refer to the relevant sections in this book.

Show the report to your instructor, who will help you to correct the points on which you failed. Listen to the advice your instructor gives, and try to get as much practice as you can before you retake your test.

Right of appeal

Although your examiner's decision can't be altered, you have the right to appeal if you consider that your driving test wasn't conducted according to the regulations.

If you live in England or Wales, you have six months after the issue of the statement of failure in which to appeal (Magistrates' Courts Act 1952, Ch. 55 part VII, Section 104). If you live in Scotland, you have 21 days in which to appeal (Sheriff Court, Scotland Act of Sederunt (Statutory Appeals) 1981).

Section seven
➔ Additional information

This section covers

- Disqualified drivers
- Traffic commissioners and traffic area offices
- Other useful addresses
- Goods vehicle licence categories
- Minimum test vehicle requirements
- Cone positions
- Glossary
- Hazard labels
- Tying a dolly knot

⊕ Disqualified drivers

Retesting once disqualified

Tougher penalties now exist for anyone convicted of certain dangerous driving offences. If a driver is convicted of a dangerous driving offence, they'll lose all goods vehicle entitlement.

The decision as to whether they'll be required to undergo an extended car driving test before they're once again allowed to drive a heavy goods vehicle (HGV) rests with the courts.

An HGV driving licence can't stand on its own. You must also possess a valid full category B driving licence (that is, a car licence). If you lose your category B licence entitlement, you also lose your HGV licence.

Applying for a retest

A person subject to a category B retest can apply for a provisional licence at the end of the period of disqualification.

The normal rules for provisional licence holders apply

- the driver must be supervised by a person who's at least 21 years old and who has held (and still holds) a full licence for the category of vehicle being driven for at least three years
- red L plates (or D plates, if you wish, in Wales) must be displayed to the front and rear of the vehicle
- driving on motorways isn't allowed
- HGVs may not be driven on a provisional car licence (category B).

Having passed a category B extended test, a goods vehicle driver must apply to the traffic commissioner for their goods vehicle licence. The return of the licence is at the discretion of the traffic commissioner, who can order a retest if it's considered necessary.

A further retest isn't ordered in all cases.

⊛ Traffic commissioners and traffic area offices

Scotland

Level 6
The Stamp Office
10 Waterloo Place
Edinburgh
EH1 3EG
Tel 0300 123 9000

Area covered
All Scotland and the Islands

North-east and North-west of England

NE – Hillcrest House
386 Harehills Lane
Leeds
LS9 6NF
Tel 0300 123 9000

NW – Suite 4, Stone Cross Place
Stone Cross Lane
Golborne
Warrington
WA3 2SH
Tel 0300 123 9000

Area covered
Blackburn with Darwen
Blackpool
Cheshire
Cumbria
Darlington

Derby City
Derbyshire
Durham
East Riding of Yorkshire
Greater Manchester
Halton
Hartlepool
Kingston-upon-Hull
Lancashire
Merseyside
Middlesbrough
North-east Lincolnshire
North Lincolnshire
Northumberland
North Yorkshire
Nottingham
Nottinghamshire
Redcar and Cleveland
South Yorkshire
Stockton-on-Tees
Tyne and Wear
Warrington
West Yorkshire
York

West Midlands and Wales

38 George Road
Edgbaston
Birmingham
B15 1PL
Tel 0300 123 9000

Area covered: West Midlands
Herefordshire
Shropshire
Staffordshire
Stoke-on-Trent

Telford
Warwickshire
West Midlands
Worcestershire
Wrekin

Area covered: Wales
All of Wales

East of England

Eastbrook
Shaftesbury Road
Cambridge
CB2 8BF
Tel 0300 123 9000

Area covered
Bedfordshire
Buckinghamshire
Cambridgeshire
Essex
Hertfordshire
Leicester
Leicestershire
Lincolnshire
Luton
Milton Keynes
Norfolk
Northamptonshire
Peterborough
Rutland
Southend-on-Sea
Suffolk
Thurrock

West of England

Jubilee House
Croydon Street
Bristol
BS5 0GB
Tel 0300 123 9000

Area covered
Bath and north-east Somerset
Bournemouth
Bracknell Forest
Bristol
Cornwall
Devon
Dorset
Gloucestershire
Hampshire
Isle of Wight
North Somerset
Oxfordshire
Plymouth
Poole
Portsmouth
Reading
Slough
Somerset
Southampton
South Gloucestershire
Swindon
Torbay
West Berkshire
Wiltshire
Windsor and Maidenhead
Wokingham

London and the south-east of England

Ivy House
3 Ivy Terrace
Eastbourne
BN21 4QT
Tel 0300 123 9000

Area covered
Brighton and Hove
East Sussex
Greater London
Kent
Medway Towns
Surrey
West Sussex

 # Other useful addresses

The Association of Lorry Loader Manufacturers and Importers of Great Britain (ALLMI)
Unit 7b, Prince Maurice House
Cavalier Court, Bumpers Farm
Chippenham
SN14 6LH
Tel 0844 858 4334
Fax 0844 858 4332
Website allmi.com

The Chartered Institute of Logistics and Transport in the UK
Earlstrees Court
Earlstrees Road
Corby
NN17 4AX
Tel 01536 740100
Website ciltuk.org.uk

Driver and Vehicle Agency (DVA)

County Hall
Castlerock Road
Waterside
Coleraine
BT51 3HS
Tel 0300 200 7861
Email dva@infrastructure-ni.gov.uk
Website nidirect.gov.uk/information-and-services/motoring

Driver and Vehicle Licensing Agency (DVLA)

Drivers' Customer Services
Correspondence Team
Swansea
SA6 7JL
Tel 0300 790 6801
(Monday to Friday, 8.00 am to 7.00 pm. Saturdays, 8.00 am to 2.00 pm)
Website www.gov.uk/dvla

DVLA Drivers' Medical Enquiries

Swansea
SA99 1TU
Tel 0300 790 6806
Website www.gov.uk/dvla

DVSA customer support (driving and riding)

Tel 0300 200 1122 (English) or 0300 200 1133 (Welsh)
(Monday to Friday, 8.00 am to midday)
Email customerservices@dvsa.gov.uk
Website twitter.com/DVSAgovuk or facebook.com/dvsagovuk

DVSA customer support (vehicles)

Email enquiries@dvsa.gov.uk
Tel 0300 123 9000
(Monday to Friday, 7.30 am to 6.00 pm)

DVSA (written enquiries)

The Ellipse
Padley Road
Swansea
SA1 8AN

Logistics UK (was the Freight Transport Association Ltd)

Hermes House
St John's Road
Tunbridge Wells
TN4 9UZ
Tel 03717 112222
Fax 01892 552360
Website logistics.org.uk

Historic Commercial Vehicle Society

Diane Taylor
Rosedene
Tilburstow Hill Road
South Godstone
Surrey
RH9 8NA
Tel 01342 894564
Email info@hcvs.co.uk
Website hcvs.co.uk

HSE

Online only at hse.gov.uk
Major incident reporting done by phone on 0345 300 9923
Monday to Friday, 8.30 am to 5.00 pm

Road Haulage Association Ltd

Roadway House
Bretton Way
Bretton
Peterborough
PE3 8DD
Website rha.uk.net

Road Operators' Safety Council (ROSCO)

Tel 01557 500680
Email admin@rosco-uk.org
Website rosco-uk.org

Road Transport Industry Training Board (RTITB)

Access House
Halesfield 17
Telford
TF7 4PW
Tel 01952 520200
Website rtitb.co.uk

Royal Society for the Prevention of Accidents (RoSPA)

RoSPA House
28 Calthorpe Road
Edgbaston
Birmingham
B15 1RP
Tel 0121 248 2000
Fax 0121 248 2001
Email help@rospa.com
Website rospa.com

Scottish Qualifications Authority

The Optima Building
58 Robertson Street
Glasgow
G2 8DQ
Tel 0345 279 1000
Fax 0345 213 5000
Email customer@sqa.org.uk
Website sqa.org.uk

Skills for Logistics
The Old Brewery
9–11 Lodway
Pill
Bristol
BS20 0DH
Tel 01179 278800
Email contact@skillsforlogistics.co.uk
Website skillsforlogistics.co.uk

⊕ Goods vehicle licence categories

Category	Description
C1	Medium-sized goods vehicle over 3.5 and up to 7.5 tonnes, with a trailer up to 750 kg MAM
C1E	Medium-sized goods vehicle over 3.5 and up to 7.5 tonnes, with a trailer over 750 kg MAM
C	Heavy goods vehicle over 7.5 tonnes, with a trailer up to 750 kg MAM
CE	Heavy goods vehicle over 7.5 tonnes with a trailer over 750 kg MAM

Motor homes and recreational vehicles come under either category C or category C1, depending on their maximum authorised mass (MAM). If used on test, they must meet the minimum test vehicle requirements for the relevant category.

For more information on licensing categories, see DVLA leaflet INS57P, which can be obtained via **www.gov.uk** or directly from DVLA (see 'Other useful addresses').

⊙ Minimum test vehicle requirements

The standards

Any vehicle, or vehicle and trailer combination, presented for use at test must meet minimum test vehicle standards.

All vehicles used for category C1, C1E, C and CE tests must have externally mounted nearside and offside mirrors for the examiner's use, a seat belt fitted to any seat used by the examiner or by any person supervising the test, a tachograph and an anti-lock braking system (ABS). Trailers don't need to be fitted with ABS.

All vehicle combinations must operate the appropriate service brakes and utilise a heavy-duty coupling arrangement suitable for the weight.

A tractor unit isn't a suitable vehicle for the category C or C1 test.

A vehicle displaying trade plates isn't suitable for a driving test, as the conditions attached to trade licences don't allow a vehicle to be used for this purpose. All vehicles should have the relevant no-smoking signs in the cab area to conform with the regulations concerning smoking in vehicles used for work purposes (see section 3 for further information).

All test vehicles must also conform to all the requirements shown in the following tables.

Load requirement

Most goods vehicles used for driving tests must meet a minimum 'real weight' requirement on the day they present for test. This will involve a load being carried on the vehicle.

This is called the 'load requirement', and it's explained in the following tables for each category of vehicle.

Medium-sized goods vehicles

Category	Description	Load requirement
C1	A medium-sized lorry with a maximum authorised mass (MAM) of at least 4 tonnes, at least 5 metres in length, capable of 80 km/h (50 mph) and with a closed box cargo compartment at least as wide and as high as the cab; tachograph, ABS, seat belts and examiner mirrors.	No load requirement.
C1E	A drawbar outfit made from a combination of a category C1 vehicle towing a trailer of at least 2 tonnes MAM with a combined length of at least 8 metres, capable of 80 km/h (50 mph) and with a closed box trailer at least as high and as wide as the towing vehicle. The trailer may be slightly less wide than the towing vehicle, but the view to the rear must be by use of external mirrors only; tachograph, ABS, seat belts and examiner mirrors.	The load requirement applies only to the trailer. The trailer can carry either • 600 kg of aggregates such as sand, stone chippings, gravel or any other recycled material packaged in sealed transparent bags. All bags must weigh at least 10 kg and be the same weight. The weight must be clearly stamped on them by the retailer. Toxic materials must not be used or • one intermediate bulk container constructed of moulded plastic or steel of 1,000 kg or 600 kg capacity when filled with water.

Heavy goods vehicles

Category	Description	Load requirement
C	A rigid goods vehicle with a MAM of at least 12 tonnes, at least 8 metres in length and at least 2.4 metres in width, capable of at least 80 km/h (50 mph). The vehicle should have a closed box cargo compartment at least as wide and as high as the cab; tachograph, ABS, seat belts and examiner mirrors.	Five 1,000-litre intermediate bulk containers full of water.
CE	There are two types of test vehicle in the CE category:	
	1. A drawbar outfit made from a combination of a category C vehicle and trailer, with a combined MAM of at least 20 tonnes, a length of at least 7.5 metres from coupling eye to extreme rear, and a combined length of at least 14 metres with a trailer at least 2.4 metres in width. The vehicle combination should be capable of 80 km/h (50 mph), with a closed box cargo compartment at least as wide and as high as the cab; tachograph, ABS, seat belts and examiner mirrors.	Load requirements apply to both the vehicle and the trailer. • The vehicle should be loaded with five 1,000-litre intermediate bulk containers full of water. • The trailer should be loaded with three 1,000-litre intermediate bulk containers full of water.
	2. An articulated lorry with a MAM of at least 20 tonnes, with a minimum length of 14 metres and a minimum width of at least 2.4 metres. The vehicle should be capable of 80 km/h (50 mph) and have a closed box cargo compartment at least as wide and as high as the cab; tachograph, ABS, seat belts and examiner mirrors.	Eight 1,000-litre intermediate bulk containers full of water.

⊕ Cone positions

To calculate the reversing area's layout, identify the length of your vehicle in the left-hand column and scan across to the right-hand columns for the relevant cone positions.

The cone positions are relative to the base line (see 'The reversing exercise', in section 6).

Rigid vehicles

Cones A and A1 should be set at three-and-a-half times the vehicle length.

Overall length of vehicle	Cone B	Cones A & A1	Overall length of vehicle	Cone B	Cones A & A1
5.00	7.5	17.5	9.75	14.6	34.1
5.25	7.9	18.4	10.00	15.0	35.0
5.50	8.3	19.3	10.25	15.4	35.9
5.75	8.6	20.1	10.50	15.8	36.8
6.00	9.0	21.0	10.75	16.1	37.6
6.25	9.4	21.9	11.00	16.5	38.5
6.50	9.8	22.8	11.25	16.9	39.4
6.75	10.1	23.6	11.50	17.3	40.3
7.00	10.5	24.5	11.75	17.6	41.1
7.25	10.9	25.4	12.00	18.0	42.0
7.50	11.3	26.3	12.25	18.4	42.9
7.75	11.6	27.1	12.50	18.8	43.8
8.00	12.0	28.0	12.75	19.1	44.6
8.25	12.4	28.9	13.00	19.5	45.5
8.50	12.8	29.8	13.25	19.9	46.4
8.75	13.1	30.6	13.50	20.3	47.3
9.00	13.5	31.5	13.75	20.6	48.1
9.25	13.9	32.4	14.00	21.0	49.0
9.50	14.3	33.3			

All dimensions are in metres.

All articulated vehicles

Cones A and A1 should be set at four times the vehicle length.

Overall length of vehicle	Cone B	Cones A & A1	Overall length of vehicle	Cone B	Cones A & A1
8.00	16.0	32.0	13.50	27.0	54.0
8.25	16.5	33.0	13.75	27.5	55.0
8.50	17.0	34.0	14.00	28.0	56.0
8.75	17.5	35.0	14.25	28.5	57.0
9.00	18.0	36.0	14.50	29.0	58.0
9.25	18.5	37.0	14.75	29.5	59.0
9.50	19.0	38.0	15.00	30.0	60.0
9.75	19.5	39.0	15.25	30.5	61.0
10.00	20.0	40.0	15.50	31.0	62.0
10.25	20.5	41.0	15.75	31.5	63.0
10.50	21.0	42.0	16.00	32.0	64.0
10.75	21.5	43.0	16.25	32.5	65.0
11.00	22.0	44.0	16.50	33.0	66.0
11.25	22.5	45.0	16.75	32.5	66.0
11.50	23.0	46.0	17.00	32.0	66.0
11.75	23.5	47.0	17.25	31.5	66.0
12.00	24.0	48.0	17.50	31.0	66.0
12.25	24.5	49.0	17.75	30.5	66.0
12.50	25.0	50.0	18.00	30.0	66.0
12.75	25.5	51.0	18.25	29.5	66.0
13.00	26.0	52.0	18.50	29.0	66.0
13.25	26.5	53.0	18.75	28.5	66.0

All dimensions are in metres.

⊕ Glossary

Abnormal load A load that can't reasonably or inexpensively be divided into two or more loads and therefore can't be carried under the provisions of the Construction and Use Regulations.

ABS Anti-lock braking system (developed by Bosch), which uses electronic sensors to detect when a wheel is about to lock, releases the brakes sufficiently to allow the wheel to revolve, then repeats the process multiple times over a very short space of time, thus avoiding skidding.

AdBlue A mixture of urea and water that is used to reduce harmful exhaust emissions in diesel engines.

ADR Abbreviation used for the European agreement stating the rules covering international carriage of dangerous goods by road.

AETR The European agreement concerning the work of crews of vehicles engaged in international road transport.

Air suspension system This uses a compressible material (usually air), contained in chambers located between the axle and the vehicle body, to replace normal steel-leaf spring suspension. It gives an even load height (empty or laden) and added protection to fragile goods in transit.

Articulated vehicle A tractor unit coupled up to a semi-trailer; commonly referred to as an 'artic'.

Axle-lift device A device permanently fitted to the vehicle, which is used to reduce or increase the load on the axles.

Axle weights The maximum permitted weights carried by each axle, depending on axle spacings and wheel/tyre arrangement. (Consult the regulations, charts or publications that give the legal requirements.)

Banksman A person who is trained to direct large vehicles.

Box trailer Normally a solid-sided semi-trailer that's loaded through rear doors.

BS EN ISO 9000 British Standard relating to quality assurance, adopted by vehicle body-builders, recovery firms, etc.

C&U (Regs) The Construction and Use Regulations, which set out specifications governing the design and use of goods vehicles.

CAG Computer-aided gearshift system, developed by Scania, which employs an electronic control unit combined with electro-pneumatic actuators and a mechanical gearbox. The clutch is still required to achieve the gear change using an electrical gear-lever switch.

CMR The main document needed when transporting goods internationally by road. It confirms that the haulage company has received the goods and that a contract of carriage exists between the trader and the haulage company.

CNG Compressed natural gas.

COSHH Regulations 1988 The Control of Substances Hazardous to Health Regulations 1988 place a responsibility on employers to make a proper assessment of the effects of the storage or use of any substances that may represent a risk to their employees' health. (Details can be obtained from the Health and Safety Executive.)

CPC for transport managers This Certificate of Professional Competence indicates that the holder has attained the standard of knowledge required in order to exercise proper control of a transport business (and is required before an operator's licence can be granted).

Cruise control A facility that allows a vehicle to travel at a set speed without use of the accelerator pedal. The driver can immediately return to normal control by pressing the accelerator or brake pedal.

Curtain-sider A popular semi-trailer and rigid load area design that has largely replaced 'flat-bed' load areas. It normally has a rigid roof and rear doors, with curtain sides that draw back on both sides of the loading area.

Diff-lock A device that forces both wheels on an axle to rotate at the same speed. (Normally they're able to rotate at different speeds – to assist cornering, for example.) This increases traction on surfaces such as mud and snow.

Double-deck trailer This has two levels of load area and can improve business efficiency by increasing load volume, cutting unnecessary mileage and reducing fleet size.

Double declutching A driving technique that enables the driver to adjust the engine revs to the road speed when changing gear. The clutch pedal is released briefly while the gear lever is in the neutral position. When changing down, engine revs are increased to match the engine speed to the lower gear.

Drawbar combination The drawing vehicle is coupled to a trailer by a rigid towing device. Also referred to as a 'lorry and drag' or 'wagon and drag'.

Drive-by-wire Modern electronic control systems that replace direct mechanical linkages.

Driver CPC The Driver Certificate of Professional Competence is proof that the holder has attained the standard of knowledge required in order to exercise proper control of a goods vehicle or passenger-carrying vehicle.

Electronic engine management system This system monitors and controls both the fuel supply to the engine and the content of the exhaust gases produced. The system is an essential part of some speed retarders.

Electronic power shift A semi-automatic transmission system, developed by Mercedes, that requires the clutch to be fully depressed each time a gear change is made. The system then selects the appropriate gear.

Fifth-wheel coupling A device that allows a tractor unit to be connected to a semi-trailer, using a 'pin' on the trailer and a plate (the fifth wheel) on the tractor unit.

Flat-bed A basic flat floor on a semi-trailer or the flat load area of a rigid vehicle.

GCW Gross combination weight, applying to articulated vehicles.

Geartronic A fully automated transmission system developed by Volvo. The system doesn't include a clutch pedal. Instead, there's an additional pedal operating the exhaust brake.

Groupage This means combining orders from several different sources or customers into efficient and cost-effective loads for onward movement.

GTW Gross train weight, applying to drawbar combinations.

GVW Gross vehicle weight, applying to solo rigid vehicles and tractor units. Also known as maximum authorised mass (MAM).

HGV (heavy goods vehicle) A commercial vehicle designed to carry goods. The combined weight of the vehicle and goods exceeds 3.5 tonnes.

HSE The Health and Safety Executive. HSE produces literature that provides advice and information on health-and-safety issues at work.

Intermediate bulk container (IBC) A water container adding weight to the vehicle.

Intermodal operations Combined road and rail operations for the movement of goods where the 44-tonne weight limit is authorised – subject to certain conditions.

ISO containers Also called intermodal containers, these are designed to transport freight by ship, truck or rail.

Jake brake A long-established system of speed retarding that alters the valve timing in the engine. In effect, the engine becomes a compressor and holds back the vehicle's speed.

Kerbside weight (KBW) The total weight of a vehicle plus fuel, excluding any load (or driver).

Laminated A process commonly used for windscreens, where plastic film is sandwiched between two layers of glass. If an object strikes the windscreen, it will indent the screen but won't cause large fragments of glass to detach.

LEZ (Low Emission Zone) A specified area of Greater London, within which diesel-engined vehicles are required to meet specific emissions standards.

Lifting axle An axle that may be lowered or raised, depending on whether the vehicle is carrying a load that needs to be distributed over an additional axle. Such axles may be driven, steered or free running.

LNG Liquefied (compressed) natural gas.

Load-sensing valve A valve in an air-brake system that can be adjusted to reduce the possibility of wheels locking when the vehicle is unladen.

London lorry ban A night-time and weekend ban on lorries over 16.5 tonnes MAM, applying to most roads in Greater London other than trunk roads and exempted roads. All vehicles other than special types or those concerned with safety or emergency operations must display a permit and exemption plate if they're to be used in the restricted areas. Note: not all London boroughs operate the scheme.

Lorry-mounted crane A lifting device mounted on the vehicle chassis to enable one-person loading and unloading.

Low loader A semi-trailer used for transporting heavy machinery.

LPG Liquefied (compressed) petroleum gas.

MAM Maximum authorised mass, also known as maximum permissible weight or gross vehicle weight, is the maximum weight of a vehicle, including the maximum load it may safely carry. This is normally shown on a plate fitted to the vehicle.

Mobile worker A mobile worker is defined in legislation as 'any worker forming part of the travelling staff, ie drivers, crew, trainees and apprentices who are in the service of an undertaking which operates road transport services for passengers or goods by road for hire or reward or on its own account'.

MPW Maximum permissible weight. Under the EU drivers' hours rules, this means the weight of the vehicle and any trailer (added together) or the towing vehicle's maximum permissible train weight – whichever is less.

Muck-away An industry-recognised term for the bulk removal of surplus or waste materials by road from a construction site.

Multi-drop A journey involving deliveries to several different places.

Operating centre Any commercial vehicle that's authorised on a goods-vehicle operating licence must be registered to an appropriate base – the operating centre.

Own account Goods vehicle operators that primarily move goods produced by their own companies.

Owner–driver A driver who's also the authorised operator of the vehicle, being self-employed rather than employed by a haulage company.

PG9 A prohibition notice issued by DVSA.

Plated weight Refers to Department for Transport regulations for recording and displaying information relating to the dimensions and weights of goods vehicles, indicating maximum gross weight, maximum axle weight and maximum train weight. In the case of trailers, the plate indicates maximum gross weight and maximum axle weight for each axle. This is in addition to any manufacturer's plate that's fixed to the vehicle or trailer.

POD Proof of delivery. This can be any of the usual delivery documents (delivery note, consignment note, waybill, etc) or a special POD document. It normally shows the delivery address, date and time of delivery and what was delivered, as well as the recipient's name and signature.

PPE Personal protective equipment. The basic set of PPE is recognised as a high-visibility vest, hard hat, steel-toecap footwear and gloves.

Range changer A gearbox arrangement that permits the driver to select a series of either high- or low-ratio gears, depending on the load, speed and any gradient being negotiated. It effectively doubles the number of gears available (frequently up to a total of 16 gears, including crawler gears).

Real total mass (RTM) The actual or real weight of the vehicle and load. For example, if a vehicle weighs 5 tonnes and its load weighs 5 tonnes, the RTM is 10 tonnes.

Red Routes Approximately 360 route miles (580 kilometres) in the London area have become subject to stringent regulations restricting stopping, unloading and loading. Red Routes are also being introduced in other major towns and cities.

Re-grooving A process permitted for use on tyres for vehicles over an unladen weight of 2540 kg, allowing a new tread pattern to be cut into the existing tyre surface (subject to certain conditions).

Retarder An additional braking system that may be either mechanical or electrical. Mechanical devices either alter the flow of engine exhaust gases or amend the valve timing (creating a 'compressor' effect). Electrical devices energise an electromagnetic field around the transmission driveshaft (this is more frequently used on passenger vehicles).

Retractable axle This is the axle raised by an axle-lift device.

Road-friendly suspension A suspension system where at least 75% of the spring effect is produced by air or other officially recognised compressible fluid under pressure. See Annex II of Council Directive 96/53/EC(a) for defined equivalents within the EU.

RPC Reduced Pollution Certificate. Specific vehicle types, registered in the UK prior to October 2006, are able to obtain an RPC. Vehicles with a valid RPC can be registered for a reduced level of vehicle excise duty.

SAD Single administrative document. This is used to transport goods between EU member states. Such goods are now classed as having community status within the EU.

SAMT Semi-automatic transmission system, in which the clutch is used only when moving off or stopping.

Selective or block change A sequence of gear changes that omits intermediate gears while correctly matching the speed of the vehicle.

Self-steering axle These are fitted to the rear of trailer bogies or multi-axle vehicles. They reduce tyre scrub, increase tyre life, aid manoeuvrability and marginally improve fuel consumption.

Skeletal trailers Skeletal trailers have a bare chassis with twistlocks, and are designed for carrying containers.

Splitter box A gearbox with high and low ratios, which effectively doubles the number of gears available.

Subcontractor Anyone who's contracted by another transport company to carry out deliveries on behalf of that company.

Supply chain The chain of suppliers, warehouses, transport and delivery to the final customer. Some companies provide a complete supply-chain logistics service for manufacturers or retailers.

'Suzie' lines These are the red air-supply line (also known as the emergency line) and the yellow brake line between a vehicle and trailer.

Tachograph A device that records vehicle speeds, duration of journey, rest stops, etc. Required to be fitted to specified vehicles.

Tare weight This is the weight of an empty vehicle or container (also known as the unladen weight). By subtracting this figure from the gross weight (laden weight), you can determine the weight of the goods carried (net weight).

TBV Initials of the French (Renault) semi-automatic transmission system that employs a selector lever plus visual display information.

TC Traffic commissioner, appointed by the Secretary of State to a traffic area so as to act as the licensing authority for goods vehicle and public service vehicle operators in the area.

Thinking gearbox The term used to describe a fully automated gearbox that selects the appropriate gear for the load, gradient, speed, etc by means of electronic sensors.

TIR Refers to a security system, specifically a cord, fitted by customs to secure a load from tampering.

TIR carnet Approved document showing full details of journey/load/packaging.

Toughened safety glass This type of glass undergoes a heat-treatment process during manufacture, so that, in the event of an impact on the windscreen (for example, from a stone), the glass breaks up into small, blunt fragments, thus reducing the risk of injury. An area of the windscreen in front of the driver is designed to give a zone of vision in the event of such an impact.

Tractor unit A vehicle that, on its own, can't be loaded with goods but can be coupled to semi-trailers that can be loaded.

Trailer swing This occurs when severe braking causes partial loss of control as the rear wheels of a semi-trailer lock up on an articulated vehicle.

Train weight This is the combined MAM of the vehicle and the trailer it's pulling.

Tremcard A transport emergency card that must be carried when transporting ADR loads. It gives detailed written instructions to the driver in the event of a crash involving a load of dangerous goods.

Turbocharged The exhaust gas drives a turbine, which compresses incoming air and effectively delivers more air to the engine than is the case with a normal or non-turbocharged engine.

Turbo-cooled or intercooled Refers to a system where the air from the turbocharger is cooled before being delivered to the engine. The cooling increases the density of the compressed air, further improving engine power and torque.

Ultra Low Emission Zone (ULEZ) A ULEZ is now in place in central London. This covers the same area as the Congestion Charge. Most vehicles, including cars and vans, must meet tighter exhaust emission standards or be liable for a daily charge to drive within the ULEZ area.

Unladen weight This is the weight of the vehicle before loading. It doesn't take into account the weight of the crew or any extra equipment such as a fridge or television for the crew's use.

Unloader valve A device fitted to air-brake systems, between the compressor and the storage reservoir, which is pre-set to operate when sufficient pressure is achieved and allows the excess to be released. (This is often heard at regular intervals when the engine is running.)

VRO Vehicle registration office, dealing with matters relating to the registration of goods vehicles, taxation and licensing.

Walkaround check It's essential that every driver carries out a thorough walkaround check before using a vehicle on the public highway (see section 3 for more information).

WTD Working Time Directive. This is an EU directive that limits the number of hours people can work and determines what breaks should be taken, minimum holiday entitlement, etc. It applies to all kinds of employees, not just mobile workers, but currently excludes those who are self-employed.

⊙ Hazard labels

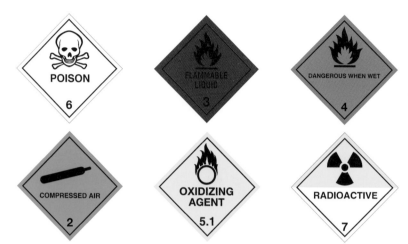

⊙ Tying a dolly knot

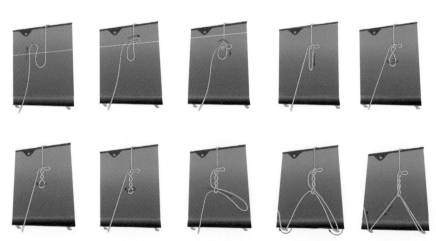

 # Index

LORRIES CAN'T LIMBO

Wise up Size up

Around 1,800 vehicles crash into rail bridges every year. Nobody wants to be a bridge basher. As a professional driver, plan your route and make sure you know the size of your vehicle before every journey.

Visit **networkrail.co.uk/wiseupsizeup** for more information

Working in partnership

Driver & Vehicle
Standards
Agency

NetworkRail

Learning to drive, ride or simply want to brush up on your knowledge?

- All the latest revision questions and answers
- Over 100 high-quality hazard perception clips
- Accessible on any internet-connected device

Visit **safedrivingforlife.info** and enter code **SD10** to save 10%.